Japan in Analysis

Also by Ian Parker

PSYCHOANALYTIC CULTURE: PSYCHOANALYTIC DISCOURSE IN WESTERN SOCIETY

CRITICAL DISCURSIVE PSYCHOLOGY

SLAVOJ ŽIŽEK: A CRITICAL INTRODUCTION

REVOLUTION IN PSYCHOLOGY: ALIENATION TO EMANCIPATION

Japan in Analysis

Cultures of the Unconscious

Ian Parker
Manchester Metropolitan University

palgrave
macmillan

First published 2008 by
PALGRAVE MACMILLAN
Houndmills, Basingstoke, Hampshire RG21 6XS and
175 Fifth Avenue, New York, N.Y. 10010
Companies and representatives throughout the world

PALGRAVE MACMILLAN is the global academic imprint of the Palgrave Macmillan division of St. Martin's Press, LLC and of Palgrave Macmillan Ltd. Macmillan® is a registered trademark in the United States, United Kingdom and other countries. Palgrave is a registered trademark in the European Union and other countries.

ISBN 13: 978–0–230–50691–6 hardback
ISBN 10: 0–230–50691–7 hardback

This book is printed on paper suitable for recycling and made from fully managed and sustained forest sources. Logging, pulping and manufacturing processes are expected to conform to the environmental regulations of the country of origin.

A catalogue record for this book is available from the British Library.

Library of Congress Cataloging-in-Publication Data
Parker, Ian, 1956–
Japan in analysis : cultures of the unconscious / Ian Parker.
p. cm.
Includes bibliographical references (p.) and index.
ISBN 0–230–50691–7 (alk. paper)
1. Psychoanalysis–Japan. I. Title.

BF173.P285 2008
150.19′50952–dc22 2008011402

10 9 8 7 6 5 4 3 2 1
17 16 15 14 13 12 11 10 09 08

Printed and bound in Great Britain by
CPI Antony Rowe, Chippenham and Eastbourne

Contents

Acknowledgements

Much of the material for this book was gathered during a research visit to Japan (and China) in 2004, during which many people gave their time to answer my stupid questions; they include Asada Akira, Doi Takeo, Kitayama Osamu, Hayashi Momoko, Karatani Kōjin, Saito Tamaki and Suzuki Junichi. I would like to thank the Daiwa Anglo-Japanese Foundation for financial support for travel and accommodation in early stages of research for this book in 2004 and 2006. In 2007, I sent a draft manuscript to colleagues, and visited Japan again (and this time also Korea). I was able to renew my acquaintance with colleagues who had assisted me during my first visit, and some of these I am able to thank again now. Those who read the draft of the book and provided invaluable comment, corrections and additions to the text, facilitated or participated in meetings with colleagues to discuss key issues included Aono Atsuko, Arakawa Naoya, Igarashi Yasuhiro, Kanemaru Ryuta, Kim Byong Joon, Kishida Ana, Kōno Tetsuya, Kotani Hidefumi, Jim McRae, Matsuki Kunihiro, Muramoto Kuniko, Muramoto Shoji, Nakakuki Masafumi, Shingu Kazushige, Sato Tatsuya, Shin Myoung Ah, Sugamura Genji, Sugiman Toshio, Suzuki Satoshi and Lynn Thiesmeyer. Although I have amended the text in line with this feedback, I have also added new material after the second visit and so errors that now appear in the book are still my responsibility. I am also grateful to the following people for their kindness and help with the project in Japan and back in the UK, and these people enabled me to bring new dimensions to the account: they are Ben Beechey, Daniela Caselli, Derek Eardley, Kristian Indries, Kawano Kiyomi, Susan Makevit-Coupland, Okada Akiko, Seki Yuri, Takemura Kazuko and Yatsuzuka Ichiro. Those who enabled me to think through some of the issues in the work in subsequent discussions include: Peter Branney, Tony Brown, Berenice Burman, Tony Cartwright, Martyn Hampton, Sattish Harbance-Singh, Ian Law, Viktoria Low and Ilana Mountian. It would not have been possible to obtain and even to begin to process the information on the visits – and so this is where I express my deepest thanks – without the help of my travel companion and co-researcher, Erica Burman.

Introductions and Preliminary Meetings

This book is about psychoanalysis in Japan, but the issues it explores have direct relevance to the way we understand ourselves now, whether we are inside or outside Japan. It is a pathway into psychoanalysis and, at the same time, a pathway into Japan. The book draws on interviews, meetings and discussions with analysts – not only psychoanalysts – from different theoretical traditions and connects the ideas that have been adapted and developed from outside Japan with indigenous systems of thought, showing what they owe to elements of Japanese culture. Distinctive patterns of child-rearing, local conceptions of self in relation to others and culturally-bound possibilities for reflection and change raise questions about the place of psychoanalysis there, and here.

The cultural resources Freud drew upon are not accidental or tangential to psychoanalysis but necessary to it and this makes every analysis into a specific kind of cultural practice. Psychoanalysis developed at the end of the nineteenth century in Europe as a form of intense self-exploration in which one person speaks to another about themselves in a peculiar, highly-charged relationship which itself comes to re-enact what they are speaking about. As they speak, the patient, or analysand – who is the one who is really doing the analysing – has to deal not only with the presence of the analyst but with the fact that hitherto private tangled experience is thereby being made public. The stuff of who they are appears in language in the analysis and in that process the analysand together with the analyst untangles the symptoms that led them to find another to speak to about their distress. Psychoanalysis is a talking cure; a cure which requires that there be some sense that things are unconscious to us, pushed out of awareness and kept at bay because they disturb and threaten to undermine what we think will make us happy. Freud homed in on what was most disturbing, especially upon sexuality as the most intimate core of who we are and around which we construct hosts of fantasies about how we might love others and find satisfaction in that love.

Already, in this most simple cluster of assumptions about the self there are complex culturally-specific images put to work about what is inside and outside us, what forms of motivation are primary and how they push to the surface, and what speaking about ourselves might cover over or reveal. While there is, of course, a focus on things Japanese in this book – at least, the things that can be rendered intelligible to outsiders – we must not forget that psychoanalysis itself is quite a bizarre way of understanding people and striking up relationships with them. Psychoanalysis exaggerates to a level of unbearable horror the ideas that people would least like to entertain about themselves, and the assumptions it makes about human nature should not be taken for granted. In this book psychoanalysis sometimes seems to operate as a window upon Japan, but we will also see how stepping into another culture enables us to find a new window upon psychoanalysis. To ask why there is psychoanalysis in Japan, then, is also to arrive at a way of unravelling the context in which psychoanalytic practitioners work.

When I started writing the book I imagined that the motif of 'Japanalysand' might be useful to highlight the way in which analytic work is undertaken by the person who makes a demand for analysis. It is the analysand who makes the most searching interpretations, and transforms themselves in the process. In much the same way, I thought, 'Japan' in this book would be our analysand; it would figure as a culture that has made a demand for psychoanalysis and has worked through some of the consequences. So, the different chapters do focus on the way Japan has absorbed analytic ideas and produced its own particular interpretations of itself.

However, at the same time we need to approach this question reflexively and turn it around so that the 'Japanalysand' is also the reader of this book, you, gazing into this other culture, a culture that has avidly consumed representations of itself as it has internalized psychoanalytic ideas. The reader as analysand will thus find something that disturbs taken-for-granted assumptions about the Western self and its limits. In that process, perhaps, it would be more accurate to say that the motif of 'Japanalyst' becomes more salient as Japan comes to function in the position of analyst to force those outside the culture to make sense of who they have become. And why should the same process not take place for those who seem at home 'inside' the culture discovering some uncanny aspects of things that may have otherwise been taken for granted or conveniently overlooked?

The scope of analysis in the book ranges from influential US American forms of 'ego psychology' to British Kleinian, object relations and contemporary Freudian approaches, as well as Lacanian psychoanalysis, Jungian analysis and psychoanalytic psychotherapy. Each of these approaches is to be found in Japan today. The book outlines the forms that psychoanalysis has taken in Japan, drawing out connections to relevant cultural-historical factors, but does this with an eye to two key tasks. One is to try and disentangle what appears to be characteristically 'Japanese' about various forms of psychoanalysis, and the other is to explore the conditions under which those kinds of psychoanalysis could arise.

One of the most dangerous moments during the writing of this book was when I tried to explain to my barber what it was about. Incredulity that I should want to devote my time to such a topic quickly turned into hilarity when I had to tell him how many analysts there were exactly in Japan. He was waving a pair of very sharp scissors around my head as he almost collapsed and fell upon me crying with laughter. What on earth could such a book be about, and who would want to read it? Eventually he regained his composure and started to rehearse for me what it might include. His construction of the book was fairly accurate. There might be some history, description of how psychoanalysis in Japan had taken on a distinctive form, and then evaluation of how well it suits that culture.

This guy may think he knows nothing about psychoanalysis and he has never been to Japan, but for sure he knows something about the format that books like this should take. But then, he did not press me further on why exactly I should be writing this book, and it is that position of the researcher that I have actually tried to put in place of the evaluation. After all, psychoanalysis never suits any culture very well and, while it may attract some enthusiasts for it as a social theory or clinical practice, there is mostly hostility to what it says and does. Psychoanalysis is always out of place, and this makes the study of it in one particular culture a curious enterprise. How are we to go about it?

This book first explores the perspectives of the ego psychologists trained in the US in Chapter 1 before moving on, in Chapter 2, to those who are more closely connected with the British tradition. Then we turn in the third chapter to Japanese Lacanian perspectives, before looking at wider cultural forces and representations of therapy and psychology in relation to Jungian analysis in Chapter 4. The final chapter reflects on the questions asked of Japanese analysts and how psychoanalysis in Japan draws attention to the conditions for psychoanalysis to have emerged in the West.

From the start we are faced with questions of language, and with the way English restructures the Japanese phenomena we try to describe. It may seem odd to the English reader, for example, that Japanese names in this book will follow the form they take in Japan, with family name followed by given name. Good. This particularity of naming is the least of it, and it is one of the aims of this book to attend to what is strange in Japanese psychoanalysis so that we may reflect on assumptions we make about psychoanalysis and thus, for a moment, become strange to ourselves.

1
Dependency in Development: 'Where id was, there ego shall be'

One powerful image of contemporary psychoanalysis is that it is primarily concerned with strengthening the ego, and in the English-speaking world it is now often commonly viewed as a therapy designed to boost self-esteem and reinforce a sense of identity. This popular image of psychoanalysis corresponded very well with the competitive individualism of US American culture after the Second World War, and it also served as a moral lesson to America's erstwhile enemy during the occupation of Japan. Psychoanalytic suspicion of the irrational unconscious driving forces that were assumed to underpin mass psychology chimed with political anxieties about the supposed collective nature of the Japanese. The development of psychoanalysis in Japan therefore had to tackle the way one might or might not be obedient to what one took human nature to be, and so as a clinical practice to some limited extent it set itself against ostensibly traditional psychiatric treatments. As part of this process a distinctive analysis of dependency and autonomy emerged in Japan, an analysis which adapted and transformed theories of the ego and its relation to others. Japanese psychoanalysis thus turned apparent weakness, its subordinate relationship to a culturally-specific system of psychology introduced from outside the country, into its strength.

I

Freud did not often refer to Japan. When he did, he treated it as an exotic site of pre-religious tribal relics and pre-scientific feudal traditions. In his 1913 work *Totem and Taboo* he briefly discussed the prohibition against touching the Mikado as an example of the 'taboo upon rulers',[1] and offered some examples of animism, magic and dramatic representation of intercourse to guarantee the fertility of the earth among the Ainu people.[2] These people, confined to the northernmost island of Hokkaidō (one of the four main islands), also figure later on in Freud's mention of totemic bear feasts.[3] Japan is therefore, in this account, a place that serves to exemplify the pre-history of psychoanalysis, but it is not a place in which we might expect psychoanalysis as such to thrive. However, even as Freud was writing this work, papers on psychoanalysis by various Japanese authors were starting to appear; 'The psychology of forgetfulness' and 'How to detect the secrets of the mind and to discover repression', for example, were published in 1912.[4]

Rival collections of Freud's writings appeared in Japan from 1929 to 1933, and the different editions of his books and papers reflected a struggle between certain individuals vying for Freud's attention and between groups interested in interpreting psychoanalysis as a literary or clinical form of knowledge. (We will look in more detail at these conflicts in Chapter 2.) An advertisement for one of the editions gives a flavour of the popular expectations of psychoanalysis at the time; 'God or devil? New, brave theory! What is psychoanalysis?'[5] The different editions of Freud's works also served as ammunition in the struggle between distinct disciplinary traditions.[6] We can see this aspect played out most clearly in the two separate translations of *Beyond the Pleasure Principle* that appeared in 1930.[7] One version was translated from the 1920 German edition (*Jenseits des Lustprinzips*) and this rendered '*geistes*' as *shinteki*, for which one literal rendition might be 'of the heart-mind'.[8] The other version, translated from the 1922 English translation of Freud's text, took the supposed equivalent term 'mental' and translated it into Japanese as *seishin* (or 'spirit'). Yet another Japanese translation ten years later rendered 'mental' as *shinri*, but this term, chosen by the leading 'lay analyst' and translator Ohtsuki Kenji,[9] has since been used to designate 'psychology' rather than psychoanalysis.[10] So, 'psychology' is nowadays referred to in Japan as *shinrigaku*, while *seishin* signifies a range of practices, from the spiritual (*seishin-teki*) to the medical (as in *seishin-byōin* for 'mental hospital' and *seishin-igaku* for 'psychiatry').[11]

This tangle of competing medical, psychological and spiritually-oriented translations conceals an even more complex contested terrain, and we cannot make sense of that terrain merely by consulting a multilingual dictionary. Instead, we first need to briefly trace how psychoanalysis developed in the US before the Second World War. Freud himself engaged in public disputes with his colleagues there who wanted to restrict psychoanalytic training to candidates who were medically qualified, and he even threatened to break completely from them over the rights of 'lay analysts' to practice.[12] The medics effectively won this battle though, and so when psychoanalysts fled fascism in continental Europe for the States in the 1930s they had to undergo medical training, in some cases to retrain if they were already doctors because their qualifications were not recognized in their new adoptive home country.[13] It could be argued that it was, at least partly, the precarious existence of the new émigré analysts that gave rise to an emphasis in American psychoanalysis on adaptation. Instead of psychoanalysis operating as a subversive questioning and unravelling of how someone had come to be who they were, it was turned into a treatment that confirmed the individual's identity and their ability to compete with others to survive.

One of the most prominent expressions of this shift in psychoanalysis was that of 'ego psychology', a focus on the core of the self as a 'conflict-free' sphere of the ego that defended itself against irrational forces. This most simplistic snapshot – of US American psychoanalysis as a form of psychology administered mainly by medically-trained psychiatrists – will help us for now to appreciate which particular psychoanalytic ideas were to become influential in Japan after the Second World War. However, as we shall see, the picture is a good deal more complicated than this, and Japanese analysts disentangled the deeper complexities of ego psychology as they applied it and made it something of their own.

In Japan the word 'psychoanalysis' is now conventionally rendered as *seishin-bunseki*, and so at the same time as there is a sharper terminological differentiation of psychoanalysis from psychology (*shinrigaku*) than in English, the *seishin* part of the term evokes something spiritual as well as allying itself with psychiatry. However, this is a psychiatric practice that also has embedded in it a specific theory of psychological development and a focus on the psychological health of the ego. The 'lay analysts' were marginalized during the formation of the Japan Psychoanalytic Society in 1955, and psychoanalysis as a clinical practice now often tends to be treated as a sub-discipline of psychiatry.[14] Just as in the US, then, there is a powerful strand of psychoanalysis that survives as a form of medical psychology.

Freud's own summary of the end-point of psychoanalytic treatment in lectures given in 1933 warranted the argument that psychoanalysis should aim to increase the domain of the ego over unruly forces:

> ...certain mystical practices may succeed in upsetting the normal relations between the different regions of the mind, so that, for

> instance, perception may be able to grasp happenings in the depths of the ego and in the id which were otherwise inaccessible to it. It may be doubted, however, whether this road will lead us to the ultimate truths from which salvation is to be expected. Nevertheless it may be admitted that the therapeutic efforts of psycho-analysis have chosen a similar line of approach. Its intention is, indeed, to strengthen the ego, to make it more independent of the super-ego, to widen its field of perception and enlarge its organization, so that it can appropriate fresh portions of the id. Where id was, there ego shall be. It is the work of culture – not unlike the draining of the Zuider Zee.[15]

This characterization of psychoanalysis raises a number of issues about what the culture of the ego must be like, and what the benefits of civilization built upon self-sufficient individuals would be. Here Freud acknowledges that 'mystical practices' might enable the same kind of insight that is aimed for in psychoanalysis, but he nuances his account so that his therapy is aligned with a scientific worldview rather than a religious one claiming ultimate truth or salvation. However, there is another aspect to this moral tale in Freud's writing on the ego and the super-ego that is also relevant here; an element of violence might also itself be necessary to subdue unconscious forces, and the path to civilized behaviour entailed the installation of the super-ego. A few years earlier Freud argued that civilization is able to gain mastery over 'the desire for aggression' in the individual 'by setting up an agency within him to watch over it, like a garrison in a conquered city'.[16]

We can start to see a logic unfolding here in which an occupying force enables one necessary step toward civilization to be taken so that the next step might then allow a civilized autonomous power to emerge that will be more independent of that facilitating super-ego.[17] This psychoanalytic logic also anticipates and echoes the cultural logic of the United States as it triumphed over Japan and installed an occupation regime that lasted from the end of the Second World War until 1953.[18]

Occupation

Emperor Hirohito, forced to renounce his claim to be a living god in the 'Declaration on Humanity' (*Ningen Sengen*) drafted by General MacArthur as Supreme Allied Commander of the Allied Powers ('SCAP'), apparently attributed Japan's defeat to underestimation of America and Britain, and to over-reliance, as he put it, 'on spirit as opposed to science'.[19] Scientific superiority of some sort was demonstrated by the 6 August 1945 atomic bomb which killed 90,000 people at Hiroshima and then 50,000 more at Nagasaki three days later (when the Japanese government did not move fast enough to comply with Allied demands). Such technical mastery was also apparent in the nature of the new administration as US rationalist conceptions of the mind and treatment for distress came to structure the mental health system in Japan over the next eight years.

Japan had earlier closed itself to the outside world shortly into the 'Edo period' (1600–1868), and this time of 'national seclusion' (*sakoku*) not only restricted entry of foreigners but also forbade Japanese to travel or trade with them. The US navy (under Commodore Perry) forced open this blockade in 1853, and the next 'Meiji period' (1868–1912) was marked by openness to the West and by rapid industrialization.[20] Many cultural movements were explicitly modelled on western European culture; individuals and fashion trends affected the dress and manners of their favoured role models in a way that anticipates many more recent borrowings from cultures outside Japan.[21] The well-known Meiji writer Sōseki Natsume commented that this pressure of competition with the West was itself creating a shallow self-centred mentality among the Japanese.[22]

If this was an individualization of experience accompanying the development of capitalist society in Japan, a process bemoaned by some Japanese, it certainly did not go nearly far enough for some outsiders keen to contrast their own individualist culture with what they saw as Japanese collectivism. The most influential account of that kind was produced by the anthropologist Ruth Benedict in *The Chrysanthemum and the Sword* which was published in the US in 1946.[23] Benedict was assigned by the Office of War Information to understand 'the most alien enemy the United States had ever fought in an all-out struggle',[24] and her work is one of the most powerful sources of an opposition sometimes drawn between Western cultures based on 'guilt' and those (like Japan) organized around 'shame'.[25] Hers really is an 'outsider' account, dependent on Japanese informants in the US who, it seems, either had reason to distance themselves from their own culture (and tell tall tales to the researcher about the enemy) or to identify all the more closely with it (and protectively romanticize it with the hope of making friendly ties with the researcher's culture); and she wrote the book without ever setting foot in Japan.

Benedict concluded her examination of Japanese 'enemy' culture with praise for her own side and the administration of the country under

MacArthur since VJ-Day, and some warnings that 'Japan's motivations' in the surrender and agreement to strive for peace were 'situational'. Even so, she argued that '[t]he Japanese have taken the first great step toward social change by identifying aggressive warfare as an "error" and a lost cause'.[26] Her discussion of the motif of the 'mirror' in Japanese childhood is designed to explain to a western reader the pattern of restraints that results from indulgence of boys by the mother and then separation; this leads the boys to yearn for a return to childhood. It 'leaves in their consciousness', she argues, 'the deep imprint of a time when they were like little gods in their little world, when they were free to gratify even their aggressions, and when all satisfactions seemed possible.'[27] There then follows a remarkable catalogue of psychological characterizations that moves very quickly from the domain of an anthropology driven by the imperative to understand and control alien populations to something more quasi-psychoanalytic:

> Because of this deeply implanted dualism, they can swing as adults from excesses of romantic love to utter submission to the family... They can prove themselves remarkably submissive in hierarchical situations and yet not be easily amenable to control from above... They are afraid of their own aggressiveness which they damn up in their souls and cover with a bland surface behavior. They often keep their thoughts busy with trivial minutiae in order to stave off awareness of their real feelings.[28]

What is most remarkable, however, is that Benedict's book has for many years been a best-seller in Japan, and her account of Japanese culture is perhaps the most powerful influence on the popular strand of *nihonjinron* writing in the country (that is, writing that revolves around theories of what the Japanese are). Her views are 'reflected in most *nihonjinron* writings by Japanese, whether they endorse or refute her claims'.[29] This will be apparent when we turn to Japanese psychoanalytic theories of child development later on. Benedict was also working within a tradition of anthropological research that drew upon psychoanalytic ideas, and so her characterization of Japanese mentality included certain assumptions about human nature which were then also transmitted to US and then Japanese readers who took her work seriously.

Psychoanalysts in Japan who had trained after the Second World War did not at any point in discussion with us refer directly to the US military occupation, which is perhaps a telling absence that indicates how powerfully this traumatic period affected the development of psychoanalysis. There are critical assessments of the impact of the occupation on academic developments by some psychologists however,[30] and an attempt to show how US-American conceptions of 'intelligence', for example, cannot be translated directly into the Japanese context,[31] and even mainstream histories of psychology in Japan typically include an account of the way Western ideas were imported after the Second World War.[32] The impact of the atomic bombs and the occupation is also clearly evident in popular culture, and the history of the *Godzilla* series of films is testimony to anxieties about the repetition of such traumatic events, particularly the US firestorms over many Japanese cities in which civilians were terrorized in a prelude to the Hiroshima and Nagasaki attacks. Even so, there is even then an attempt in the films to downplay the existence of the US troops in the country at the time.[33] Later, some leading figures in psychoanalysis were (as we shall see in the next chapter) actively involved in the anti-war movement during the 1960s and 1970s.[34]

1950, five years into the occupation, saw what the Japanese Prime Minister of the time referred to as a 'gift of the gods'; during the Korean war the US Army made 'special procurements' (*tokuju*) of billions of dollars over the next three years amounting to around a third of foreign income. Some industries that were dependent on raw materials were then able to double production. In addition, Japanese forces were rearmed to maintain security in Korea in a force that was to become the 'Self-Defence Forces' (*Jietai*) in 1954, and Japan was still able to keep its own defence spending to around a miniscule 1% of gross national product (that is, roughly a sixth of the proportion of that spent during peace-time by other nations).[35] The reorganization of the educational and state mental health systems during this time was, as a consequence, heavily influenced by US military requirements, and many young psychiatrists learnt their craft with the US administration in Japan. These included key figures who went on to study psychoanalysis in the United States and then return to Japan to build a Japanese Psychoanalytic Society that looked to Chicago (by then the home of the International Psycho-analytical Association, the IPA) for recognition of their right to practice as psychoanalysts.

The US administration was not only worried about what it saw as a revival of Japanese nationalist mass psychology, but also acted fast to stop the activities of the socialist and communist movements. The Japanese Communist Party, at that time guided by Moscow, did actually endorse the occupation, but the favour was not returned by the SCAP-led regime;[36] in 1948 labour legislation outlawed strikes in the public sector, and from 1949 to 1950 during the 'Red Purge' about 12,000 communists were sacked. Against Western images of the Japanese workforce being compliant and company-oriented, there was much active challenge and the Communist Party had about 5% of the seats in the Diet (the Japanese parliament) from 1949 until very recently.[37] This kind of organized Japanese opposition to free-enterprise capitalism not only threatened economic links with the 'free world', but raised the spectre of alien collectivist forces hostile to individuality as such. It is just too glib to say that communist organization in Japan is 'heir to the same habits of Japanese political thought and behaviour as the mainstream components of the System',[38] and this kind of account smothers over the internal differentiation of Japanese society and of the opposition movements, repeating older US suspicions that Japanese communism might be worse than the civilized modern capitalism they aimed to develop during the occupation.

Groupism

Many of the recent popular representations in the West of the Japanese – as being more defined by groups they belong to than by individual personal qualities – are actually a function of labour management practices that were introduced from the US in the 1950s and imposed and enforced in the 1960s. The reshaping of the workforce through 'quality control' measures applied to small groups in industry and the expectation that workers would show life-long loyalty to their own 'company world' met bitter resistance. The concept of 'quality control' itself was introduced into Japan from the United States at the end of the 1950s by the Japan Productivity Centre. The feigned admiration for the group spirit of Japanese employees among US American entrepreneurs is mingled with resentment that their own workers would not buckle under in the same kind of way.[39] Far from continuing an ancient tradition of collectivism in Japanese culture, the company world required the atomization of radical working-class organizations so that each individual would then be intimidated by 'real and objective systems enmeshing all aspects of the worker's life'.[40]

There has been a significant shift in the last 50 years in the relationship between the 'group' and the 'individual' that also produces an objective grounding for the anxieties about individual purpose and social relationships. These are the kinds of relationships that psychotherapy typically addresses. And there is, of course, a class dimension in this shift whereby middle-class professionals more directly attuned to therapeutic notions of the self in the West could advertise those notions to working-class clients, and then find confirmation that therapy will be more likely to work for those who have become more genteel, more 'civilized'. An individualist ethos among entrepreneurs, professionals and academics, together with new forms of alienation among the working class that accompanied industrialization, meant that the 'collectivism' of the Japanese now operates more as a nostalgic and ideological cultural practice than as the reality of lived experience.[41]

This does not mean that such collectivism was not then also materially effective as an explanatory resource or an ideal (both for those who admired and feared it). The supposed 'groupism' used to explain the Japanese character thus serves to cover over and obscure some of the most interesting distinctive patterns of subjectivity that underpin the practice of psychotherapy in general and psychoanalysis in particular.[42]

In the early 1950s, however, Japanese psychoanalysts faced a difficult task in persuading their colleagues in the US that they really took the 'individual' seriously enough. The theoretical stakes were immense, and there were serious practical consequences if the International to which they looked for recognition and accreditation would not accept that what they did counted as psychoanalysis. In 1953 *The International Journal of Psycho-Analysis*, the flag-ship journal of the IPA, published a broadside by James Moloney which argued against the very idea that there could be such a thing as 'Japanese psychoanalysis'. Moloney suspected that the MacArthur regime had only brought about the most superficial changes, and his article was designed to show that whatever the Japanese analysts said they were doing, it could not really be psychoanalysis aiming at individual freedom because they, the Japanese, insist upon 'insensible and unconscious submissive conformity to the existing culture'.[43]

Moloney argued that while they claim to follow Freud in wanting to free the individual, they merely 'pay lip-service' to his ideas; in reality Japanese analysts are loyal to the authority of Japan as a 'national entity'.[44] The complaint that they must merely be pretending to be engaging in a practice that is antithetical to their culture is rounded off in a stinging accusation:

> ...the whole Japanese nation is, and should behave as, a single individual. National entity is analogous to the occidental concept of the individual. Thus it is reasonable, to the Japanese, that the idea of the Freudian id can be syncretized into the Japanese national entity principles. The amorphous id, like Japan, is timeless and without

> boundaries, and hence fits the concept that the Japanese nation, having neither beginning nor end, is coeval with heaven, earth and the Mikado. It follows logically that the Japanese identify the superego with the unlimited power and person of the emperor.[45]

One of the ironies of Moloney's paper is that he charges the Japanese analysts with being rather like Western psychiatrists in wanting not to free the individual but endeavouring to 'adjust him to his environment'.[46] This is at a time when US American psychoanalysis was dominated by psychiatry (against Freud's express wishes, a medical training had become a prerequisite for psychoanalytic training there) and when the main theoretical tradition was precisely concerned with the process by which individuals adapt themselves to society. The Japanese psychoanalysts were therefore being encouraged to adapt to an American practice, a practice that had itself departed from psychoanalysis in Europe around Freud. The relationship between Japanese and US conceptions of psychoanalytic training and treatment thus exemplify contradictions that have riddled every institution that has tried to define exactly what psychoanalysis is.

Psychiatric practice in the US after the Second World War was also starting to emphasize the role of group psychotherapy and 'therapeutic communities' as contexts for the individual to learn to relate to others. A generation of Japanese psychiatrists in the late 1940s and early 1950s, including those who later trained in psychoanalysis, were working in therapeutic communities based in psychiatric hospitals before they focused on individual work. This history then informed their own conceptions of the relation between the individual and the group in the wider culture. In this respect, paradoxically, the Japanese group psychotherapy and Group Analytic traditions that emerged more recently are actually more explicitly individualist than forms of psychoanalysis that work only with individuals.

For example, the main defining features of the 'developmental tasks' one of the leading US-trained group psychotherapists advocates (in an article devoted to counselling and psychotherapy with 'difficult adolescents') are focused on individually-oriented goals. The three developmental tasks are 'physical joyfulness of working', 'joyfulness of the phallic performance' and 'joyfulness of psychological working',[47] and while these tasks are referenced to the US-American psychoanalytic tradition, the overall thrust of the article is designed to connect with a person-centred approach that appears to sidestep psychoanalytic questions of the unconscious and transference in favour of a genuine, warm and empathic relation to the client that will encourage them to find themselves.[48] This is not to say that psychoanalysis is wholly dissolved into humanistic group therapy; quite the opposite. Kotani Hidefumi, who first trained as a psychologist and then underwent group psychotherapy training in the US, has now made the Institute for Advanced Studies of Clinical Psychology at the International Christian University (ICU) in Tokyo the base for a 'Psychoanalytic Systems Theory' that reformulates aspects of ego psychology linked to General Systems Theory.

The context for the development of this approach is the 'flood of useless data' that besets people in the age of information technology and makes it difficult for them to engage in an open 'relational dialogue' with others, including with therapists at times of crisis and distress. In this approach the aim is to enable clients to make a free 'safe space' in their psyches and so also to make psychoanalytic practice more akin to Zen meditative space, and so the hope is that 'the psychological space is a subjective experience that can be reproduced in the inter-subjective field between therapist and patient'.[49] It is in this context, in therapeutic work in Kotani's Institute at the ICU, that 'phallic activeness' and an 'initiative ego' can also become the focus of psychoanalytic work with women working within a therapeutic 'safe space'.[50]

There are a number of intriguing aspects of this work that we might view as symptomatic of the context in which they have developed, and which have some consequences for other forms of psychoanalysis in Japan to be addressed in later chapters. The first is the role of psychology as a disciplinary resource as an alternative to medical psychiatry, and this new tradition of work at ICU thus claims to bring the 'organism' back into the relationship between stimulus and response; in this way a version of ego psychology is being configured to address the concerns of humanistic practitioners who will also be mindful of resources from Zen Buddhism without wanting to buy into it as an archaic religious belief system. The second aspect is the motif of 'safe space' which resonates with the mission of ICU, founded by US Americans on the site of an old Japanese air force base; the ICU states in the publicity brochure '21st Century Center of Excellence Program: Research and Education for Peace, Security and Conviviality' that the University was 'established for the promotion of world peace'.[51]

A third aspect, which returns us to the question of the role of the individual and group psychology, is to notice how this group psychotherapy is the setting for individual enlightenment. In Kotani's view, the Japanese find individual therapy more comfortable than group therapy, and this can be an all too convenient for them to avoid some of the more difficult aspects of interpersonal relationships that are addressed in a group setting. And it is precisely because of stereotypical images of the Japanese as group-oriented, and an attempt to circumvent these stereotypes, that the educational establishment has been reluctant to tackle the group dynamics that come into play in the bullying and suicide as individual responses to alienation that is endemic in Japanese schools. The argument that group psychotherapy is the most challenging and so most effective way of addressing the way individual identity is formed through relationship with others was also made by 'group analysts' in Tokyo. The British 'Group Analytic' tradition, which is ostensibly more social than US American varieties of group psychotherapy, is represented in Japan, though even here there have also been strong connections with the US American group analysts.[52]

Popular Western diagnoses of the group-oriented character of the Japanese thus reflect, and indeed make more visible, a potent Western fantasy about what an individual is, and that image of the individual underpins the image of what the group is in Japan. Moloney, for example, in his vicious attack on the possibility of there being such a thing as Japanese psychoanalysis, employs the motif of the 'occidental concept of the individual' to make sense of the way the 'national entity' operates: 'eighty million Japanese citizens are eighty million living cells which constitute the single body that is the person of Japan.'[53] It is little wonder, then, that Japanese analysts looking to the IPA would be very careful in asserting that there must be something distinctively Japanese about their practice.

Obedience

One way of making an alliance with psychoanalytic institutions outside the country has been facilitated by Japanese analysts explicitly distancing themselves from home-grown forms of therapy.[54] In contrast to the topic of the impact of the US occupation, which they avoided, Japanese psychoanalysts during our research visits took great delight in caricaturing and ridiculing Naikan therapy and Morita therapy. These therapies claim an essential affinity with traditional culture, and they have also been taken up in the West by those who idealize what they see as the Japanese access to unsullied nature and spiritual purity.[55] In both cases these therapies have also operated as therapeutic community options within the context of psychiatric treatment.[56]

Naikan therapy consists of isolation (in which the patient will be instructed to meditate) and 'counselling' (in which the patient is encouraged to develop their own understanding of problems of living). The approach was developed by Yoshimoto Ishin in the 1950s, and draws on Buddhist ideas concerning the interdependence of self and others (*nai* means inner, and *kan* observation and introspection). Yoshimoto was a devout follower of the Jodo Shinshu Buddhist group, and there are clear and explicit connections between Naikan therapy and Buddhist conceptions of self. Observation needs to be focused on the inner world in such a way that it does not reinforce the symptom. During guided meditation the therapist will periodically open the folding screen around the patient's tatami mat, bow in formal greeting and ask what the patient is thinking about. The three key questions to be asked of the patient concern: first, what they have received from others; second, what they have given to them; and third, what troubles and difficulties they have caused them (and 60% of the time is specified for this question). These questions revolve around the interminable indebtedness one owes to others, evoked by the Japanese word *on*. The patient is expected to begin with expressing gratitude to their mother, a first key goal of the therapy, before moving on to think about what they owe to their father, family and community.[57]

Morita Therapy was so-named after Morita Shōma, a doctor who developed an approach in 1919.[58] For a Moritist, it is the focus on undesirable traits that needs to be tackled rather than the 'symptom' itself. Inpatient Morita Therapy has four stages; absolute isolated bed rest, light work, intensive work, and preparation for daily living. The first stage of isolated bed rest is what Morita called the 'agony period' (and was the main focus of the amused scorn of analysts who described Morita therapy). The use of a mental hospital bed rather than traditional tatami-mat floor for patients is itself something that distinguishes this more psychiatrically-oriented practice from Naikan therapy (and Morita is also much more hostile to psychoanalysis, which is seen as deviating too far from psychiatry). Patients may become more anxious in this stage of the therapy because, apart from being able to use the toilet, washing the face once a day and brushing teeth after meals, no recreational activities are permitted (no television, reading, smoking, talking with friends and so on). Light work in the second stage might involve picking up dead leaves, and then heavier more intensive work follows which typically includes chopping wood. In the fourth stage the patient is permitted to leave the hospital on errands and then gradually return to their lives at home.

During the course of the treatment, '[t]herapists generally ignore patients' complaints about their symptoms', and in this way 'they help the patient redirect his attention from self-scrutiny towards the outside world'.[59] The shift of focus away from the symptom, away from an obsessive worrying away at what is wrong toward an acceptance of the necessary flaws and discomforts of living, is compatible with Buddhist philosophy. This fundamental pain of living is something that was also emphasized by analysts who were more sympathetic to Buddhism (and we will turn to these accounts in more detail in Chapter 3). The giving up of selfish attachments and the questioning of one's self-centred life in both Naikan therapy and Morita therapy is a goal that psychoanalytically-oriented analysts anywhere would also be concerned with.

What is striking about Morita therapy (and this applies also to the more extreme and marginal Naikan therapy) is how careful its founder was to engage and debate with Western psychiatry and even with psychoanalysis.[60] For example, it claims to treat '*shinkeishitsu*', which, Morita says, is 'anxiety disorder with hypochondriasis',[61] and the therapy comprises techniques designed to shift attention from physical pains to an experiential reengagement with reality. Here Morita departs from Zen meditation techniques to focus on the positive impact of activity in 'practical events'.[62] This focus on practical tasks also, of course, makes Morita sceptical about the value of psychoanalysis as a talking cure (something that is to him rather too close to confession), though he does see some 'cathartic' release of emotion as useful. This, he claims, is where there is a similarity with psychoanalysis, but it is a version of psychoanalysis that Freud actually abandoned quite early on, for it supposes that repression is something that bears on 'emotion' rather than the ideas (representations that are the main focus of a psychoanalytic account of the relationship between conscious and unconscious).[63]

In addition, Morita claims he can lead the patient from their faulty thinking – the 'contradiction by ideas' that he terms *akuchi* in order to evoke the 'misplaced knowledge' Zen Buddhism refers to – to 'obedience to nature'. Acceptance of nature and death thus allow him to extrapolate from *shinkeishitsu* as a specific, perhaps culturally-bound disorder, to broader questions of suffering that are also relevant to physical illnesses:

> ...since the client has an emotional preoccupation with her or his abnormal condition, any attempt to deny or remove this attachment contradicts the obedience to nature. It is only by means of providing the client with an appropriate ecological environment that destruction of her or his contradiction by ideas can be accomplished and the client can realize experientially the state of obedience to

> nature. It is not until clients master this state that they can be liberated from pain and agony.[64]

While this statement of the approach appears to resonate with Buddhist precepts, the medical psychiatric orientation of the approach is clear in the attempts to define 'diagnostic criteria' for *shinkeishitsu*. The 'treatment model' of Morita therapy has, according to some advocates, changed from a traditional behavioural one to a 'cognitive-emotional' technique in which there is now more attention to symptoms and what the client makes of them, an attention to the emotional experience of therapist and client, and attempts to bring about 'cognitive-emotional change'.[65]

Naikan and Morita therapies show us what psychoanalysis in Japan is not, but they also reveal suppositions about the nature of suffering and enlightenment that some forms of psychoanalysis there have tried to take on board. The rigidly structured system of the treatments and overt moralizing were the main problems in the practice of such therapies for many of the mainstream psychoanalysts, and the links to Buddhism as a spiritual belief system were sometimes also seen as problematic. Recent attempts to elaborate Zen Buddhism as a therapeutic practice concerned with 'mindfulness' have tended to steer clear of the Naikan and Morita approaches and also avoid mainstream psychoanalytic debates (though we will see attempts to connect Lacanian and Jungian perspectives with Buddhist ideas in Chapters 3 and 4).[66] There are important questions raised in the practice of these therapies about the role of the 'ego' – whether it is an organizing centre of the self to be strengthened, or an obstacle to obedience to nature to be dissolved – and there are underlying theoretical motifs of passivity and dependence that Japanese psychoanalysts have articulated in their own theories of childhood development.[67]

Amae

The most well-known Japanese psychoanalyst outside Japan is Doi Takeo, who trained first as a psychiatrist and studied with US military psychiatrists during the occupation, and then travelled to America to train at the Menninger Clinic in Kansas as an analyst. Doi's work has been concerned with elaborating the concept of *amae* as an emotion or feeling state of dependence on others specifically named as such in Japanese, but which also has application to other cultures. *Amae* plays a crucial role in all relationships, including, of course, in therapeutic relationships in which the patient will experience, and try to resist, dependence on the analyst. His best-selling book *The Anatomy of Dependence* was first published in Japan in 1971,[68] and is one of the favourites in the *nihonjinron* tradition.[69] The 'surprised recognition' he remembers experiencing when he read Benedict's *Chrysanthemum and the Sword* together with the impact of Moloney's dismissal of the Japanese analysts have led Doi to champion a distinctive psychoanalytic view of child development. Whether it is distinctively 'Japanese', however, is another question.

Doi's book opens with an anecdote about a psychiatric scholarship visit to the US in 1950 that throws into relief not only Japanese expectations about relationships of dependency on others but also US American assumptions about the nature of the individual. Doi recounts how he was asked to a colleague's house and was then faced with a bewildering array of choices that required him as guest to make decisions; the etiquette designed to make him feel at home actually made him ill at ease, a problem summed up by the injunction that he should help himself. The message, so alien to him as guest, was that he was alone and responsible for his decisions at the very moment when he expected that others, his hosts, would look after him.[70]

The sub-text of Doi's writing, in fact, is often a reflection on the form of the Western 'self' as disconnected and alienated, reduced to the ego, and this is perhaps because, for him, the West shows a direction that the Japanese will have to travel but also serves as a warning that they might travel too far. Psychoanalysis as a necessary individualizing practice is thus tempered with the sense that Western psychoanalysts also need to learn about other forms of selfhood (and here the universalizing impulse of psychoanalysis is matched by an equally universalizing message sent back to it from Japan):

> The West as we see it today is caught in a morass of despair and nihilism. It is useful to remember here that the Japanese experience long ago taught the psychological impossibility of freedom. For the Japanese, freedom in practice existed only in death, which was why praise of death and incitements towards death could occur so often. This occurred, of course, because the Japanese were living according to the *amae* psychology, but it is equally true that all the attempts of modern Western man to deny or to sidestep *amae* have not been enough to transcend it, much less to conquer the lure of death.[71]

Most social-scientific research on *amae* does not acknowledge that Doi is a psychoanalyst or that his main interest is in how it plays out in the clinical setting.[72] Instead, *amae* is usually presented as a case example of the 'social construction' of emotion, as something that can only be evoked for inhabitants of other language systems by citing the way it is used in popular culture.[73] Sometimes it is re-conceptualized in communication studies with the aim that it may be understood by Japanese and European-American researchers alike as 'one of the primordial emotions for successful intercultural interactions between peoples from slightly dissimilar countries and cultures'.[74] The focus on *amae* as a motif in cross-cultural developmental psychology in the West has tended to reduce it to operating as a mere variable in child-rearing practices in which Japan functions as a 'limit case' in order to test what are presumed to be universally applicable theories of attachment.[75]

There is a shift in Doi's writing from his first book *The Anatomy of Dependence* to the later *The Anatomy of Self*;[76] from seeing *amae* as a peculiarly Japanese emotion to claiming that it is a universal human emotion that other languages do not normally attend to. There does also seem to be a tactical shift of emphasis between these positions in different papers for different audiences.[77] Doi's first position – that *amae* is peculiar to the Japanese – provides a basis for thinking of psychotherapy in Japan as different from the West,[78] while his second line of argument aims for a rapprochement with Western traditions.[79] In a recent account of *amae*, for example, he takes great pains to point out that '*amae* by definition is something that takes place non-verbally',[80] and he then links it with work from within the British tradition of psychoanalysis as well as from US-American work.[81]

For Doi, *amae* (the noun form here designed to characterize dependence) is to be found first in the infant's relationship with the mother, and the awareness that the child has of its surroundings and its dependence on the mother leads it to *amaeru* (the verb form describing how someone seeks another to indulge them in their state of dependence). This clinging dependence – *amaeruing* to others – lives on in a mentality that is at root 'the attempt to deny the fact of separation that is such an inseparable part of human existence and to obliterate the pain of separation'.[82] This then also leads to a number of irrational attempts to be dependent on others in adult life – to *amaeru* to them – which may be intolerable to others, may even be viewed by them as 'egocentric'; Doi uses the notion to describe pathological cultural and political processes (and we will return to these in the next chapter). On the other hand, however, there is also a more positive potential in *amae*, and an interpretation that could be made that would bring it close to the Zen tradition of *satori* (enlightenment), which could be interpreted either as 'filial piety' or a relation to the mother as one that receives her unconditional love.[83]

Doi is a member of the Japan Psychoanalytic Society (JPS) – *Nippon Seishin-Bunseki Kyokai* – the officially recognized IPA group, but is now a rather marginal figure within that organization. We will say more about the JPS and its troubled history with the IPA in the next chapter – it is a history that itself exemplifies something of the tension between respect for Japanese particular circumstances on the one hand and adherence to Western 'standards' on the other – but for the moment suffice to say that there is a sharp differentiation between the JPS as the organization of accredited 'psychoanalysts' and the Japanese Psychoanalytic Association (JPA) which brings together a range of different practitioners who agree to call themselves 'psychotherapists'. However, as we have seen, some recent developments in psychoanalytic group psychotherapy that build upon the legacy of ego psychology have taken place outside the JPS, and those developments then constitute a new context in which the JPS analysts take forward their own debates.[84]

Masochism

Nakakuki Masafumi would certainly be recognized as a psychoanalyst in most countries of the world, but his position in Japan is rather different. As someone who practices psychoanalytically as a member of the JPA but outside the JPS, his role is symptomatic of the particular historical dependence of Japanese psychoanalysis on the institutions that govern it in the English-speaking world. Nakakuki, who is now in his late 70s, did his psychoanalytic training in the US after working in Tokyo as a psychiatrist and, like Doi, brought ideas about therapeutic communities from the US into Japanese mental hospital wards. However, Nakakuki told us that he did not carry out the second supervised analytic case that is a requirement for training of psychoanalysts in the IPA training organizations based in the US. This meant that he could not then be eligible for membership of the officially-accredited IPA group in Japan, the JPS.

We have played out once again, in this difficult sensitive discussion about rights to membership of the JPS as an IPA-recognized psychoanalyst, a fraught history of the relationship between the US and Japan, and echoes of the years of occupation. This is a relationship between the barely-trusted Japanese psychiatrists and the Western bodies assuming authority to decide what really counts as psychoanalysis, and the history of decisions to submit to that external authority is still alive today. In some respects Nakakuki is one of the most dedicated adherents of

US-based ego psychology, more so than most other psychoanalysts in Japan who have borrowed from other traditions of work inside and outside the IPA. At the same time his marginal position has given him the freedom to develop theories of the development of the ego that are specifically rooted in Japanese child-rearing practices.

Now Nakakuki runs his own ego psychology psychoanalytic group in Tokyo, and is one of the leading figures in the mainly Westerner expatriate therapist group the IMHPJ (International Mental Health Professionals of Japan) – Kanto Chapter which has its own registration requirements and meets every month in the Aoyama district of Tokyo.[85] Nakakuki agrees with Doi that *amae* represents key characteristics of Japanese culture, but reformulates it as a personality formation that arises in 'narcissistic, oral, anal and genital' psychosexual development 'all of which have in common the individual's "sweet" behaviour'.[86] Aggressive and defensive strategies in therapy need to be conceptualized as involving psychic states that not wholly included in *amae*, and so although Nakakuki differentiates his account from a Kleinian description (in which 'the child's self is primarily invested with aggressive drives which are projected and split off', a description we will take up in the next chapter), he does provide a bridge between Doi and theories which attend to the violent underside of apparently compliant dependence on others.

Nakakuki takes a clinical perspective that works right at the borderline between an attention to 'transcultural psychiatry' which values difference and the attempt to define 'normal mental functioning' which appeals to commonality, and he elaborates this perspective with reference to 'traditional' Japanese culture and US-based 'psychoanalytic theories of development'.[87] In this model, the Japanese mother is accorded prime responsibility for the development of what Nakakuki terms 'normal masochism', a relationship that relies more on appeals to feelings than to explicit appeals to authority. Of course, although the focus is on the relationship between the dependent and masochistic son and his mother in these accounts, the development of girls into mothers is just as crucial to the reproduction of the meshwork of relationships in which both women and men are positioned as suffering. The poor mother who devotes herself to the care of her son is thus described in other accounts from within the JPS as a 'wounded caretaker' who is expected to indulge others and enjoy the martyrdom she subjects herself to.[88]

There is a long tradition of psychoanalytic work on 'normal masochism' going back to Freud, who made a distinction between pathological varieties and a necessary dependence of the infant on others.[89] The particularly intense relationship with the mother helps 'sensitize the child to the feelings of others and helps the child internalize maternal expectations effectively'.[90] There are explicit references here to one of the first Japanese challenges to Freud, to the suggestion that an 'Ajase complex' which emphasizes the relationship between mother and child may be at least as important in Japanese childhood development as the Oedipus complex. And there hangs a tale.

Standard accounts of the Oedipus complex require that there be three elements to the structure of childrearing; mother, child and father. While Freud was wary about specifying that a specific psychological complex would operate as a universal template, and agreed to use of the term 'complex' only in 1910 (under the influence of Jung), he did often refer to the story of Oedipus. That convoluted story, in which Oedipus actually tries to avoid the prophecy that he will murder his father and marry his mother, is then condensed into a formal structure which emphasizes that the first love relation between infant and carer must be broken by a third figure who represents the existence of other people and adult love relations. Psychoanalysts in the West often flesh out that formal structure with culturally-specific content (that the carer must be the mother, that the third figure must be the father, and so on), and the first psychoanalysts in Japan responded with another myth which filled out the content in a different way.[91]

The first most influential suggestion was made by Kosawa Heisaku who unsuccessfully tried to persuade Freud that the Hindu myth of the prince Ajase might be more relevant than the story of Oedipus to explain patterns of Japanese childhood:

> Queen Idaike, feeling her beauty and husband's love fade, was anxious to have a child, and a soothsayer told her that a hermit living in the woods would be reincarnated in her womb in three years. She could not wait this long and killed the hermit, who imposed a curse as he died that he would, as her son, kill her husband. She feared her future son Ajase, and as she gave birth dropped the child from a high tower so that he fell, but he survived with a broken finger. The adolescent Ajase was told that his mother had tried to kill him by an enemy of the Buddha, and tried to kill her, but guilt overcame his rage and manifested itself in an illness that covered his body with sores. Queen Idaike confided in the Buddha and devoted herself to caring for her son, and so he recovered and became a good king.[92]

Kosawa argues that 'The most archaic sadism is oral. To bite to pieces is the most primitive violence and the most awful sin, because it means to bite the "mother" to pieces, who is the origin of life itself', and here the Kleinian tenor of the account is quite evident; 'Ajase's violence was awful as awful can be, in that it meant to injure his mother.'[93] Three key themes were elaborated from this rendering of the story by Okonogi Keigo (a student of Kosawa who became one of the most important emissaries of Japanese psychoanalysis to the IPA): 'the mother's desires both to have the child and to kill her child', 'prenatal rancour and child's desire to kill the mother' and 'two types of guilt'.[94] We can notice here that the queen's husband (King Bimbashara) disappears from the story quite early on, and the emphasis is on the relationship between Idaike and Ajase, between mother and son.[95]

Although Nakakuki draws on the argument that an 'Ajase complex' may be important, and this is evident in his account of the 'introjection and identification with the masochistic mother', he also retains key elements of the Oedipus complex and emphasizes the 'narcissistic power struggle between father and son'.[96] The narcissism that is provoked by the relationship between mother and child is then transcended, and '[a]s narcissism grows to a sound self-esteem and a healthy ambition with an idealized self, so does masochism grow to an objective self-criticism and a realistic self-discipline with a prohibitive self'.[97] The clinical implications of the treatment of this masochism are then framed in terms that would be recognizable to any US-American ego psychologist. So, when a masochistic patient provokes the therapist and risks repeating childhood experiences of being rejected or abused, the therapist is encouraged to give 'consistent care and concern and persistent attempts to understand the patient's problems in the context of therapeutic structure without the retaliation', and this response to the transferential display of masochism is designed to provide a model of care which 'is gradually internalized into the patient's self-representation'.[98]

Nakakuki, while drawing on US ego psychology, is nonetheless sometimes acutely critical of US-American culture, finding a positive value in the way that 'masochism is quite openly manifested in Japanese culture in normal and sublimated forms'.[99] The 'cultural narcissism' that has been diagnosed by US-American cultural critics is cited, for example, as functioning as a defence against 'cultural masochism'.[100] On the other hand, the actual therapeutic technique that is employed is dependent on US-American developments of theory and technique in psychoanalysis. What the Japanese psychoanalysts indebted to US American ego psychology draw attention to is the psychic consequences of the child's relationship to the mother. There are, then, profound consequences of this early relationship for the fabric of culture as the relationship between men and women is transformed in Japan.

Psychoanalytic ideas implanted in Japan in the course of the US occupation therefore emphasize the value of individual agency, and it is the aim of clinical work to bring the analysand to the point where they will indeed be able to separate themselves from the chains of command that enmesh them in patterns of obedient behaviour. In this way psychoanalysis endorses a view of the development of Japan as proceeding from a 'pre-modern' state of unmediated power relations into a more differentiated, and hence civilized society. Political theorists in Japan had also been offering exactly this kind of diagnosis of the predicament of the Japanese after the Second World War, and the influential writer Maruyama Masao had argued that there was no sense of 'despotism' as a concept against which could be pitted a progressive alternative political movement.[101] These arguments, to the effect that there was no sense of self in Japan that could enable a critical sense of responsibility or agency, and the implication that such critical ideas must be introduced from outside Japan, have been endorsed more recently by writers like Karatani Kōjin.[102] We will be taking up these arguments in more detail in Chapter 4, but their particular relevance to the account in this chapter and the next pertains to the question of gender.

Japanese feminist writers have pointed out that the image of society that is perpetuated in such ostensibly critical accounts is of it as homogeneous, as if there were not existing differentiation between the position of men and the position of women.[103] In addition, such accounts privilege a stereotypically masculine ideal of autonomous individuality at the very same time as they rule women out of public space as active participants. As relations between men and women are transformed, then, it has been necessary to develop an analysis of the 'feminization' of Japanese culture which attends to the way women continue to be derogated at the very same time as their nurturing qualities are idealized, treated as essential unchanging aspects of their identity and nature. As we will see, debates in Japanese psychoanalysis in the next wave of work after the arrival of ego psychology are intimately bound up with these questions about the role of mothers and the nature of femininity.

2
Institutional Politics and Cultural Intervention: 'They were killing their mothers'

Psychoanalytic ideas were first taken up in Japan when Freud was still the leading force in the movement, and so a visit to the father of psychoanalysis was assumed to be crucial if the ideas were to be accurately represented in the country. And, right from the start there were attempts to interest Freud in culturally-specific creation myths so that the re-creation of psychoanalysis on home ground might be easier to develop, creation myths that have borne fruit in new conceptions of desire, how it is incited and prohibited. These new conceptions developed after the Second World War while profound transformations in psychoanalytic accounts of childhood were taking place in the British Psycho-Analytical Society. So, here – from Britain – were theoretical resources for Japanese analysts to shift attention from the father to the mother in psychoanalysis and, at the same time, resources to comprehend growing generational conflicts and political violence. In the process, psychoanalytic accounts which could be used to interpret the culture – in motifs of motherhood, security and sexuality – were becoming common currency. The cultural-political profile of psychoanalysis thus started to intersect with images of the self and with the sense that psychoanalytic notions could become authentically Japanese.

Fathers

Kosawa Heisaku, 'the father of Japanese psychoanalysis' whose photograph now adorns the back wall of a teaching room in the Japan Psychoanalytic Society in Tokyo, set off for Vienna in December 1931.[1] Kosawa had been attending seminars on psychoanalytic theory at Tohoku University in Sendai (in the north east of Honshu island), but needed to know more about the practice of psychoanalysis first-hand.

A *Journal of Psychoanalytic Psychopathology* was already being published by the 'Tohoku School', but Kosawa wanted to know more about how it could be developed as a therapeutic approach. This would also circumvent some obstacles to the implantation of psychoanalysis in Japan, two alternative trends in Freudian thought that threatened to sidetrack attention away from clinical practice.

The first obstacle was the appearance of a psychoanalytic group in Tokyo, the Tokyo Psychoanalytical Association, led by a US-trained psychologist Yabe Yaekichi and then (after his death in 1945) by a writer and 'lay-analyst' Ohtsuki Kenji. Yabe had undertaken a (very brief) training analysis during a visit to London in 1930 with Ernest Jones and Edward Glover, and he met Freud in Berlin (who was apparently delighted to hear that *Beyond the Pleasure Principle* was chosen to be translated into Japanese because the idea that life tended toward death seemed to accord so well with Buddhism).[2]

This group in Tokyo already styled itself as a branch of the IPA, and Yabe had the authority of the then IPA president (Ernest Jones) to set up the group. A 'Tokyo Institute of Psychoanalysis' was also set up by Ohtsuki with the main aim of translating all of Freud's writing into Japanese. However, the fact that Yabe was a psychologist, not a psychiatrist, and, even worse, that Ohtsuki was a mere literature graduate, meant that there were worries that the clinical basis of psychoanalysis was being undermined.

Some of the fiercest battles in psychoanalysis after the Second World War were fought around the question of medical authority, and when rival groups merged to form the JPS (which was approved for membership of the IPA in 1955), Ohtsuki and the lay analysts were excluded.[3] The psychotherapy sister organization with over 2000 members, the Japanese Psychoanalytic Association (JPA) – sometimes referred to by the JPS analysts as the 'fan club' – nominated Ohtsuki as vice president but this was seen as a slight, and so he refused.[4]

The second obstacle was the character of the Tohoku School under the leadership of Marui Kiyoyasu, for although Marui was interested in promoting psychoanalytic theory, it was still treated as a version of a system of clinical diagnostic classification heavily influenced by German psychiatry. One of the reasons Freud supported the right of non-medical lay analysts to practice in the German-speaking world was precisely because the German medical establishment operated on assumptions about psychopathology that were antithetical to psychoanalysis.[5] These same medical assumptions were also influential in the

US, and we know that Freud lost the argument there. Marui had already in 1918 gone to study in the US with the German psychiatrist Adolf Meyer (who himself attended Freud's introductory lectures at Clark University in 1909), and then got permission from Freud in 1927 to translate Freud's writings.

However, it seems that because Freud did not then hear again from Marui he assumed he had lost interest and so Freud also granted the translation rights to Yabe in the Tokyo group.[6] Marui travelled to Vienna in 1933, just after his pupil Kosawa left, but now it was too late (even though it is said that Marui impressed Freud's daughter Anna, who commented that he looked like Ernest Jones).[7] His pupil had seized the initiative, bypassed Marui and the Tohoku School, and now the lineage is traced back directly from the present-day JPS to Kosawa, and so to psychoanalysis as a distinctive strand within medical psychiatry. Kosawa opened a clinic in Tokyo after he returned to Japan in 1933, and conducted a struggle on two fronts; against the lay analysts, who were eventually sidelined completely, and against his former teacher Marui, who died in 1953 (two years before the JPS was founded).

The visit to Freud enabled Kosawa to undergo analysis himself and undertake some clinical training, and it was clear that the imprimatur of the master – personal agreement over translation rights of key texts and approval of plans to set up local organizations – was now necessary to take psychoanalysis forward in Japan. A phone call to the Freud house at Berggasse 19 failed to get him an audience, but a Japanese friend studying medicine in Austria helped him get a letter of introduction from the former president of Vienna University (who had once done some teaching at Tohoku). This letter, along with a letter from Marui (who had also arranged for Kosawa to be promoted from lecturer to associate professor to enable him to undertake the trip), did the trick. Kosawa was delighted:

> Now I could meet with the world famous Professor Dr. Freud. I could not still my heart! ... And then Dr. Freud talked to me in a mumbling low voice. Sometimes he asked me with his hand behind his ear 'what?' I felt his sharp and analytical mind. Dr. Freud was hard of hearing. ...the meeting with Dr. Freud ended in an atmosphere of relaxation. Dr. Freud saw us to the door. By mistake, he switched the light off instead of ringing the bell. The little parapraxis very much pleased me. If you had a smattering of psychoanalysis you could understand the degree of my joy at the moment.[8]

An interpretation of the Professor Dr.'s Freudian slip – the 'parapraxis' – Kosawa seemed to be hinting at here is that Freud turned the light off because he had an unconscious wish that his young visitor would stay the night.[9] Eventually, after some haggling over fees for a prospective analysis – Freud offered to reduce the amount charged to ten US dollars from the 25 he originally stipulated during the meeting – Kosawa was passed on to Richard Sterba for analysis and was supervised by Paul Federn (then President of the Vienna Psychoanalytic Society). Kosawa sent a German translation of his paper on the 'Ajase Complex' to Freud while he was in Vienna, but Freud's peremptory response was not encouraging.[10] Recognition of the importance of this work has only come later as psychoanalysis has developed in Japan under Kosawa's guidance.

Kosawa practised psychoanalysis throughout the Second World War at a time when the practice was viewed as a 'dangerous, Jewish system of thought', and the security services kept him under surveillance.[11] After the war one of Marui's other students intended to study psychoanalysis in Germany, but his application was rejected on the grounds that 'it was not good to learn Jewish knowledge'.[12] Kosawa succeeded Marui as director of the IPA Sendai branch in 1953, changed the name of the organization to the Japan branch and relocated it to Tokyo, and he then remained president of the JPS until 1968. The Ajase Complex has (as we have already seen in Chapter 1) been an important conceptual alternative to the Oedipus complex and it shifts attention from rivalry with the father to a deeper more painful relationship with the mother.

Prohibition

Okonogi Keigo, who was for many years until his death in 2003 the diplomatic representative of the Japan society to the IPA and responsible for implementing internationally-agreed training requirements, argued that there was no necessary contradiction between western and local accounts of the self: 'Indigenous Japanese patterns of thought merged with the imported theory of psychoanalysis'.[13] However, this merging had to manage some important tensions, creative tensions that still characterize psychoanalysis in Japan today.

A first tension was that Buddhism might provide a worldview that was incompatible with psychoanalysis. Early followers of Freud in Japan had already come under pressure from Morita therapy, which did develop an approach that promised the best of scientific psychiatry and aspects of Zen Buddhism (as we have seen in Chapter 1). Buddhism was at that time also attractive to those analysts, like Ohtsuki and Marui, who separated from mainstream psychoanalysis after the Second World War. Ohtsuki went on to develop an approach known as 'Life analysis', for example, in which there should be a stabilization of experience as one comes to terms with one's nature organized through an 'unconscious synthetic principle'.[14]

A second tension arises from the interpretation of Buddhist texts, and there is some disagreement among scholars in Japan as to whether either the original Ajase story or the later versions of the story do actually prioritize mother-son relationships as Kosawa claimed, and whether they really offer an alternative to themes of father-son rivalry and parricide. Buddhism arrived in Japan via China and Korea in the 6th century, but it was not until the 12th century that a distinctive Japanese Buddhism developed.[15] Okonogi claims that the popularization of this variant of Buddhism was closely connected to the enlightenment of women as mothers, in particular to 'assuaging the guilt of mothers who had killed or aborted their infants'.[16]

A third tension – between an account specific to Japanese culture and a conception of development that is universally applicable – runs even deeper, and it throws into question the civilizing aims of Western psychoanalysis. These aims were predicated on the recognition of what is most primordial in human nature and the acquisition of a position in culture from which to reflect on that nature. The Oedipus complex was described by Freud as something primal, and his studies in *Totem and Taboo* grounded the experience of each particular human individual in a general pre-history of humanity thought by him to have been excavated by anthropologists.[17] At the same time, though, the passage through the Oedipus complex enables the infant to separate from the mother and come to terms with the role of the father, and it is he who stands apart and outside the first relationship to provide a more objective mediated standpoint from which to view it. The father's standpoint is thus one we identify with when we look dispassionately (and scientifically) at the world. One might then say one of the outcomes of 'positive oedipal relationships' is that the therapist's role 'is similar to that of the father in that he has to mediate between the aggressively demanding child and the vulnerable, masochistic caretaker that coexist in the patient'.[18]

While the Ajase complex might also 'possess a universal character', focusing on 'questions linked to one's origins: the identity of one's parents and the circumstances of one's birth', as Okonogi has claimed, it begs a question as to whether that is enough for the development of individual identity to take place.[19] Strict Freudians will ask where the external vantage point is with which we might identify and which will enable us to separate from the mother.[20] It is this principle of mediation that was crucial to early psychoanalytic accounts of development.

Perhaps Kosawa's reading of the Ajase story as an underlying 'complex' that would be more genuinely Japanese than Freud's Oedipus complex was a little idealistic, borrowing too quickly from a Buddhist legend without explaining the material conditions in which Buddhism took root in Japan.[21] Kosawa's student Okonogi corrects this and sets out reasons why it may be relevant in a 'maternal society' like Japan, and why it might also become more relevant to societies that have seen the impact of feminism.[22] With respect to the three key themes that appear in the story of Ajase – 'the mother's desires both to have the child and to kill her child', 'prenatal rancour and child's desire to kill the mother' and 'two types of guilt' – Okonogi explores how the position of women in contemporary Japan may exacerbate the problems they have faced historically.

There are, for example, reasons why the mother may desire both to have the child and to kill her child that lie with the demands placed on women and the lack of support – from an extended family or from men – when child-rearing has seen increasing 'nuclearization' and when men are still mainly absent from the home.[23] The theme of 'prenatal rancour and child's desire to kill the mother' can be located in the transmission of conflicts from one generation to another, and the child's 'empathy for the mother's suffering'.[24] Okonogi points out that it was upon reaching adolescence and faced with the conflicts over his birth that Ajase is overcome by 'prenatal rancour' (and his mother had been under intense pressure to have a child when she felt her husband's love lessen with her fading beauty). Properly speaking, then, this 'prenatal' rancour is something that is activated only after the original event in classic psychoanalytic fashion.

Psychoanalytic conceptions of causality are quite different from everyday commonsensical linear notions, and an incomprehensible event becomes 'traumatic' as the result of a second event which recreates the earlier event, and so turns the earlier event into the trauma which will then 'cause' later events to also be experienced as traumatic.[25] Ajase then suffers the rancour he experiences towards his mother as if it were always already there, from before his birth. With respect to the 'two types of guilt' that appear in the story, Okonogi points out that the tragedy of the tale is that the mother Queen Idaike is forced to take responsibility for her child, and it is in this context that 'a split appears between the idealized mother who wields all-powerful love and control and the frightening mother who wields the right of death'.[26] But then, how does the child escape from the mother if the father is absent? An answer is provided by an analyst of the next generation, Kitayama Osamu.

A psychoanalytic alternative to the role of the father as an agent in development, one that would introduce some mediation in the relationship between mother and child, was eventually provided by Kitayama in a new articulation of 'prohibition' that drew on Japanese folk tales. This move bypassed Buddhism to some extent, for the Japanese traditional stories he refers to were older and could provide an account of indigenous 'patterns of thought' that did not either buy into another worldview or get entangled in debates as to what religious scriptures really said.

For Kitayama the key prohibition is one he terms 'don't look'. In the popular story 'Urashima Taro', for example, the fisher-boy Urashima is carried by a tortoise to an undersea palace where he meets and marries a beautiful princess. When he wants to return home she gives him a box which she tells him not to open. He returns home to find that hundreds of years have passed, and feeling bereft of his family he opens the box and then suddenly becomes old and dies. A series of folk tales include the same motif: a 'snake wife' forbids her husband to look at her when she gives birth, but he does, to find that his wife is a snake; a 'fish wife' tells her husband not to look while she is having a bath, and when he looks and discovers she is a fish, she leaves him; and a 'clam wife' forbids her husband to look at her when she is cooking, but he disobeys and finds her urinating in the pan, upon which she goes back to the sea. And, in the myth of Izanagi-Izanami who created the islands of Japan and Shintō deities, Izanami dies after having given birth to a fire god who burns her genitals and then prohibits her husband Izanagi from following her into the land of the dead; he disobeys the prohibition 'don't look', she wreaks revenge, and he only just escapes with his life. In sum:

> ...Japanese folk tales, differing from western fairy tales, which end happily, reveal a tragic failure in the integrative process; they keep only a good part or a good product, casting away its animalized producers, some of them having been injured. The infantile hero's demanding nature, which seems innocent, is obviously connected with the oral demand towards the mother's breast which may be extended to her body to rob it of its good contents. His breaking of

> the prohibition *don't look* confronts him with what he had been attacking or what he should feel guilty of; something he cannot accept.[27]

The prohibition 'don't look' and the transgression of it then leads the hero on a tragic path in which there will be no prospect of reconciliation. Instead, the outcome is closer to Freud's original psychoanalytic argument that there can be no complete cure; that instead the most that can be hoped for is to transform 'hysterical misery into common unhappiness'.[28] This also serves to show how the relations in which the individual is entangled right from the start as a condition for becoming human will always linger on, a form of 'debt' or 'obligation' that is captured in Japanese in the word *'on'*.[29] It is concept that much preoccupied Ruth Benedict in *The Chrysanthemum and the Sword*, and for her it was to be found in range of everyday expressions, such as one of the expressions of regret, *sumimasen* for which a literal translation might be 'this never ends'.[30] The interminable debt that one experiences throughout one's life is also, in Kitayama's account, a way of specifying how it is that each apparently separate individual is intimately enmeshed in relations with others.

Relations

The turn to Buddhist legends and folk myths in Japanese psychoanalysis involved much more than a simple replacement of the Freudian story of the child's relation to its father with an earlier and, by implication, deeper account of the child's relation to its mother. This was no mere debate about different cultural contents that would flesh out the story. It involved a fundamental shift in the formal structure of psychoanalytic explanation, to one which was (as Kitayama acknowledged in his account) 'a two-body relationship rather than a typical triangular situation'.[31] A shift of this kind had already occurred in European psychoanalysis in the 1940s, and nearly split the British Psycho-Analytical Society. The differences that had exploded between followers of Anna Freud and Melanie Klein were patched over after 'controversial discussions' in an agreement that there be separate trainings co-existing in the same organization (which lasted until 2005).[32] Anna Freud made alliances with the US ego psychologists (who were following a similar trajectory to her in emphasizing the role of the ego and the defences used to protect it) and worked within a grouping that is now known as the 'contemporary Freudians' (originally the 'B group').

Klein and her followers delved deeper and earlier into primitive fantasy in her 'A group'. A third 'middle' or 'independent' tradition also emerged led by former Kleinians who emphasized the 'object relations' that structured the infant's experience of their mother.[33] The Kleinian and object relations traditions have provided valuable theoretical resources for the Japanese analysts, and there have been increasingly close ties forged that have, to some extent, displaced the hitherto influential US American analysts from centre-stage. The profound shift to the mother in British psychoanalysis sidestepped Freud's universalizing claims about the role of the Oedipus complex as a triangular structure and enabled Japanese analysts to find wider application for their 'two-body' account beyond Japanese culture. Perhaps now there was a way of articulating an account of the relationship with the mother that would be even more universal to human development than Oedipus, and so it would actually be Freud's theory that could then be understood as providing a limited description that was itself culturally-specific.

Japanese psychoanalytic studies of the relationship between mother and infant provided a particular way of understanding developments in British psychoanalysis, for here was a culture in which the rather bizarre speculations of the Kleinians and object relations theorists might immediately make sense. For Klein, the pre-Oedipal infant is already torn between love and hatred for first objects – most important of which is the breast – and the 'paranoid-schizoid' position is marked by a frightening oscillation between unconscious fantasies of omnipotence and persecution. The infant's boiling cauldron of spoiling spite can only be assuaged by a shift into a 'depressive position' in which they understand that those they aim to destroy are the same objects as those they desire so ruthlessly.[34] Donald Winnicott broke from Klein, refusing this grim picture of the infant's mind, and was one of the leading 'independents', but even though there was fundamental disagreement over the role of the 'death instinct' much-vaunted by Klein, his focus on the way the mother manages to withstand the unremitting demands of her child complements Klein's work. He describes, for example, the many reasons why a mother hates her baby – 'even', he says, 'a boy'.[35] The mother must thus 'contain' her infant, much as an analyst will contain the aggression of an analysand, and she thus provides 'good-enough' care that facilitates development; for Winnicott it is as if 'Where the Id of the infant is, there the mother's Ego must be also'.[36]

It is understandable that accounts of the Ajase complex and the 'don't look' prohibition made convenient and then enduring connections with

Kleinian theory. Okonogi points out that in the Buddhist sutras, resentment directed at one's origin is *mishōon*, a 'prenatal rancour' that Ajase experiences toward his mother (who, remember, tries to kill him by dropping him from a high tower but only succeeds in breaking his finger). This prenatal rancour then give rise to a fear of retaliation very close to the 'persecutory guilt' Klein describes, and this kind of guilt can only be surmounted through experiencing remorse, something close to Kleinian 'reparative guilt'.[37]

Kitayama's discussion of folk tales of marriage between humans and non-humans also draws comparisons with Klein's account of 'the infant's painful development of loving and hating the mother ambivalently and losing her as a whole object'.[38] The still influential descriptions of *amae* are less amenable to a Kleinian reading – and we know that Doi was more influenced by the US tradition in psychoanalysis – but there are still significant connections made in this strand of work with the British independent tradition.[39] There are a host of explicit references to Kleinian, Winnicottian and other British-based theories of child development in the JPS 50th anniversary volume, and there is discussion of current research in Britain that reflects some of the authors' histories of training at the Tavistock Institute in London.[40] There are book-length Japanese introductions to Kleinian and object relations theory published by leading JPS analysts, and translations of contemporary British tradition texts.[41]

While there are still many references to US-based analysts, there are also more recent references to contemporary globalization as being equivalent to 'Americanization'.[42] The increasing influence of British psychoanalytic theory can be illustrated by the discussion in one of the JPS anniversary book chapters on prenatal rancour and the Japanese term '*en*'.[43] *En* is an elusive concept that may be defined in at least three ways: as 'An indirect condition that contributes to bringing about an outcome'; 'relationships'; and 'edge and/or brim'.[44] The term can be used to mean relationship and also destiny (with this sense of the term derived from standard Chinese translation of the Buddhist notion of *pratyāya*), and so will refer generally to 'relations as determined by fate'; 'In conversation it is often used, especially by people of strong Buddhist inclination, to refer to the good fortune of having met someone. To marry, in particular, is to join *en*, and to divorce to "cut" it'.[45]

The clinical case discussed in this contribution on prenatal rancour concerns a female patient who attempted suicide, resented therapeutic support and then came to terms with her dependence on the therapist and so also on her mother.[46] (The therapist is a woman, but this is not explicitly attended to in the case discussion.) The point at which the patient comes to a point of no return – that is, to the 'edge' (as the third definition of *en* given at the end of the last paragraph) – also brings her face-to-face with conditions and relationships (the second definition) in which she makes decisions that have seemed up to then chance occurrences, out of her control (that is with reference to the first definition of *en*). And so, *en* is also a different framework from traditional Western psychoanalysis for understanding chance:

> Nothing stands of itself, everything is carried out by 'en', and moreover, it does not exist in the inner world of an individual. If we go by that principle and blame everything on 'en', one's self will never work as a decisive factor and responsibility is dispersed. If so, there is no common ground with psychoanalytic thinking. However, the term 'en' has a deep significance embedded in Japanese daily life, and is not to be used lightly. In fact, I may safely say that we are already deeply embedded in something we consider 'en'. It is something absolute beyond the reach of the individual, sometimes the object of rancour, and at other times the mechanism that enables us to accept what cannot be helped. It is also the object of gratitude since it is perceived as something that directs good fortune.[47]

Relations of interdependence of self and others – the *en* in which selves are embedded – thus pose questions to an individual undergoing psychoanalysis, so that a sense of obligation would not then call forth destructive resentment, but would rather be contained, comprehended and worked through.

Mothers

Japan is a very safe country, and Japanese who travel abroad are often fearful that they may encounter violence.[48] This is a powerful self-representation of Japanese culture and, regardless of whether it corresponds to reality or not, it structures how peaceful home life and a dangerous outside world are counterposed and experienced. And it structures how Japanese psychoanalysts understand the relationship between home and abroad. The current secretary of the JPS, Kitayama Osamu, described how so many Japanese – those who travel to study at the Tavistock Institute for example – return because the country is so much safer than others, and even how the world may eventually succeed in becoming a peaceful place by following Japan as an example. Kitayama may have been teasing us when he suggested this idea, but his hope for a peaceful world was certainly sincere and at least some elements of the truth about the way the Japanese see themselves and others were conveyed in his playful description. He writes in his preface to the JPS anniversary volume of the great possibilities for the future development of psychoanalysis, noting that Zen and a variety of musical instruments were apparently imported into Japan around a 1,000 years ago and they have been perfected in this country while having become extinct in their countries of origin: 'I predict that, for our psychoanalysis to become truly a Japanese original, it will require a long period of time – perhaps close to 1,000 years – for it to be ranked on a par with Buddhism.'[49] The JPS president Nishizono Masahisa embellishes this theme with specific reference to the family as the model of harmonious space, place of '*wa*': Here *wa* – often evoked as consensual negotiation that maintains stability of relationships – is contrasted with the conflictual individualism of the West:[50]

> To Europeans and Americans, assertion of the individual, personality of nomadism, severance between individuals, contracts aiming at resolving it as an actual problem and love transcending it as a problem of humanity, appear to be essential qualities. To the Japanese up until the present, experiencing such love is said to have been difficult. The Japanese are said to have given first priority to 'wa', sum or harmony or linkage in existing as a family community or family group. To that end, they adopt an attitude of restraining themselves and following others, while reading the expression and attitude of the other party.[51]

Nishizono's discussion of changes in child-rearing practices and the position of women explores spatial relations in which children appear to be pampered in traditional 'patriarchal' culture but are actually controlled, and in which the father is only apparently the protector of the family, and in turn is also subject to control. At stake here is the continuity of '*ie*', the family unit maintained by way of succession through the male line, sometimes through arranged marriage, and strongly infused with religious values. From this arises a sense of 'fate or relationship' which Nishizono sees manifest in *amae*.[52] The man who seems to be a source of power is actually, then, playing a 'false self' role as father, and Nishizono uses this Winnicottian notion of the 'false self' (in which one becomes trapped by a version of one's self adopted for others) to explain how this father is strong but also at the same time fragile.

It would be possible to read this account – and also Okonogi's historical analysis of the Ajase complex – as sympathetic to feminist accounts of the contradictory position of men as they relay patriarchal power relations through culture, but there are particular complications here, and resonances with an influential strand of what has been termed 'maternalist feminism'. This version of Japanese feminism emphasizes the role of woman as mother, and relations of caring and dependence can then be easily extrapolated to describe the whole of the culture as being in some sense 'feminine'. Some feminists in Japan have argued that Japanese national identity is constructed as a kind of 'feminine identity', in contrast to the US as stereotypically 'masculine'. This means that the onus is often placed on women to guarantee and protect authentic Japanese characteristics – such as *wa* – and to be blamed when things go awry.[53] Japanese psychoanalysis is thus navigating difficult political territory when it attempts to sum up what it is to be Japanese and to root that account in the relationship between mothers and children. How is one to account for political conflict when a new generation refuses to obey the meshwork of obligations that were supposed to enable consensus and healthy dependence?

Feminism has disturbed some traditional assumptions about authority and the place of '*ie*', but there are other more momentous political events that have been more disruptive, and they have impacted on the illusory but functional 'consensus' rebuilt during and after the US occupation. The first was a wave of student radicalism in the 1960s that outdid the movement in most other countries in its violence and impotence. There had already been mass protests from 1960 when several million people mobilized against the US-Japan Mutual Security Treaty Revision, but the *Zengakuren* student federation protests intensified violence not only against the universities and the state but also provoked deadly conflict within the movement.[54] Firebombs on campuses were accompanied by sectarian attacks, murders of political opponents on the left and then the formation of the Red Army (*Rengō Sekigun*) followed by a series of terrorist outrages; these events left a lasting disillusionment with radical politics among those who were involved.[55] An active left-wing movement organized around the Sanrizuka activities against Narita airport lasted until after the airport finally opened in 1978, but this protest saw six dead and 7,000 wounded.[56]

Doi's response was to emphasize collusion rather than conflict between the youth and their parents, and the problem lying at a more fundamental level than a mere generation gap; there was, he writes, '*amae* and the permitting of *amae*, with no feeling of paternal authority.'[57] But if there was, as he says in a later commentary on this analysis, 'nothing to convey a true sense of authority',[58] there were still appeals to their mothers to hear their protests; he interprets a placard raised at Tokyo University protests that read 'Don't stop us, Mother, the ginko [sic] trees are weeping' as indicating that 'the students felt that their mothers, if no one else would know how they felt.'[59]

The second major eruption of conflict, a second trauma that was to charge the earlier conflicts with an even greater intensity, was the sarin gas attack by the Aum Shinrikyō sect on five trains on the Tokyo underground in 1995. Some Western analysts have linked Aum with the earlier student movement protests, claiming to find in both 'struggles with *totalized group involvement* and ... *death centred macho*'.[60] Another response was provided by the popular novelist Murakami Haruki who published an extraordinary collection of narratives of people caught up in the gas attack together with reflections on how such episodes of violence in Japanese history are disowned and projected into others. Murakami's analysis itself employs quasi-psychoanalytic motifs to argue that the phenomenon of Aum was so disturbing because '[i]t shows us a distorted image of ourselves in a manner none of us could have foreseen'.[61]

For Kitayama 1995 marked a turning point, and the reasoning he employs here repeats and exemplifies the way in which childhood dependence and the enduring relation to mothers figures in the Japanese psychoanalytic imagination. At least in the student protests it was possible for Doi to detect an appeal to mothers. In stark contrast – a sharp break with the past – those who put the gas on the trains must have known that those they loved might possibly have been travelling that day. This is why it is so shocking and significant to psychoanalysts like Kitayama that it is no small exaggeration to say that 'they were killing their mothers'.[62]

Culture

The attention to structure – to the conditions that will give rise to certain forms of experience – makes Japanese psychoanalysis, and any psychoanalysis worth the name, unwilling to turn to underlying human nature or archetypal cosmic forces.[63] In this respect, representations of children and their underlying nature in Japan are already more congenial to psychoanalysis than popular representations in the West. One only has to compare *Lord of the Flies* – in which the children regress to barbarism and play out rituals of exclusion infused with Christian imagery, as if such predispositions bubbled away beneath the thin veneer of civilization – with Ōe's *Nip the Buds, Shoot the Kids*.[64] In Ōe's 1958 book the reformatory boys sent to a remote village during the war are clearly influenced at every point by the actions of adults, ranging from punishment to war, to the evacuation and to the response of the peasants. The options open to the kids are structured by an adult world, and so their actions throw light on social arrangements rather than bypassing and obscuring those arrangements with appeals to deeper more mysterious and immutable explanations.

This means that the interpretation of culture by Japanese psychoanalysts deals with material that is often more immediately amenable to analytic interpretation, the kind of interpretation that traces out structural conditions for experience. Kitayama's analysis of *ukiyoe* – 'pictures of the floating world' which are wood-block print representations of the relationship between mother and child from about 200 years ago – show, for example, 'joint attention' that facilitates certain kinds of emotional bonds.[65] This kind of developmental bond is studied and valued in Western studies, but Kitayama shows how Christian representations of Virgin and Child typically show more distance between the two, distance which may 'express individualism and the triangular situation involving the father in the West'.[66] It would seem that cultural representations then frame how mothers and children actually relate to one another.

Kitayama includes clinical case material in which a young woman analysand describes how she is labelled by her family as dependent; they tell her 'You are an Amaenbou (meaning a "child of Amae")'.[67] A relationship is then brought to light in which the mother as someone 'big' to whom this analysand would look for love is also for her now someone more fragile, and so 'she feels guilty for her poor mother becoming small and losing power'.[68] Kitayama then uses the relationship between dependence and size to explore the construction of Henry Moore sculptures (one of which – 'Draped reclining mother and baby' – stands in front of the station in Fukuoka). In a further elaboration of the motif 'don't look', he argues that the holes in these sculptures pull us toward 'the secrets of a woman's body'; 'Being invited to look into the secrets inside may lead us to the tragic revelation of something terrible, since it breaks the taboo against looking'.[69]

Western representations of Japan have often focussed on violent sexualized resistance to dependence, one notorious condensed image being the nationalist antics and ritualized suicide (*seppuku*) in 1970 of Mishima Yukio.[70] Some of these themes are tackled by the Japanese analysts using object relations theory to uncover pathological child-rearing practices that may have given rise to this suicide.[71] A contribution to the JPS anniversary volume, for example, describes how the grandmother of the young Mishima took him away from his mother and raised him on a bed in her sick-room until he was 12 years old until she became too sick to care for him and handed him back to his mother. A strictly regulated feeding schedule combined with restrictions on playing outside, and then only with girls selected by the grandmother, led to the development of 'a quite, obedient, sensitive, precociously intellectual child who had never expressed his feelings'. Feelings were, instead, in classic Winnicottian 'false self' fashion, concealed 'as if behind a Noh mask' (and Mishima is indeed well-known for his early book *Confessions of a Mask*, in which his homosexuality is explored).[72]

The representation of the grandmother thus assumes importance in the constellation of 'objects' that populate Mishima's internal world, but she is still not blamed for her actions, and the rest of the family is complicit in their relationship with her as a bad object that cannot be acknowledged as such:

> ...the badness of the parents in the sense that they could not have protected their son from the invasion of his grandmother was diminished by their becoming a victim together with their son. This situation will make it difficult for a child to develop the whole object relationships with the mother. This means that Mishima had been in the state of part object relationship throughout his life, splitting into the bad relationship with his grandmother and the good relationship with his mother, in which he cannot bear rage or hatred towards his mother... There was no bad person in this family. Consequently, Mishima could not find any channel for his aggressive discharge, except towards the objects in his fantasized world or himself (provoking suicidal wishes).[73]

Mishima always got his mother to read his writing, which functioned as an 'intermediate area' that was invaded and undermined by his literary success, and this resulted in an 'identity crisis' that was only resolved when he found a new intermediate area. This replacement for the writing read by his mother was a 'language of the flesh' in his concern with a muscular body, which itself collapsed as Mishima felt himself growing older and frailer and so he eventually led his own private army 'The Shield Society' to the Ichigaya base for the final act.[74]

Mishima's writing invites psychoanalytic interpretation, and raises a question about how far notions of unconscious fantasy and desire were available to him to make sense of his sexuality. Contemporary Japan is, perhaps, more infused with such notions, and some of the newer writing by young women indicates that psychoanalytic interpretations may be even more potent now. Kanehara Hitomi's prize-winning little book *Snakes and Earrings*, for example, is a best-seller that has the 19 year-old girl protagonist Lui work her way from getting pierced for over-sized earrings to masochistic sex relationships.[75] But even then there are reminders of relations of dependence in the midst of the violence. When one of her lovers bursts into tears, Lui experiences a temptation to allow him to amaeru to her, for her to be a mother to him, but she then draws back: 'Seeing him like that made me want to respond to his feelings, but whenever a tiny seed of hope took root in me and began to grow, it was always crushed by a heavy downpour of self-loathing'.[76]

Another prize-winner in the same genre is Akasaka Mari with her novel *Vibrator* following the journey of young bulimic woman who hears voices, and here the narrative is more explicitly therapeutic, involving something that we might even interpret as a 'corrective emotional experience'.[77] The young woman Rei tags along with a lorry driver, and there comes a point quite late-on in the book where she has become totally dependent on him; she takes the mike of the CB radio on the truck and can only come out with 'baby talk'.[78] This is quickly followed by an increasing urge to vomit and then a demand to her partner, 'beat me', but he does not; instead, he tells her 'I like you. I can't beat you'.[79] Soon after he allows her to drive the truck, and in this new-won emergent state of engagement with the world the voices disappear. Even as rebellious young women fight back, then, there appear to be resources to allow them to thrive that are culturally-located even at the same time as those resources owe much to the globalization of images of an independent self.

Folk

The JPS website characterizes psychoanalysis as a 'practice in which an analyst interacts with an analysand in a special way', and this practice enables the analysand to understand unconscious parts of themselves so that they will be 'free from captivity'.[80] To be qualified as a psychoanalyst, the site informs visitors, there is a 'basic academic and clinical requirement' that candidates are already 'a medical doctor and/or a clinical psychologist',[81] but it also then points out that psychoanalysis will not only benefit 'medical, psychological or social assistance professionals' and those in 'educational positions', but also 'those with creative careers, such as scholars and artists'; this is because through 'a search for the depth of oneself, creativity can gain depth, breadth and liveliness'. There is a pitch to a constituency that has always been important to psychoanalysis around the world, but here the appeal is made quite explicit: 'Minds which were becoming easily trapped during the pursuit of artistic or academic goals can regain some free space for creation'.

There are branches of the Society's Psychoanalytic Institute in Tokyo and Fukuoka, and there are around 20 candidates training at present, which is just less than the total number of full members. There are about the same number of full members listed, though some of these analysts are now quite old, and it seems that there are effectively 15 active full members; and this does not mean that they are full-time practising analysts.[82] There are 11 'training analysts' currently listed among these; in the IPA tradition a candidate is required to have analysis with a training analyst (which is a rule that some other psychoanalytic traditions reject on grounds of confidentially and institutional regulation of trainees). If one takes that into account, and we assume that analysands really are being seen for at least 'four times a week',[83] the number of people undergoing psychoanalysis must be very small. (This also explains why a number of the contributions to the JPS anniversary volume concern psychiatric classification, psychoanalytic psychotherapy, group psychotherapy, or weekly sessions of free association.)

Notwithstanding this, the tiny number of active practitioners does not at all give a measure of the impact of psychoanalysis. In fact, it has often been the case that the weight of psychoanalysis in a culture is in inverse proportion to those actually involved in clinical practice. This then raises a question about the degree to which Japanese psychoanalysts participate in the cultural processes they analyse. The answer is, quite a lot.

When the secretary of the JPS reports that a young woman who was referred to him 'looked happy to see me, a psychotherapist',[84] this is surely only the half of it, as can be easily seen if the name 'Osamu

Kitayama' is tapped into Google. What come up are masses of entries for CD listings rather than psychoanalysis, and this is because Kitayama has been famous for many years as a folk singer, often appearing with the band 'The Folk Crusaders'.[85] The music was designed to support protests against the US war in Vietnam, and there is a strong 'peace' theme running through many of the songs.[86] While some of the Japanese analysts do not seem sympathetic to radical politics,[87] there is a liberal or left ethos in the background of quite a few of those involved now in training the next generation.

Many practitioners of psychoanalysis in Japan inside and outside the JPS point to the increasing public profile of psychoanalytic arguments, even if the term 'psychoanalysis' or the name 'Freud' is not always directly mentioned. The writings of Murakami Haruki, for example, are evidence of a reworking of magical realist themes that are also attuned to the unconscious desires and fantasies of the protagonist.[88] Oedipal themes are even woven into the text of his books alongside other Western cultural material, sometimes explicitly, as in the prophecy one character repeats to another that 'Some day you will murder your father and be with your mother' in *Kafka on the Shore*.[89] The explorations of mourning and encounters with apparitions from the dead in the stories of Yoshimoto Banana are also compatible with psychoanalysis, at least laying the ground for people to make sense of their own experiences in therapeutic fashion.[90] Psychoanalysts in Japan often refer approvingly to these cultural expressions of interest in ideas about the unconscious, and those images of the self are necessary for psychoanalytic training organizations to thrive.

The *Nippon Seishin-Bunseki Kyokai* was established, the JPS website states, by 'Psychiatrist Heisaku Kosawa', 'the only Japanese who practiced psychoanalysis faithfully to his master Freud'.[91] The history of psychoanalysis practised in Japan has since, as we have seen, been characterized by attempts to turn it into something that is not only a Western import. However, this has been the trajectory of many imported cultural practices concerned with transformations in subjectivity. It is sometimes said, for example, that while Murakami is a popular Japanese novelist, his writing actually borrows the form of the US novelists – Scott Fitzgerald, Capote, Irving, Carver – he has translated. Those influences are much more apparent in his first book *Hear the Wind Sing*, and there is an intriguing account of the protagonist as a boy being taken to a stupid psychologist; he tells the boy a story about a billy goat with a heavy gold watch round his neck that does not work who is brought a brand-new watch for his birthday by a rabbit, which makes the billy goat very happy, and then comes the moral, the psychologist's interpretation to the boy: 'You are the billy goat, and I am the rabbit and the watch is your mind.'[92]

The quasi-psychoanalytic diagnosis Murakami offers of the Japanese psyche as a kind of beautiful soul that refuses to own up to its own involvement in the Aum underground attacks is deliberately linked by him to his explorations of the 'underworld' disturbed in earlier novels.[93] Perhaps it is possible to absorb the diagnosis because it is embedded in culturally-available representations of the self and the unconscious and also because he is speaking from somewhere on the margins, inside yet at the edge of Japanese culture. Murakami's first successful novel, readers will know, was published after he spent a time running his own jazz club in Tokyo.[94] In similar vein, what is striking to a western audience for 'The Folk Crusaders' will be not so much that it is in Japanese, different, but that the form of the music – cadences, choruses, crescendos – is so typically recognizable as western folk. The formal structure of the music thus signifies something not quite Japanese at the same time as it signifies something counter-cultural, and possibly radical in Japan.

Psychoanalysis is therefore set against a background of cultural, and counter-cultural, interest in popular Freudian imagery combined with Japanese motifs relayed through folk legend. Allusions to cultural heritage then become worked into accounts of the self that draw on quite different motifs. One significant example of the way the contradiction between stories of development of the self from the past and present coexist is in the representations of the Ajase story. In the original Indian story Ajase does try to kill his father, imprisoning him so that he will starve to death. Ajase's mother, Queen Idaike, secretly takes food to the king, which enrages Ajase, who then develops the abscesses that express his guilt.[95] Kitayama comments upon this as follows:

> Although Ajase does not kill his mother, she is so devoted that she is likely to kill herself for her child. The expression 'killing oneself' in everyday Japanese is a metaphor which refers to self-sacrifice, and its literal meaning seems worth analysing. It seems to me that the child's guilt feeling is generated not only by the infantile 'killing' demand but also through the self-sacrificing mother who tends to kill or hurt herself, feeling sorry for the child she so deeply loves. She cannot stop it for 'killing herself' can be amusing as well as exhausting. She is usually conscious and even proud of this self-

> injuring behaviour or self-devaluation and its hidden masochistic fantasy, which she may hide from those she takes care of.[96]

It seems that it is the function of the myth that is most important to Kitayama and JPS analysts before him, and here insofar as it aids psychoanalytic interpretation of patterns in Japanese culture. Psychoanalysis itself has been maintained as a theoretical system that has been modified, the most dramatic transformation here being not so much the introduction of specific cultural contents from local folk tales as a shift from a triangular (Oedipal) childhood structure to a 'two body' conception to describe the relationship between mother and child. This body modification has still, nonetheless, insisted on its allegiance to Freud and this has resuscitated the role of the mother in the JPS. A British psychoanalytic Freud that throws into question the importance of the father in the development of an individual subject has come to shape psychoanalysis on the other side of the world. But, as one Japanese analyst commented when questioned about the links the JPS has with a European tradition of thought, is it really the case that Freud himself was European?[97]

3

Civilization and its Contents: 'Buddhistic cyberspace in Kyoto'

Transformations in cultural identity in Japan – rapid economic growth and semiotic mutation as rapid industrialization and technological expertise displaced and submerged apparently ancient traditions – have been accompanied by a questioning of this identity, and then the arrival of a type of psychoanalysis that questions identity as such. Lacanian psychoanalysis, working with a distinctive notion of the unconscious structured like a language, provides a paradoxical resource to analyse a people who are assumed to speak a language that renders them, it is said, 'unanalysable'. But the paradoxes in this ostensibly most modern version of psychoanalysis also permit an unravelling of the self that eventually coincides with the very 'emptiness' that venerable forms of Buddhism aimed at. This psychoanalysis from France is designed to operate on the kind of individual subject and knowledge produced by scientific revolutions, but it also addresses forms of rationality and irrationality that call for another concept of subjective truth altogether. On the one side this psychoanalysis can be used to interpret the forms of identity that tie young alienated men to technology, and it seems to speak their language. On the other side it provides a way of conceptualizing new eroticized identities, new modes of being feminine in Japan.

Identification

Japanese analysts have often questioned the assumption that they should aim to become the same as the leading figures from European psychoanalysis they admired, as if the transmission of the theory into another culture should require some form of identification. There is an additional unpleasant association to such a notion of identification when we are considering Japanese psychoanalysis, for Freud's own ideas about identification were elaborated in the context of work on mass psychology.[1]

Each member of a group of any kind, Freud argued, identifies in their ego with the ego of other members of the group, and what they then have in common is a leader or an abstract 'leading idea' that they have each put in the place of their 'ego-ideal'. The ego-ideal here can be seen as a fore-runner of what Freud was later to refer to as the 'super-ego', though it also has a more positive role than the purely punitive function with which the super-ego is usually associated.[2] The ego-ideal can also be seen as the heir to infantile narcissism – the love for oneself grounded in the illusion that child and mother were once fused together – which is how some strands of IPA psychoanalysis in France have maintained it as something conceptually distinct from the super-ego (which is treated as heir to the Oedipus complex).[3] What would be worse than to see Japanese followers of Freud falling in line with a kind of mass psychology in which they were simply putting him in the place of their ego-ideal?

France was the place where one of most bitter drawn-out splits in the psychoanalytic movement took place, eventually culminating in the 'excommunication' of Jacques Lacan in 1963.[4] The theoretical and clinical stakes of the dispute could be said to turn around the question of identification. Lacan and his followers argued that US-based ego psychology (of which one of the leading figures, Rudolph Loewenstein, was once Lacan's own analyst) aims to bring about identification between the ego of the analysand and ego of the analyst. If the analyst is well-analysed, the reasoning goes, then their perception of reality would surely already be cleansed of illusion and their ego should provide a perfectly good model for someone who wanted to become a healthy well-adapted citizen like them. Against this, Lacan saw the end of analysis as entailing 'absolute difference' – new freedom of movement in the 'symbolic' register – and identification is thus seen as a function of the 'imaginary' register that lures the subject into the comforting idea that they do indeed have a self-contained 'identity'.[5]

Little wonder that Lacan was sympathetic to Klein's descriptions of unconscious fantasy that tore the infant's mind into warring part-objects and in which 'projective identification' was a frightening and inescapable part of human experience; 'madness' lies at the heart of every individual subject. And Klein actually lies at the origin of Lacanian psychoanalysis in Japan. Shingu Kazushige, the author of the 1995 best-selling and widest-read introduction to Lacan's work in

Japanese, describes his own strange trajectory from Klein to Lacan through an encounter with a woman patient during the course of his work as a psychiatrist. At that time Shingu was planning to go to England to study Kleinian psychoanalysis, and the woman was studying French. By the end of her treatment she had switched to English literary theory, and in this '*mutual* psychoanalysis' (as he puts it) Shingu changed places with her to learn about French psychoanalysis, as if her 'madness' was also to become the 'cause' of Shingu's book on Lacan's psychoanalysis *Rakan no Seishin-Bunseki*.[6]

Shingu introduces the Lacanian notion of the 'desire of the Other' to explain how the interests of each partner had swapped places. As with object relations theory, and in line with Freud's own account, each individual's 'desire' is for another desire – we desire that an other desire us – and it is conditioned by another desire, is derived from the desire of the first significant other. The relation between this doctor and his patient had thus introduced a desire for Lacan into Japan:

> To use an old psychoanalytic term, what happened to us could also be called an exchange of 'ego ideals'. Ideas like 'France' or 'England', which have to some degree been symbolized, can include within them a mark that guides the subject along its path to socialization. This is the ego ideal, and it is what we had exchanged between us. There is a very close relation between the desire of the Other and the ego ideal, and it is because we carry the desire of the Other that we end up on the wild goose chase for an abstract ideal in the first place. The desiring heart, to some extent, already belongs to the other.[7]

Psychoanalysis in Lacan's work – a tradition that now informs the practice of most analysts outside the English-speaking world – aims to 'return to Freud' by reading it through a series of innovative concepts. These include the registers of the 'symbolic' (into which the individual is inducted as they learn to speak), the 'imaginary' (an illusory channel of unmediated communication between self and other) and the 'real'.[8] This 'real' dimension is, as Shingu points out, 'impossible' – a 'spatial paradox' as he puts it – and Lacan treats objects of fantasy as impossible objects that he defines as objects of the other or '*objets petit a*'.[9] Shingu focuses on the object of the other – *objet petit a* – and how it might be specified logically rather than experientially in his introduction to Lacan's ideas in Japan, translated into English with the title *Being Irrational: Lacan, the Objet a, and the Golden Mean*.[10]

Just as US analysts like Moloney had tried to fathom the mentality of the Japanese and puzzled over the role psychoanalysis might play in such a completely different culture, so Lacan had things to say about the uptake of his ideas in Japan. He visited Japan twice and wrote a special preface to the 1972 Japanese translation of his writings in which he commented on the relevance of psychoanalysis in that culture.[11] Like other French structuralist intellectuals who were fascinated by the exotic character of this place as an 'empire of signs',[12] Lacan was not at all negative about Japan. Precisely the reverse, for here was a living laboratory space in which it might be possible to identify the distinctive characteristics of language that rendered psychoanalysis possible in the first place. Psychoanalysis as a talking cure relies on a theory of language and upon the connection that a speaking subject makes between 'word presentations' that structure conscious thought and 'thing presentations' that form the contents of the unconscious. For Lacan, these 'thing presentations' are still organized in such a way that the unconscious is structured like a language.[13] Perhaps Lacanian psychoanalysis would flower in Japan because the relationship between words and things was different here, and to say that psychoanalysis was therefore impossible would be a way of remaining true to it as something that had often already characterized itself as an 'impossible profession'.[14]

Language

A paradox riddling psychoanalysis imported into Japan is that the theoretical framework is often used to interpret a people who are supposed to be 'unanalysable'. Lacan's comments on psychoanalysis in Japan, particularly in his preface to the Japanese edition of his *Écrits*, can be read as making of Japan once again a limit-case in which psychoanalysis breaks down, in which it is as if psychoanalysis in Japan is 'neither possible nor necessary'.[15] Here it seems that Lacan's interest is in the 'materialist dimension' of the Japanese language, in which the Chinese *kanji* characters (which are both ideograms and phonograms as components of the Japanese writing system) are read both phonetically (*on-yomi*, with sounds imitating the original Chinese) and semantically (*kun-yomi*, with Japanese sounds layered into the character).[16]

For example, the word 'Lacan' is represented in Japanese script using *katakana* (one of the scripts used for transliterating foreign loan words, a script that runs alongside the *kanji* characters). Japanese names, however, are written in *kanji*, and this means that when someone says their name, their interlocutor will also want to know how it is written – what the *kanji* is – so that the meaning of it can be grasped. If there is no clear link established between the sound and the *kanji* there is an ambiguity, and this ambiguity is the source of refined punning in poetic forms like *haiku*. So, when 'Lacan' is given a *kanji* script notation in some of the playful internal discussions among Lacanians, this will be one that has a close enough conventional sound to match the sound that is usually captured in *katakana*. One favourite way, not at all the only way, of representing 'Lacan' is with the *kanji* that signify 'Buddhist master'. The important point here is that there is an indeterminacy of meaning built into the operation of the script, and the Japanese subject oscillates between the 'word' (the stuff of consciousness) and the 'image' (the stuff of the unconscious).

As Shingu puts it, 'the Japanese language balances between *on-yomi* and *kun-yomi* (two ways of reading and pronouncing the ideographic characters, or *kanji*, of written Japanese)'.[17] This then 'frustrates the process of true repression' and the Japanese subject 'is born and exists in a state of being pinched between these two ways of reading and pronouncing.' And there is more:[18]

> Divided not only in speech and writing, the Japanese subject is fragmented in the formality system of the Japanese language, in which a variety of modal expressions indicate social situation, and grammar requires different declensions according to these modalities; there are also multiple terms for the first-, second-, and third-person pronouns. Notwithstanding this fragmentation, or more correctly, owing to it, the Japanese subject maintains unity through a principle of constellation: the Japanese see themselves reflected in the social-institutional hierarchy, which they perceive as being as eternal as the celestial bodies. Thus, the Japanese seem to be exempt from the anxiety of aphanisis [annihilation of self][19] that arises at certain times in life. For such people, psychoanalysis is neither necessary nor possible.[20]

One consequence of this division – a double inscription of subjectivity in ways of reading the Chinese *kanji* characters – is that the unconscious, if it is to be treated as a system of hieroglyphs (as Freud did in his conception of it as a system of 'thing presentations'), is also viewed as available to conscious awareness. The element of signification that should be repressed – through 'primal repression' that constitutes the relationship between consciousness and the unconscious – at the very moment the subject starts to speak is exposed, public, and is present to consciousness. If this is so then we might also expect that what is the case for 'psychotics' (as defined in Lacanese) would also be the case for the Japanese, that psychoanalysis as such is impossible; that 'Japanese *écriture* could thus be seen as a historical product of the Lacanian "foreclosure" of primal repression'.[21]

Lacan did, around the same time as writing the preface, describe Japanese as 'the perpetual translation of the events of language', and he contrasted this view of an 'empire of semblances' with Roland Barthes' account of Japan as an 'empire of signs', arguing that for the Japanese 'there is nothing to defend against the repressed, because the repressed finds itself lodged in this reference to the letter'.[22] Perhaps this proposition does then indeed provide warrant for the claim that 'their writing system does not make room for the installation of primordial identification'.[23] But whether psychoanalysis in Japan is impossible and unnecessary or not is another matter.

On this point Lacan, again in the preface to the Japanese translation of his writing, tentatively makes a more nuanced claim that for those who inhabit the Japanese language there may not be a need for psychoanalysis save to regularize relations with the machinery of their enjoyment.[24] It is possible to read this statement as a reiteration of the notorious US-American claim by Moloney 20 years earlier that psychoanalysis in Japan must actually necessarily be concerned primarily with adjustment to be possible as a culturally-appropriate clinical practice. At the very least, the question of translation of psychoanalytic concepts from the West (whether from German or English, or now from French) is intimately bound up with the internal process of translation from script to script, and within the forms of script used for speaking and writing.

A crucial aspect of the directly visible characteristic of writing in *kanji*, Shingu argues is the way that certain traits – what Lacan described as the 'unary traits' – come to signify the subject. The particular positioning of the Japanese subject in relation to the characters is 'manifested in the lines (*traits*) of Japanese orthography', and so 'Japanese subjects are visible to themselves in the form of their written characters'.[25] Nevertheless, Shingu argues, it is still possible to discover certain 'traits' that do signify the Japanese to themselves, and these are traits which also enable them to find a place from which to view who they are. One way of characterizing the 'ego-ideal' is to say that it is the 'ideal' point from which we would like to be looked at, the point from which we are loveable (and the 'ideal-ego' is the point which we try to occupy to nestle into that loving gaze). Here Shingu turns to Barthes' observations in one of his little essays on the line that defines the shape of the Japanese eye.[26] This line, Shingu argues, 'appears on the faces of the Japanese, foreigners to Barthes, but is a place from which he can behold himself'.[27] Such a trait, a position with which we identify and from which we become aware of ourselves is something that was noticed by a foreigner in this case, but a trait of this kind is a 'structural necessity for humans' and when Japanese experience that 'foreignness' themselves, then analysis is put on the agenda.

This 'foreignness' which provokes questions about the nature of personal and cultural identity is not resolved by any simple identification with the trait, but it should open the way to 'absolute difference', precisely that by which Lacanians define the end of analysis. In Lacanian analysis everything that is solid melts into air and all marks of a substantial identity and fixed objects of desire are revealed to be fantasy constructions. The key lesson from Lacan in this account is that desire itself is illusory,[28] and this lesson has profound implications for psychoanalysis and for the role of the analyst. If Shingu is right, then 'the subject who "wants" to teach this truth must himself be elided as an illusion, but just before vanishing can appear as an object of desire for others'.[29] The relationship between analysand and analyst is therefore impossible, and this is why the analyst functions in the place of *objet petit a*. Lacan himself often addressed the impossible nature of psychoanalysis, and not only for the Japanese.[30] Perhaps it is impossible for the Japanese not because they cannot undertake analysis that will lead them to realize that the seemingly substantial objects that structure their lives do not exist, but because they have already absorbed this lesson of analysis and it is therefore simply unnecessary to them.

Nothing

A Japanese Lacanian visiting Ireland encountered a Buddhist riddle: What is it, a small boy asked him, that you can eat, that the poor have, that the rich do not want, and that is more powerful than God? Lacanian psychoanalysts and their analysands arrive at the same answer as they systematically desubstantialize every single Freudian concept or come to realize that the *objet petit a* that they circle around was constituted by them and amounts at the end of analysis to nothing. This nothing is also, as other Japanese Lacanians have pointed out, what differentiates Kleinian analysts who search for substantial objects and find them in the mother's body from analysts attending to the kind of space which a shape encloses a particular kind of absence.[31]

Ultimate reality in Buddhism is not 'God' or 'being' or 'substance' of any kind, but *śūnyatā*, which is often translated as 'emptiness', but the process of arriving at such emptiness is easier said than done (and not even easy to speak of). Like psychoanalysis, which is interminable because the subject is compelled to repeat the reification of categories and objects that they desire as they must still speak a language outside the language that is necessarily saturated with reference to such principles,[32] the attempt to attain emptiness of self never ends. This *śūnyatā* is emptiness that 'itself must be emptied by rejecting any attachment to emptiness' for it is 'a dynamic function of emptying everything, including itself'.[33] There are signs for some outsiders that this concern with nothing is not confined to the intricacies of Japanese Buddhism but is itself a function of Japanese culture.

Roland Barthes, in one of the essays on bowing in his little book on Japan, *Empire of Signs*, notes that there are certain ontological assumptions about the nature of a person in the West that call for specific rituals of recognition: 'Topologically', he writes, 'Western man is reputed to be a double, composed of a social, factitious, false "outside" and of a personal, authentic, "inside" (the site of divine communication)', and so a person is a site 'girdled, closed by a social envelope'.[34] Bowing in Japan does not, he argues, call into play the motifs of condescension and humiliation that the Westerner attributes to those who bow and those who are bowed to, for it is an empty form rather than being, as it is in the West, a sign of communication between 'two personal empires (each ruling over its Ego, the little realm of which it holds the "key")'.[35] And such forms that operate as signs, functioning as such in relation to each other, are to be found everywhere, Barthes claims; so in the essay on packages he comments:

> ...there is in Japan a profusion of what we might call: the instruments of transport; they are of all kinds, of all shapes, of all substances: packages, pouches, sacks, valises, linen wrappings (the *fujo*, a peasant handkerchief or scarf in which the thing is wrapped), every citizen in the street has some sort of bundle, an empty sign, energetically protected, vigorously transported, as if the finish, the framing, the hallucinatory outline which establishes the Japanese object destined it to a generalised transport. The richness of the thing and the profundity of meaning are discharged only at the price of a triple quality imposed on all fabricated objects: that they be precise, mobile, and empty.[36]

Japan was very heaven for French structuralists; for it seemed that here explanation could really proceed with reference to organizing principles, formal properties, rather than with reference to particular entities inside or underneath what could be observed.[37] Writers like Barthes were taken with what was most ancient about Japan, while more recently the Lacanian anti-psychiatrist Félix Guattari became fascinated by the construction of forms of subjectivity in the advanced technological spaces of modern Japan.[38] Karatani Kōjin, a political theorist who has engaged with Western structuralist and 'post-structuralist' arguments, provides a critical twist to this fascination of Western writers with 'nothingness' in Japan, arguing that the fact that the 'self' did not exist in Japan was crucial to it becoming 'a cutting-edge super-Western consumer and information society'; Indeed, Karatani notes, 'there was no self (subject) or identity, but there was a predicative identity with the capacity to assimilate anything without incurring any shock or giving rise to any confusion'.[39] It is a truism, the worn-coin of cliché mobilized by Western observers, that Japan is simultaneously older and newer than many other cultures.[40] Some Lacanians in Japan do work theoretically at the intersection between tradition and technology, and Buddhism here once again holds the key to a link that locks the two together.

Shingu guided us, his visitors, around more ancient layers of Kyoto and explained elements of Buddhism and Japanese mythology. The tour began with a sheet of paper he had prepared that had the heading 'Buddhistic cyberspace in Kyoto', but it soon became clear that the 'cyberspace' to be explored was really spiritual space. This 'spiritual' dimension is very different from that of the Jungian 'Kyoto school' (we will meet in the next chapter), however, and the relationship that a mortal being has with a dimension beyond physical death draws on Buddhism in such a way as to retain the 'atheist' stance of psychoanalysis.[41] Reference to concepts that at first seemed to be from modern psychiatry, such as 'metempsychosis', turned out to be at root spiritual. As his leaflet explained, '[m]etempsychosis is a fundamental pain for all beings and the emancipation from it is *jōbutsu* (becoming Buddha),' and then continued that '[i]n order to do *jōbutsu*, we need the final enlightenment (truth) through the power of Buddha. Nehan (nirvana) is the place beyond metempsychosis'. The tour also included visits to the district of Kyoto inhabited by Geisha, where the signs on the lanterns outside the houses where they worked comprised three inter-locking circles; here, Shingu pointed out, was Lacan's Borromean knot, a figure often employed to indicate the intersection between the orders of symbolic, imaginary and real.

Shingu described how Buddhism in medieval Japan was underpinned by belief in the agony of transmigration through six realms, which include the realm of *Gaki* where people have been turned into demons. In Kyoto today 'Brocade Street' (also known as 'the stomach of Kyoto') is the name given to a place that was once covered with excrement from *gakis*, but which appeared at the time to come from Seitoku, a thirteenth-century bulimic monk who was later revered as a saint (but the emperor decided that to call that place 'Shit Street' would have been a bit unseemly). Today on that street vegetables and *miso* (soybean paste), as would have been eaten by the saint, are still sold and a popular current saying has it that failure to differentiate is 'to confuse *miso* and shit'. The past is still present, then, and can be interpreted employing psychoanalytic themes of mourning, which typically proceeds by way of forms of 'oral introjection', and through this interpretation it is possible to see how traditional Freudian categories are also still alive in the newer Lacanian versions of psychoanalysis.[42]

These accounts do not, of course, need to be taken literally. Psychoanalytically-speaking they symbolize through use of metaphor and conventional imagery deeper themes about origins and loss, and in Lacanian psychoanalysis there are theoretical resources to comprehend how 'truth' operates on different levels which have some correspondence with Buddhism. In Buddhism there are two levels of truth; representations of transmigration (or *samsāra*) operate as forms of 'conventional truth' but it is necessary to go beyond attachment to the realm of transmigration to arrive at 'ultimate truth'; 'In this detachment, the trans-samsāric realm is opened up, and ultimate truth is fully realized'.[43] This is rather similar to the distinction Lacan makes between the speech of a 'subject of a statement', in which discourse produced may or may not be conventionally or empirically true, and that speech which appears in analysis as the 'subject of the enunciation' in which the process of speaking coincides with what is spoken about as the 'truth of the subject'. The differentiation between these two forms of truth is both logical and experiential. Here the ultimate truth of the subject entails detachment and expresses *nothing*.[44]

Logic

The 'experience' that someone has of going through psychoanalysis is not sufficient to relieve them of their attachment to their fantasy objects or to desire. The process of 'working through' involves tracing through the logic of the unconscious choices that led to an individual subject becoming who they are, and the most that can be hoped for is that there might be a different relation formed with objects that will provide more freedom of movement. One might connect this conception of analysis with the discussion of the concept *en* in the JPS anniversary volume.[45] The term *en* (as 'relation) is often connected in everyday speech with *in* (as 'cause'), and so the word *innen* which combines the two 'represents a way of understanding one's own fate in one breath', and so there is a close link between this concept, a Lacanian logic of unravelling relations of cause and effect in psychoanalysis, and Buddhism; 'The familiar Buddhist dictum is that our sufferings will disappear when we comprehend the causal relationship – innen – of what we are'.[46]

This does not, however, mean that Lacanian psychoanalysis can be reduced to commonsense, and there are important respects in which it defies everyday understanding of the self. For example, in popularized Buddhism in Japan ordinary people were encouraged to believe in an afterlife, tenets of Buddhism as if it were a religious belief system to subscribe to that contrasted with authentic Buddhist thought which maintained that an acceptance of death in that 'afterlife' should precede the physical death of the individual in this early life as a condition of enlightenment. In like fashion, Lacan can be interpreted – and is interpreted thus in Japanese psychoanalytic commentary – to be arguing that it is acceptance of 'symbolic' death as the subject gives up attachment to their objects of fantasy and elements of their identity that must precede and is the condition for a peaceful physical death.[47] Symbolization in Lacanian analysis is not primarily experiential or intuitive, and the logic of psychoanalysis is predicated on the existence of a rational subject who is divided, who has pushed away what then appears to them to be things that are 'irrational'. As Shingu puts it, 'At a certain point in the history of science, then, the human subject thus conceived of an apparatus known as psychoanalysis in order that it might find itself in the form of the *objet a*'.[48]

We can go further than this, to say that if there was no history of science there would be no history of psychoanalysis, that 'psychoanalysis was not possible before the advent of the discourse of science'.[49] There are consequences of this argument for the way we use logic in psychoanalytic theory; if 'science assumes that there exists in the world the signifier which means nothing – and for nobody', which is why psychoanalysis is the only practice that could truly be called atheist, then this takes us well away from the search for any intuitively-right harmonic unity of things.[50] There are two aspects of psychoanalysis that call upon logic that are relevant here; some notion of 'ratio' through which the human subject is symbolically mapped (and maps themselves through analysis), and some notion of 'disjunction' which permits the mediated sense of self that facilitates the self-questioning that psychoanalysis requires.

It is through the process of becoming Other that we meet the *objet a*, and it is this object around which Shingu's introduction to Lacan for a Japanese audience revolves; '*object a* is the support that is necessitated when I comes to see itself from a transcendental perspective'.[51] But there is a specific quality of the relation of the I to the *objet a* that is also the relation of the Other to the I, and this relation is something that is reiterated time and again through the course of his book; 'the *objet a* thus expresses the value of the I that thinks it is human, seen from the viewpoint of the One'.[52] The relation is expressed through the 'golden mean', or what Lacan fleetingly refers to as 'a basis for this little *a*', 'the irrational number known as the golden number'.[53] For Shingu, then, the equation that is used to calculate the golden mean is 'also the equation of the symbolization process',[54] and 'the Symbolic includes within itself the golden mean, as the logical end-point of the extension *ad infinitum* of reflexive selfhood'.[55] It is the golden mean that provides the compass for Shingu's book, and which allows him to place each of the elements into a rather neat relationship with each other, to the point, for example, where it can be used to describe religious experience: 'at the moment when I perceives the *objet a* in its neighbour, I itself is seeing its I with the eyes of God'.[56]

The necessary mediation that makes self-awareness possible, the ability to step back and reflect upon oneself, is crucial to psychoanalysis. However, Shingu argues that while this is indeed an accomplishment of scientific rationality, this 'self-containing' structure of the mind – that we are simultaneously subject and object, container and contained – is a point where the modern subject of science meets the much older subject of Japanese spiritual reflective practice (and in reading this account we must remember that the Oedipus complex for Lacanians means the entry into symbolic as the child learns to speak and acknowledge the existence of others outside the 'imaginary' dual relationship between itself and its mother):

> ...traditional Buddhism joins Lacanian psychoanalysis in viewing the human mind as inseminated with madness. For Lacan, the inception of human existence occurs not at biological birth, but rather at the introduction of signifier into subject with the onset of the Oedipus complex. In my opinion, what occurs at this period of

> human development is equivalent to the construction of the self-containing structure. Owing to the signifier, the subject comes to comprehend whatever goes on in the mind in terms of language. The innovative horizon of language informs the subject with the characteristically dual-natured self-containing structure. It renders the subject of language omnipotent, and the subject of existence abject.[57]

There is a complex history to the arrival and development of Buddhism in Japan that has left its traces in the way that Buddhist myth might come to operate in psychoanalytic interpretation. These cultural-historical traces will govern the logic of enlightenment just as surely as will the personal-historical background of an individual undergoing psychoanalysis. Indeed, it is the recognition that culture and personality are intertwined in the history of the individual subject and the history of Japan that has powered debates over the role of Buddhist myths in psychoanalytic theory.

This history bears on the relation of the Japanese subject to language. To briefly anticipate the argument to be spelt out in more detail in the next chapter, the arrival of *kanji* characters from China via Korea (for many years occupied by Japan, during which time the Korean language was prohibited by the authorities) poses a problem in which the individual subject who uses the language 'is represented by a foreign signifier'. One response to this perceived tyranny of *kanji* was the development of '*kana*' script in which calligraphic writing displayed the skill of the Japanese, particularly the aristocracy; this writing of beautiful letters has been referred to as 'a triumph of the parochial individual subject over the universal system of signifiers'.[58]

There is another dimension to the structures of power relayed through the use of Buddhist mythology and the relation of the subject to language that is as important as the colonial relationship; that is, the question of gender. In spoken Japanese there is an elaborate system of honorific terms for the self and other so that, in addition to class status hierarchies being represented by the different forms of 'I' that are used by the speaker, different linguist forms were once commonly used by men and women. Although many of these forms have now fallen into disuse, there is a revival of certain terms for the self that mark class status and gender differences.[59] The formulation '*watashi wa*' to define oneself, for example, is the preferred one for girls and adults, and boys will have to abandon the distinctive formulation they used to use and might still use informally, which is *'boku wa'*; this means that as a boy becomes an adult he must in some sense mark himself as 'feminine' when he refers to himself. One prominent psychoanalytic psychotherapist told us of the quite conscious choice he had to make not to say *'washi wa'* (a particularly macho form) and to accept that he must say *'watashi wa'* as a kind of 'castration' he had to undergo in order to be an adult. Other male psychotherapists told us that they might still say *'boku wa'* to their wives at home, but in formal interaction they had to say *'watashi wa'* (and so the feminization of every Japanese of whatever sex is accomplished in public space). Some young women transgress these rules now by using the formulation *'boku wa'*, and one feminist therapist told us that she had come across this among clients, but had not interpreted it.[60]

In writing the more patriotic genuinely Japanese 'Kana' script was known as *Onna-de*, or 'women's hand', which poses a problem for the gender identity of those Japanese keen to assert themselves against a foreign language that they may then feel emasculates them. The ambiguity in forms of reading and pronunciation – between *on-yomi* and *kun-yomi* – is therefore only one aspect of the problematic relationship the Japanese subject has to the signifier. A human subject, whether she or he likes it or not, is always sexed. A crucial disjunction in Lacanian psychoanalysis is summed up by Lacan's statement that 'there's no such thing as a sexual relationship',[61] and Shingu cites this Lacanian dictum in order to lay bare 'an ontology lodged at the heart of the Oedipal subject'.[62] A translator's footnote in the book points out that the 'relation' or '*rapport*' that Lacan is referring to also evokes the 'ratio' or 'mathematical constant' that we might suppose to exist in nature.[63]

There is a close connection between the discussions of the 'ratio' of sex and that of nature in Lacan's work; for example, he anticipates his later well-known formulation about the impossibility of a sexual relationship with the statement that 'there is no place possible in a mythical union defined as sexual between man and woman',[64] and shortly afterwards, in the same session, he points out apropos the 'proportional mean' that appears in such mathematical forms as the Fibonacci series that there appears to be 'some kind of intuitive harmony', and then 'a romanticism that still continues to call it the golden number and wears itself out finding it on the surface of everything'.[65] If there is some powerful mathematical attraction to this ratio, then, it needs to be treated not as the site of harmonic resolution of difference but as the ideal point which will be impossible to attain. This tension is captured in Shingu's comment that 'the symbolization process also holds out the sweet promise that one day the self will be expressed as one, fixed, beautiful number – the golden mean – somewhere on the far side of infinity'.[66]

The 'golden mean' in Shingu's reading of Lacan for a Japanese audience thus provides a way of conceptualizing symbolic mediation necessary for a subject to locate themselves in relation to others and an account of how an external vantage point is developed so that the subject may reflect upon who they are. The 'passion' of language is something that makes us human, but it is also something that we suffer. For Lacanians this alienating function of language enables us to think, but it also introduces a technology of communication that sabotages the meaning we would like to share with others. Changes in society invariably open up and close down means of communication and provoke new fantasies by which we can escape the predicament we face as speaking beings. New technologies of the self in Japan, as we shall see, open up new forms of alienation and new disjunctions between men and women.

Otaku

The sexual landscape of youth in Japan has been transformed by new technologies, and the idea that it might now make sense to speak of 'Buddhistic cyberspace in Kyoto' must also be seen in the context of changes in the old 'electric town' district of Akihabara in the capital. Tokyo has undergone a dramatic semiotic revolution that impacts on the organization of public space and of individual subjectivity, and Lacanian psychoanalysis in Japan has provided one of the theoretical resources to conceptualize this revolution. One focus has been on the 'Otaku'. The word 'otaku' was 'originally an overpolite salutation used by housewives to mean "you and yours"', and was first used by a journalist in 1983 to describe the *otaku-zoku* (otaku tribe), who avidly consumed and circulated *anime* and *manga* comics, computer games, films and models.[67] The term became more widespread after the arrest in 1989 of a young man for serial murder and cannibalism; his collection of otaku comics and videos drew attention to 'otaku culture' as a problem. The label is supposed to capture the 'distant' character traits of *anime* fans, and the psychiatrist Saito Tamaki has become well-known for offering a defence of the otaku, using some Lacanian concepts to characterize them.

Otaku imagery in *anime* is dependent on computer graphics, even when the representations are hand-drawn, and it would be possible to argue that otaku-culture is a new 'cyber-culture' that hosts a new 'cyberpsychology'. The peculiar modes of interaction that take place in multi-user domains and in virtual worlds – some of which now have millions of inhabitants worldwide – call upon cognitive and emotional structures that are quite different from those studied by real-world psychologists. Cyberspace is a new anthropological space that illustrates the plasticity of human subjectivity and the necessary role of 'technology' in culture.[68] The impact of new technologies upon psychotherapy is immediately apparent in the key metaphors for networks of relationships that are used by 'group analysts' in Japan. While the concept of the 'matrix' in western Europe (where group analysis as a specific therapeutic modality developed) often evokes organic images of the womb and the mother by virtue of the semantic resonances with its Latin language roots), in Japan the first associations in therapy groups to the term 'matrix' are to the science fiction film series, and so to virtual worlds that offer a semblance of reality that may or may not be accurate.[69] There is also an uncanny repetition of the transmission of cultural forms into Japan from neighbouring states; now it is South Korea that has been in the forefront of building online otaku communities, with even some consequences for political processes, and these developments are now being replicated in Japan.[70]

The Japanese pavilion of the 2004 Venice Biennale, a prestigious architectural exhibition, was devoted to otaku culture, and here the impact of cyberspace on the real-world city-space was emphasized. The subtitle of the 'Otaku' exhibition spelt out the conceptual links in the rubric 'persona=space=city'. There it was claimed that the shopfronts of Akihabara have become 'otaku shrines' and that otaku icons are now 'determinants of the urban fabric'; 'Like wounded souls drawn together by a strange similitude of loss, the otaku converged on Akihabara'.[71] In this way we can see how '[n]et-based interest communities are restructuring real places'; it is not so much that cyberspace is replicating the city, rather that 'the city has begun to mimic cyberspace'.[72]

Otaku culture is sometimes characterized as comprising young people who retreat into technological imagery and lack social skills. However, even those who acknowledge that '*manga* is a low-cost, solitary expression requiring only minimal equipment' also describe vast networks of enthusiasts for the form; there is mass-participation in the '*dōjinshi*' self-produced fanzine circles, of which there are about a hundred-thousand throughout Japan.[73] Saito's description of otaku in a contribution to the Venice Biennale exhibition catalogue is as follows:

> ...otaku remain profoundly attached to their chosen 'objects of transference' well past adolescence into adulthood. Such behaviour is frequently regarded as escapist, hence the cliché criticisms that otaku are 'immature as individuals' or 'confuse fiction and reality'. This despite the fact that, to my knowledge, few can distinguish shades of fiction and reality as exactingly as they. Accordingly I would characterise (not define) otaku as persons who: (1) Exhibit an intimate familiarity with fictional contexts [;] (2) Resort to fictions as a means of 'possessing' love objects [;] (3) Live via multi-orientations, not merely bi-orientation [;] (4) Take fictional constructs for sex objects.[74]

There has been a shift in *anime* imagery in the last ten years from *kinmirai* ('near-future') apocalyptic scenarios, and there is speculation that those once-popular 'armageddon fantasies' incited the Aum attacks on the Tokyo underground in 1995.[75] Minakawa Yuku, the author of Kodansha's *Gundam Officials, Limited Edition* guide to one of the best-selling series of robot 'Mobile Suit Gundam' manga, is reported as saying that viewers did not identify with the armoured power of the robots so much as with the security of being in a mother's womb. The robot's armour becomes the body, and so being inside it is to be in 'a safe place in which you can *interact* with the world'.[76] This form of 'unification' with a mother figure that facilitates interaction is something that does not necessarily entail aggression toward others,[77] but even so the trend in otaku sub-culture is now, in a new development that contrasts with and complements machine-imagery, 'toward love-fixation' upon *bishōjo* or 'nymphs'.[78] These figures are part of the now-dominant '*moe*' imagery, one definition of which is that it 'expresses a rarefied pseudo-love toward fictitious characters and their related embodiments'.[79] Here there is an emphasis on erotic relationships with the images, the kind of relationships that Saito refers to as evidence of the predilection of otaku to 'take fictional constructs for sex objects'.

There is still a certain degree of panic over otaku culture, although the term 'otaku' as such has been rehabilitated because of the huge niche market it represents, and the negative aspects have been displaced onto young men who withdraw from society and lock themselves in their rooms. While otaku are engaged with the world through participation in sub-cultural activities, the *hikikomori* – who are often eldest sons – are completely isolated but exercise control and even inflict physical violence on their families, particularly the mothers.

One of Saito's recent books is *How to Rescue Your Child from Hikikomori*, and he argues that in Japan 'mothers and sons often have a symbiotic, co-dependent relationship'.[80]

In the Japanese press the *hikikomori*, who may number about one million, are treated as those who have 'a bit of their personality that clashes with Japanese society', though Saito points out that it is usually the children of more wealthy parents who become *hikikomori* because it is difficult to withdraw from society if the parents will not provide support.[81] The JPS analyst Kitayama has also argued that it seems to be the present trend to pathologize and 'treat' such children, these children 'who are prisoners of their family, rather than their domineering caretakers, usually one or both parents'.[82] Outside Japan the *hikikomori* are now often lumped together with *Yu-Gi-Oh* cartoons, cults, paganism, violence and ambiguous sexuality that are supposed to characterize Japanese culture. In one lurid account a Japanese psychiatrist is quoted as saying that these young adults are a mirror of the society; 'Japan, as a nation itself, is becoming hikikomori'.[83]

Yaoi

Male fantasy in otaku *anime* cyber-culture – whether it is structured around assertion of the self in the Armageddon, around unification with another through containment in the mother's womb or of possession of a passive nymph love object – begs a question. What is the nature of the woman who this fantasy revolves around, and how are the positions of women changing? Freud saw feminine sexuality as a 'dark continent', and the construction of femininity was a riddle for him.[84] Sometimes the psychoanalytic tradition has treated women as less than men, with the motif of 'penis envy' operating as the sign that woman could only ever aspire to what men already had; and sometimes analysts retreated to the rather pre-psychoanalytic line that men and women were just created different by god, and there was little more that could be said about it.[85] Lacanian theories of sexual difference have also tended to insist that there is a necessary disjunction – a structural lack of rapport – between men and women (though this argument is always qualified by the insistence that biological men and biological women might exist on one side or other of this 'impossible' relationship). To have or to be the 'phallus' for Lacan was not something that could be settled with reference to a little bit of flesh between the legs.[86]

This means that Saito's argument, outlined in his book *Psychoanalysis of Armoured Cuties*, addresses a crucial issue about what male otaku might desire about images of 'little girls armed with heavy weapons', and then about what young women might desire for themselves in those images. The term 'phallic girl' is used by him here to explain how it is that these 'armoured cuties' have a 'potential fighting power', a 'power which is their phallus and core of their jouissance'.[87] Here there are two key terms that signal Saito's Lacanian framework. First, the French term 'jouissance' is used by Lacan to describe a form of enjoyment that is (with reference to Freud's phrase) 'beyond the pleasure principle';[88] it is a driving force that is always 'too much' to bear, the point at which pleasure turns into pain. Secondly, Saito uses the term 'phallus' in a Lacanian sense, and its manifestation in the identification with the 'phallic girl' as a principle of power clearly does not refer to the penis.[89] This means that the focus of male attention – affection described by the term *moe* – is upon particular characteristics such as cat-like ears or tails; Saito gives the example of '*meganekko-moe*' which refers to an otaku whose favourite is a girl who wears futuristic glasses.[90]

There is still a well-worn psychoanalytic story of fetishistic perversion lingering in the background here, and this becomes evident when Saito discusses possible 'ancestors' of otaku culture in the West. The case in point is that of Henry Dargar, the reclusive Chicago janitor whose 15,000-page novel *In the Realms of the Unreal* discovered after his death describes the rebellion of little girls against child-enslaving men, a novel which was accompanied by fantastic murals in which the girls' naked bodies are equipped with little penises. Perhaps, Saito suggests, 'Dargar was a solitary otaku who had no company because his style of love was too much ahead of his time'.[91] The question though is still not what the penis actually is, but what it signifies.

That question then opens a different kind of psychoanalytic window on the internal mental life of the female otaku, who are often much taken by a fantasy genre known as '*yaoi*', which also has its correlates in the West in 'slashzines' produced by women in which characters like Captain Kirk and Mr Spock are coupled in lovingly drawn explicit sexual embrace.[92] As with the rather 'dissociated' sexuality of male otaku, Saito notes, there is also dissociation at work in *yaoi* sub-culture, for the young women who love these images 'do not desire homosexual men in real life'.[93] *Yaoi* is a complex phenomenon, as the entry on it in the Venice Biennale Otaku catalogue indicates: 'Originally an acronym for the words *yamanashi* "no climax," *ochinashi* "no punch-line," and *iminashi* "no meaning," the term refers to taking existing male characters from *anime/manga* and pairing them together in a romantic relationship.'[94] It is clearly more than simply boy-on-boy erotica, and for Lacanians it is recognizably on the side of 'feminine enjoyment'.[95]

Those beings who are stereotypically 'men' (though they may not necessarily be biologically male) aim for something more beyond mere pleasure that can be specifically localized in a part of the body (usually the penis) and has a climactic end point (the erotic punch-line that gives the whole act meaning). This, Lacan defines as 'phallic jouissance'. The 'woman', however, is after something more numinous, perhaps even mystical, something Lacan describes as 'enjoyment of the Other'.[96] Saito's diagnosis is quite explicit in its use of these terms (and of the way these new forms of subjectivity depart from what he still seems to assume to be a normal grid for sexual relationships). It has been noted that there is a sharp differentiation of roles in yaoi literature between the 'attacker' and the 'receiver', and this may function not so much as an endorsement and reproduction of traditional heterosexual gender roles as an ironic commentary on those formal relationships in the dominant culture; in yaoi 'we frequently see a scenario that a boy and a cunning girl scramble for a man and finally a boy's pureness wins'.[97]

Saito argues that 'Sexual desire of males is always toward having or possessing the sexual object itself', and so 'many male otaku want to collect visual data of their favourite girls'. This means that they 'always need a position of identification in the fiction like a young boy as a hero, because they always want to be a subject of their desire':

> Male otaku don't like Yaoi fiction because of their homophobic tendency. The cause of this homophobia is a fear of an unstable position as a subject of desire. In other words, the male otaku's desire is toward the phallic enjoyment (*la jouissance phallique*). But the sexual desire of females is completely different. Their desire is toward becoming the object. They always try to identify with the sexual relationship itself. Female otaku don't need the girl's position to identify in the fiction because their enjoyment reach[es] a climax when they abandon the position of the subject of desire. In other words, female otaku's position is toward the enjoyment of the Other (*la jouissance de l'Autre*).[98]

This also means that if there is any reality to this eroticized cyberspace as something spiritual – as a 'Buddhistic cyberspace' – its inhabitants would, it seems, necessarily be 'feminine'. This twists further the argument that 'transgender' and 'genderqueer' practices are tolerated more in Japan than in the US,[99] for it not only introduces a fluidity in gender categories – in the ability of biological males and females to cross the boundaries between those categories – but it also treats 'femininity' as something constituted through a process of oppression and repression in patriarchal society, and now as something that returns as the repressed without making any claim to provide a substantial essential identity for women or men. This 'feminine' state of being, then, is oriented to forms of sexuality that question 'phallic enjoyment' as such and these new forms of 'feminine' sexuality reveal the phallic obsession with defining and fixing objects of pleasure as resting, in a most thorough-going analysis, on nothing. In this way cyberspace provides a link between Buddhism and Lacan that unravels the idea that there are particular 'contents' in the unconscious or in a civilization that must be contained and treasured, particularly the alluring and captivating content that usually defines 'sexual identity'.

The representations of women in the otaku and yaoi literature indicate that Japanese feminists, allied or not with psychoanalysis, face many obstacles. It should be noted, for example, that Buddhism is not necessarily one of the allies that they could rely upon. This much can be illustrated with reference to a widespread and visible phenomenon that enrols many women as subjects who suffer, must suffer. The *mizuko jizō* – stone representations of the Buddha with little red bibs placed in temples or at roadsides for the protection of travellers, children and the unborn – appear innocent enough as manifestations of a devotion to the well-being of others. However, these statues condense a struggle over the control of women's bodies; at the same time as abortion has been legalized for many years as a form of contraception, some right-wing Buddhist temples encourage women to pay them to erect and maintain the *jizōs* to atone for the guilt of having killed their unborn child. The martyrdom of the suffering mother is thus perpetuated by such 'memorialization' strategies for every woman who has been pregnant.[100] This is just one case where the liberal free market – here the selling of *jizōs* as a form of indulgence by temple authorities – complements traditional values and prescriptions for the role of women as good mothers.[101]

Nevertheless, Lacanian forms of psychoanalysis combined with feminist critique may also be uncannily congruent with contemporary forms of sexuality in this highly-technologized society (and perhaps not only in this one).[102] This is not to say that such subjects of cyberculture would necessarily be biologically female, but that whatever sex they were they would be psychically feminine, even perhaps a new version of the feminized subjects that some Japanese feminists have described as constituting modern Japan.[103] Whether this process of feminization condemns women and men to a condition of traditional 'femininity' or whether it takes them beyond that feminine position, to something that approximates what a Lacanian would anticipate as a possible end of analysis, remains to be seen. Contemporary representations of sexuality, analysed and stretched further by Lacanians in Japan as part of a subversive logic that questions categories of gender identity, may at least show that the relation between men and women need not necessarily be a binary one that assigns biological males and females to one side of the divide or the other and essentializes the inner natures of those who inhabit each realm.

Lacan, like Buddhism, shows a way out of such dualism, a binary logic that has bedevilled Western systems of thought, including psychoanalysis. That binary logic insists on a separation between mind and body, and attempts to find the 'contents' of the mind which will facilitate connections between the mind and the body. And, in psychoanalysis, that binary logic was repeated in the attempts to describe mother-child relationships and then to puzzle over how the child might escape that suffocating dependence on one other. While Lacan's version of the Oedipus complex is sometimes read by Western psychoanalysts as merely substituting the symbolic for the imaginary – the 'complex' traversed as the infant learns to speak and escapes the dual relation with the mother to enter the realm of the 'law of the father' that structures systems of meaning – Lacan in Japan actually shows how symbolic, imaginary and real are knotted together in three registers that together give the illusion that there is something rather than nothing.

4
Religion, Cohesion and Personal Life: 'A homogeneous culture'

The divided subject of psychoanalysis calls for a view of each ostensibly unified culture as riven with contradictions, a view which poses a challenge to the idea of an authentic self rooted in tradition and to popular versions of analysis that ground individual experience in archetypes of a 'collective unconscious'. In Japan there is a paradoxical relationship between the most influential versions of this kind of analysis looking to cultural traditions on the one hand and modern scientific psychology on the other, both imported and each mobilized in governmental policy. Psychoanalysis reveals how images of 'others' that have been historically maintained at a distance, outside the culture, come to mould the internal shape of indigenous psychologies. Internal conflicts have always driven the development of theories about psychology and the management of the self, driven these developments in particular ways concerning specific 'internal others' in Japan. This attention to internal contradictions then poses questions about how psychoanalysis itself as a historically marginal practice functions in this place, and the marginal identities it attaches itself to. Psychoanalysis is then divided, between something that is already non-European and something that cannot ever be at one with a unified Japanese sense of self.

Archetypes

Freud's invention of the unconscious opened up an irreparable division in each individual subject,[1] and the longing for wholesome unity at the level of the self or society was from then on something to be interpreted by psychoanalysts rather than celebrated. Some of the earliest splits in the psychoanalytic movement in Europe revolved around the attempt to reclaim the self as centre and meld the contents of personal and collective life. Jung, to take the most pertinent example, recognized that his search for a harmonious resolution of conflicts in modern life – a search connected with a return to a deeper historical consciousness accessed through anthropological studies from around the world – broke from key tenets of psychoanalysis, and so termed his own approach 'analytical psychology'.

The return of some Jungians and 'post-Jungians' to the field of psychoanalytic debate has led to a tension at the heart of approaches to the unconscious.[2] On the one hand, the Jungian tradition is closely intertwined with the history of psychoanalysis, part of that history, and its perspective intensifies theoretical conflict in a discipline concerned with psychic conflict. On the other hand, Jungians aim to integrate the archetypal images that make up the personal and collective unconscious, to resolve conflict, and to bring a sense of closure to the divided subject. This tradition in Japan accords well with a vision of the culture as homogeneous, but the character of its own perspective, as something partial that has an uneasy relationship with mainstream psychoanalysis, actually serves to undo the claim that the culture is as unified as some would have it.[3] Japanese Jungians have an edge in the debate over every other approach to the unconscious however, access to the ear of government.

Kawai Hayao, lately professor emeritus at Kyoto University and director of the International Centre for Japanese Studies,[4] was the first Jungian analyst in Japan, training first as a psychologist in California and then undertaking his analytic training in Zürich, the Mecca of analytical psychology. Kawai is seen as one of the key figures in the *nihonjinron* tradition which devotes itself to puzzling about what makes the Japanese Japanese, and fits well in a tradition that maintains what has been termed the 'hegemony of homogeneity'.[5] As Commissioner for Cultural Affairs, Kawai has been a key figure implementing cabinet policy on the 'cultural power' of Japan; as his forward to a recent public policy document puts it, 'Channeling energy into various forms of culture and the arts does not only restore spiritual enrichment and self-confidence on the individual level, but will also have a positive effect on the economy'.[6] He was also active as a Japanese representative at the United Nations, working with UNESCO and participating in cultural initiatives as part of the reconstruction of Iraq in 2003 after the US invasion. Now, with serious illness threatening his life, and absent from his post since November 2006, he has had to give up being head of the Cultural Affairs Agency, and the Jungian group in Kyoto has been taken over by his son Kawai Toshio.[7]

He is also known publicly by way of a little book *Murakami Haruki goes to see Kawai Hayao* which reflects on the consequences of the 1995 Kobe earthquake and Aum subway sarin attacks.[8] The title reflects something of the status accorded Kawai as a sage with analytical insights into the state of the Japanese psyche, and it also provides an insight into the nature of the 'psychoanalysis' to be found in Murakami's own writing. Murakami had encountered Kawai when they were both in the United States and two dialogues (from 1997 and 1998) were published alongside interviews with Aum followers in a second volume of Murakami's *Underground*, designed to follow-up and complement the first volume composed of accounts of the victims of the sarin attacks.[9]

The 1995 events prompted Murakami to return to Japan after four years absence to explore the culture anew, and the dialogues with Kawai are often represented as marking a turning point in Murakami's writing. His early novels are read as evincing a 'detachment' that also speaks of the influence of US genres and some distance from Japanese culture, and the post-1995 books are said (by Murakami himself as well as by devotees) to show 'commitment'.[10] Other Jungian analysts have then discovered deeper resonances between Murakami's writing and themes from analytical psychology, and it is possible to find many representations of depth as something that pertains to the psyche in his books. Motifs of a 'well', for example, often figure in his writing as a place of depth and darkness into which one ventures to attain wisdom.[11]

One interpretation of Murakami's writing suggests that he presents a vision of modernity in which 'the reified structure of second nature is beginning to take on the features of a non-oppressive archaic nature'.[12] This is not merely to say that Murakami's main characters are able to survive their encounters with mysterious phenomena quite well without knowing exactly what is going on, but to point to a way of living modernity not as a series of 'shocks' or disruptions to the fabric of life; rather it is as if modern life stories 'have the calm of fairy tales, in which fantastic events come forward as natural'.[13] This kind of interpretation emphasizes the importance of fantasy elements in everyday life, but now as archetypal forms that can potentially be integrated into the self, and we thus arrive at something that marks an even deeper congruence with Jungian conceptions of culture.[14] It looks like psychoanalysis, and it functions to draw attention to the importance of the unconscious, but it provides a more benign view of the possibilities for healing divisions in society and the self than psychoanalytic clinical work would ever dare to promise.

Kawai's book *Buddhism and the Art of Psychotherapy* traces his journey from what appeared to be a fairly orthodox Jungian approach back to Buddhism again.[15] Here there is a concern with 'wholeness' and unity, something Kawai discovers in the figure of the feminine, an essential underlying quality of human experience that every individual of whatever sex should ideally be able to connect with. This also gives a Jungian edge to feminist arguments about masculinity and femininity in Japanese culture;

> ...the essence of Japanese fairy tales can be seen better through *female eyes* rather than *male eyes*. ... To look at things with *female eyes* means, in other words, that the ego of a Japanese is properly symbolized by a female and not by a male. The patriarchal social system that prevailed in Japan until the end of World War II obscured our eyes to this fact. In fairy tales, however, '*female heroes*' could freely take an active part. The investigation of those female figures will cast much light on the psyche of the Japanese.[16]

The complementary relationship between male and female that serves to guarantee the unity of a culture is thus underpinned by concepts of 'male' and 'female' that are themselves treated as essential unitary aspects of the self.[17] To discover the 'maternal' character of Japanese culture, as Kawai aimed to do in his popular writing for a Japanese audience that lies full-square in the *nihonjinron* tradition, is to affirm the way each gendered individual may become whole in a relationship with the larger whole of the nation.[18]

The Jungian twist on Buddhism that Kawai provides is summed up in one of his contributions to UNESCO publicity in 1998 in which he contrasts Western 'scientific' approaches, which break up the world into separate components viewed from a detached point of view, and his own emphasis on interconnection. No being has its own independent innate nature, he argues, and he then turns to the Buddhist conception of 'nothingness' to elaborate his argument. However, this is not an empty nothing, but something that might be thought of as full; 'This whole being is called Nothingness because it has no name, but actually one might say that it is Everything'.[19]

Individuals

The presence of Kawai in the Japanese government – a professor of clinical psychology as well as being a Jungian 'analytical psychologist'

– gives another twist, another important inflection to the historical dominance of medical psychiatry here in the fields of psychoanalysis, psychoanalytic psychotherapy and psychodynamic counselling. Also important was the fact that Kawai was first trained as a mathematician, and so he was able, upon his return from Zurich, also to train psychologists in statistical techniques (which they often, as in other countries, poorly understand); this expertise in the quantitative tradition then gave him the edge when he wanted to push more experiential approaches in clinical psychology.[20] Psychiatry has enjoyed a dominant position in many countries, particularly so in the United States, Britain and France, and this has made it possible for doctors to argue that 'lay people' should be prohibited from training or be barely tolerated as practising psychoanalysts.[21] The Japan Psychoanalytic Society modelled itself on this history (as we have seen in Chapters 1 and 2), but it also has specific reasons to be wary of psychology. The role of psychology as a separate discipline and recent attempts to regulate psychologists in Japan, have consequences for all the other participants in the 'psy' professions.

A Jungian-influenced notion of cultural unity also provides a particular context for psychology as a discipline concerned with the unity of the individual, even if the methodological approaches of the two levels of study are often very different. Kawai's own practice is within the non-interpretive strand of Jungian work, and the 'sandplay therapy' for which he is internationally known as a clinician, for example, is designed to provide the setting in which analysands will provide the interpretations themselves, or even arrive at a deeper intuitive understanding of who they are and how they might proceed through a process of 'individuation' without any interpretations being offered to them at all.[22] The Jungian analyst in this tradition often does not proceed to interpret play, jokes, dreams, slips of the tongue and transference as the psychoanalysts would.[23] However, the latest generation of Jungians who have returned from Zurich and now influence the new training institute in Kyoto tend to use interpretation much more than Kawai.

Psychologists, on the other hand, devote themselves to a good deal of interpretation of data about individual behaviour, and the idea that people should themselves interpret and come to an understanding of who they are is anathema to the experimental approach, which likes to think of itself as scientific. Here it is assumed that the observer should be detached and uninvolved in the activities that they describe, precisely in the way that Kawai sees western science proceeding. It has only been fairly recently that 'qualitative' approaches in psychology have appeared in Japan as alternatives in a discipline that has been concerned with the quantification of behavioural observations.[24]

Psychology as an experimental discipline appeared much earlier than psychoanalysis in Japan.[25] The first psychologist, Motora Yujiro, studied philosophy at Boston University for two years before working for his doctorate in psychology with G. Stanley Hall at Johns Hopkins. Hall had just returned from Leipzig, where he spent time in the laboratory of Wilhelm Wundt, the father of experimental psychology, and founded his own laboratory upon his return to the States. Motora obtained his PhD – with a dissertation entitled *Exchange, considered as a principle of social life* – in 1888 and returned the same year to teach psychophysics at the University of Tokyo.[26] Psychophysics is concerned with detailed measurement of sensation and perception, and Motora carried out research on the way that children's lack of achievement at school can be explained by way of problems of attention rather than 'mental retardation'. A leading first researcher in what is now termed 'cognitive psychology' and 'learning disability', Motora also carried out statistical studies on rhythms in Japanese classical poems and performance on word association tasks, and he produced the first textbook on psychology in Japan in 1890.[27] Together with his student Matsumoto Matataro he founded a 'psychophysical' laboratory at the University of Tokyo in 1903, in effect the first psychological laboratory in Japan.[28] A dedicated 'scientific psychologist', even so Motora presented a paper at the 5th International Congress of Psychology in Rome in 1905 on the 'Idea of ego in the Eastern philosophy' which reflected on his experience of Zen meditation at a Buddhist temple.[29]

The concern with problems of attention, which can be remedied, rather than 'mental retardation' which would be seen as enduring traits, marks Japanese psychology off from dominant US perspectives. Although there was some influence of psychological ideas about heredity from the US – including the formation of a Japanese Eugenics Society in 1924 (following the introduction of Galton's ideas in 1881)[30] – Japanese psychologists were more concerned with how child development might be facilitated than with categorizing children (so that they would then be doomed to fail because nothing could be done about them). Japanese psychological research on individual performance of perceptual tasks and cognitive processing has always been very detailed, providing painstaking description of the minutiae of responses.

Personality inventories were developed in the 1920s – and this is still before the arrival of psychoanalysis in Japan – which included a

'Morality Test', an 'Emotional Stability Test' and a 'Personality Adjustment' scale. Despite the efforts of psychoanalytic pioneers Kosawa and Marui to bring Freud's ideas about child development to Japan in the 1930s, most academic psychologists and psychiatrists were, a recent historical survey notes, 'too conservative to accept psychoanalysis as their theoretical standpoint, though many cultured persons outside of the academic institutions, especially those with a taste for literature, showed much interest in it'.[31] It is worth noting here the implication, even in this history of the discipline by psychologists, that psychoanalysis is positioned as something too radical.

The ethos of focusing on possible change against the attempt to discover innate individual differences has also marked Japanese research on 'intelligence'. A recent review of research on intelligence testing in Japan highlights crucial cultural assumptions about what 'intelligence' is. It is noted, for example, that in research on genetic and inherited factors in intelligence, 'Japanese samples tended to show a more substantial amount of shared environmental contribution to intelligence than have the Western samples'.[32] One reason offered is that 'family coherence and educational efforts tend to be emphasized in Japan, and therefore, the effect of family environment could make the intellectual performance of family members more similar'.[33] There is thus an appeal here again to the homogeneity of Japanese culture, this time at the level of the family within psychological research, but there is also an attention to 'educational efforts'. This emphasis on effort runs against assumptions about intelligence in much Western psychological research:

> The Japanese (except for psychologists and test-favoring educators) seldom refer explicitly to one's own or another person's general and stable ability. Even when they compare people in terms of intelligence, aptitude, or talent, they do not verbalize their judgements. Instead, they often discuss who is diligent, works hard, and so forth, on academic and occupational tasks... They are reluctant to select candidates using measures that apparently cannot be changed by the candidates' effort. The belief-in-effort implies that everyone can achieve a very high level of performance in any domain, if he or she engages in exercise or deliberate practice for an extended period of time.[34]

Even though 'psychologists and test-favoring educators' are singled out here as exceptions to the rule, the rule that 'belief-in-effort' should provide the main explanation of differences in ability is also the context for much Japanese psychological research, as well as what the authors of this rebuttal of Western conceptions of intelligence refer to as 'examination hell'.[35]

It is worth noting that, despite this emphasis on contextual issues in child development and education, there has been a rapid uptake of US studies of 'Attention Deficit and Hyperactivity Disorder' (AD(H)D), and the medicalization of childhood is proceeding apace in Japan as in many other countries. The formation of 'health psychology' specialist organizations will be a mixed blessing for those wishing to keep psychology separate from medicine.[36] The only feminist bookshop in Tokyo (the Crayon House) for example, is filled with self-help books (even though Japanese feminists have not often seen psychotherapy, still less psychoanalysis, as an ally of their vision of social and personal change), and psychiatric diagnostic and management texts on AD(H)D figure prominently on the shelves.[37]

Analytical psychology and empiricist experimental psychology might together have threatened to propagate and enforce cultural unity and individual conformity, linking and closing up any possible space for psychoanalytic concerns with contradiction and division of the subject. However, the forms they have taken in Japan have actually ended up providing the conditions in which psychoanalysis would be acceptable. While Jungians and empiricists each have their own reasons to be suspicious of psychoanalysis, and provide theories that are antithetical to it, there has been an emphasis on interpretation that has been quite facilitative – studies of the meaning of myths and fairy tales, for example – and this encourages transformation at the level of personal 'effort' and self-understanding.

Outsiders

Buddhism in Japan is but one component of the national culture, and it coexists with other belief systems that make explicit claims to define what it is to be Japanese. While it is sometimes claimed that '*nihonjinron* is Japan's civil religion',[38] it is Shintō that has traditionally provided the conceptual resources for defining Japanese nationalism and asserting the 'primordial homogeneity of the ethnic Japanese'.[39] Shintō, 'the way of the *kami*', provides an account of the formation of the islands and people of Japan and a warrant for the power of the emperor who is descended directly from Amaterasu, the sun goddess who sent her grandson to found the dynasty. Alongside the 'great tradition' recorded in the *Kojiki* (Record of Ancient Matters) and *Nihon Shoki* (Chronicle of Japan) that date from the eighth century, is a 'little tradition' that revolves around the *kami*, gods. As a blend of animism and polytheism, together with elements of ancestor worship and shamanism, it venerates millions of *kami* who live in mountains, rivers, trees, rocks and other natural features.[40]

Kitayama Osamu, the Winnicottian Folk Crusader, offers interpretations of folk tales that are more closely connected with the Shintō tradition, though he does not name this as such in his account.[41] On the one hand, Shintōism operates as an animistic religious system that includes creation myths that only apply to Japan and so it was an ideological resource for nationalists before the Second World War.[42] There are perhaps only about three million dedicated devotees of Shintōism as a great as well as little tradition, but it provides a conceptual frame for other 'gods'. Incarnations of the Buddha or Jesus can thus be contained within this religious system as *kami*, and Shintō 'Torii' can be found inside the grounds of Buddhist temples. While it might well operate ideologically, providing a primordial homogeneity that also necessarily excludes those who are not ethnically 'Japanese', Shintōism provides an eclectic contradictory representation of deities into which images of 'gods' from other religions could be incorporated and thus be tolerated.[43]

The journey of Buddhism from India and through China and Korea before it arrives in Japan accumulates a range of different cultural values, and the turn to Buddhism in Japanese psychoanalysis has been attentive to these different sources.[44] However, psychoanalysis is concerned with a form of 'history of the present', the way an individual makes sense of their past as their personal truth rather than the way an empirical truth about origins could be dug up from the ground of their being by an ostensibly objective observer. A psychoanalytic approach to culture also needs to attend to the way history is constructed for present purposes and the way this history of a culture enables individuals to understand their place within it. There is an important cultural question here about the relationship with outsiders – the 'Other' to the culture – that has a bearing on the psychoanalytic question that each individual inside the culture needs to address as they discover how they have become who they are.

Chinese classics and Chinese classical writing – the array of *kanji* characters that are still the core of Japanese script – became a compulsory part of the school curriculum in the Meiji period, the opening which lasted from 1868 to 1912.[45] This education centred on a system of elements of Chinese culture, *kanbun*, and this served as a necessary conceptual apparatus for making sense of the Chinese *kanji* characters. It was not long into the Meiji period before resentment surfaced however, and there were even suggestions that all reference to Chinese should be dropped from training in written Japanese.[46] Moves to abandon *kanbun* were eventually replaced with a recasting of the relationship to Chinese that would not require meddling with key elements of Japanese script. Nationalists then comforted themselves with the thought that it was the Japanese who were able to appreciate the sophistication of *kanbun*, as against the Chinese from whom they had retrieved it for safekeeping, for posterity.

Karatani Kōjin, one of Japan's leading leftwing political analysts and activists, addresses the paradoxical way that incorporation of alien concepts into a culture presumed to be homogeneous operates at one and the same time as a toleration of diversity. He does so using some quite specific theoretical coordinates that draw on psychoanalysis and that have profound consequences for the way psychoanalysis can be conceptualized in Japan. Here the relationship between Japan and its 'Others' is absolutely crucial to the argument, and these others are China and, crucial to Karatani's argument, Korea.

There is a fraught historical relationship with Korea that is very much alive today, and that is now fuelled by revelations that North Korea abducted Japanese civilians to serve as informants after 1945. Japanese ambitions to conquer China in the sixteenth century necessitated invasion of Korea and subjugation of the population along the way, and Korea was annexed to Japan three centuries later, from 1910 to 1945. There is a geopolitical question here concerning the role of Korean resistance in frustrating plans to invade China as well as the role of Korea as a barrier to China's ambitions to invade Japan. As Karatani points out, the existence of Korea has 'determined Japanese political and cultural formations'.[47] (Japanese nationalist endeavours to prove that Japan has had its own distinct culture from prehistoric times are now matched by Korean theories that 'Japan is a mere appendage to Korea, which supplied virtually all Japan has'.[48]) The 'psychoanalysis of Japan' that Karatani aims at requires attending to the representations of these material relationships, and attending to those representations as themselves having material effects.

The first step in the argument is to attend to the way early fluid conceptions of cultural production, denoted by the term 'becoming' are overlaid by technological procedures in which things are taken as given, as 'made'.[49] The civilizing process thus replaces primordial relationships between being and nothingness – exactly what we find valued in Buddhism, for example – with knowledge operating as a kind of grid in which phenomena are always already categorized. Another aspect of this first step (though it is one that Karatani does not explore) is that early infantile experience could be conceptualized psychoanalytically as a state of 'becoming' before structured patterns of relating are layered in that enable the child to comprehend what 'others' are. These patterns transform the infant's lifeworld into something 'made' which it must accept and explore.

The next step is to note how early stages of colonial expansion often operated by way of the imposition of a knowledge of the world as 'made' upon cultures that may have once prioritized 'becoming'.[50] In this way 'heterodoxy' is suppressed as 'systematic thinking' is laminated upon it, categorizing and interpreting experience. In Korea, for example, 'Chinese systematic thinking has been so radically interiorized that the ancient layer is almost completely forgotten', but in Japan, Karatani claims, 'the substratum of becoming was not oppressed'.[51] Now, the key question for Karatani, as for psychoanalysis, is not to try and return to that primordial state of 'becoming', but to attend to the particular way that Japan relates to its past, how Shintō permits patterns of thought from the outside world to be dealt with so as to never impinge on the Japanese; in Japan, then, 'imported thoughts just cohabitate spatially'.[52]

Karatani argues that it is necessary to tackle the relationship between Japan and Korea at the level of *writing*, with the 'writing system' conceptualized as a material practice rather than as some numinous national mentality.[53] Attention to the writing system as a material practice will thus enable analysts of the culture to unearth the historical relationships that are still present today. Here we return to the specific role of *kanji* in the Japanese writing system, in which the Chinese ideograms are read in two ways – phonetically, in a reading that is similar to the Chinese sound (*on-yomi*) and semantically in a reading that is taken from Japanese native sounds (*kun-yomi*) – but now there is another loop to the argument.

In Korea the *kanji* were read phonetically, and these script elements have now been dropped and replaced by a completely different writing system.[54] However, Karatani suggests that the semantic reading was imported via Korea into Japan, where it now functions in a contradictory way which permits the incorporation and preservation of external concepts inside the Japanese writing system. As the *kanji* travelled from China to Korea to Japan a series of mutations occurred in the translation (even though up to the Chinese revolution and the reformation of *kanji* script under Mao, Japanese visitors could still understand many *kanji* in China). The difference in pronunciation between Koreans and Japanese of *kanji*, for example, also means that a particular sound might be anchored in quite different *kanji* when it is written. The sound 'Lacan' might have the *kanji* 'Buddhist master' in Japan (at least for Japanese Lacanians), but in Korea one popular informal inscription is as 'joyful river'. (One member of the Korean Society for Lacan and Contemporary Psychoanalysis works as a traditional Chinese herbalist, and has the old *kanji* for 'Lacan' as the sign for his herbal medicine practice.) In Korea, this is but a playful reminder of what can be accomplished in different forms of writing, but in Japan – because of the double-reading of the *kanji* – the semantic aspect to the reading haunts every speaking subject. While the *hiragana* script is supposed to be 'the most natural Japanese' form of writing, *katakana* script is used most explicitly to write foreign loan words, and *kanji* is itself, Karatani argues, still the mark of something foreign. This tripartite division in the script thus contains within it a history and structure of Japanese political and cultural institutions, and a relation to the Other 'materialised in the system of letters';[55] this Other is Korea as the conduit, bridge and obstacle to China:

> The *kun* reading of *kanji* using Japanese native sound indicates, first and foremost, an internalization of the foreign *écriture, kanji*. Today Japanese do not think that they read Chinese ideograms using their own sounds, but simply that they express Japanese in Chinese ideograms. For Koreans the sense of *kanji* is the opposite: it remains external because it is read only in imitation Chinese sounds, phonetically [*on*]... Secondly and more importantly, *kanji*, though absorbed into Japanese, remains something external. In Japanese, the part written in *kanji* is always deemed foreign and abstract... In speaking, the foreignness of foreign words does not come into consciousness, but in writing, the fact that they are inscribed in *katakana* makes the foreignness explicit... It is thanks to this immune system that anything whatsoever can be introduced.[56]

Such an 'immune system' provides a form of defence which protects a subject from the outside world, from a symbolic system that threatens to impose itself, and if we link this account explicitly to psychoanalysis, as Karatani does, it can be conceptualized as a form of defence that actually prevents the subject from engaging fully with the outside world. On the one hand, the *kanji* can be thought of as operating visually, and their material reality in a writing system can be equated with the hieroglyphic characters that make up the unconscious. We have reviewed the argument (in Chapter 3) that the Japanese subject is faced with a writing system in which something of the unconscious is already present to them, and so psychoanalysis is unnecessary for such a people for, as Karatani puts it, 'Japanese always expose their unconscious (hieroglyph) – they are always telling the truth'.[57]

Now Karatani supplements this argument with the suggestion that those hieroglyphs that are always already necessarily present to the Japanese are from outside Japan, but that the Japanese maintain a fantasy of staying true to a pure primordial 'becoming' against the 'made' world. This defence of something that never actually existed as such is, psychoanalytically-speaking, a defence against the necessary limitation of infantile omnipotence that the infant must undergo in order to speak a language that is 'castration'. If the infant is to realize that words cannot simply mean what they want it to mean, it must accept such castration. Castration is understood here in its symbolic sense, as the process by which a child learns what power independent of itself is as it goes through the Oedipus complex.[58] The refusal of such castration in the symbolic sense that Karatani is using the term here is a type of defence which is sometimes termed by psychoanalysts 'foreclosure'.[59] It is so drastic in its refusal to accept the existence of symbolic systems – the world as 'made', as it were – that it threatens to end the delirium of creative 'becoming' that the subject is unwilling to give up as it enters language, so drastic that the defence may lead eventually to psychosis.

This does not mean that Japanese society is 'free', but that there are forms of power operating in the culture that are not Oedipal, and it is that unmediated power which means that it cannot be free. These are forms of power that do not operate through forms of mediation in which individual subjects are able to separate from others and then constitute themselves to knowingly accept or challenge calls by authority and calls for participation in nationalist fantasies. Here again, Karatani is drawing on the work of the political theorist Maruyama, who complained back in 1946 that there was no free, decision-making agent or sense of subjective responsibility for those enmeshed in the chains of power that operated without a space of mediation in 'premodern' Japan.[60]

Karatani argues that it is necessary to acknowledge the way nationalist fantasies are built around historical relationships with those the 'nation' pits itself, principally China and Korea.[61] This is why the difference between Korea and Japan with respect to their confrontation with China is, for him, 'not one among many other differences, but *the* difference through which all other differences are expressed, and the one which is still producing differences at this very moment'.[62] In Korea, 'when people accepted *kanji*, castration was inevitable', and this is, Karatani argues, 'a common phenomenon when one civilization encounters another, more advanced'.[63] But in Japan, 'the foreclosure of castration was the formation of *écriture*. If there is anything Japanese, it is this system'.[64]

Insiders

Psychoanalysts from different traditions questioned about the role of difference often made the same claim, that Japan is 'a homogeneous culture', yet the contradictory relationships with other cultures outside the islands is now increasingly visible inside. Conflict between generations along with changes in family patterns and sexual mores is also making visible the heterogeneity of the culture.[65] In fact, if there was no difference to start with, psychoanalysis as such would be impossible. There is, as we have already noted (in Chapter 1) a history of intense class conflict in Japan that already throws claims about the homogeneity of the culture into question. There is also longstanding political resistance to abuses of power in psychiatry by users of services that also lays the ground for non-medical approaches (approaches that could include clinical psychoanalysis were it not so expensive and so confined to the middle classes).[66]

Karatani provides his own conceptual response to the problem of symbolic mediation – the necessity of opening a space for critical distance so that we can encounter systems of representation as something other to us – in his account of the role of 'parallax'. Here his concern is not at all with the predicament of an infant encountering the existence of a symbolic system independent of it and submitting to the 'castration' necessary to move around in the symbolic. Instead, he has been exploring the relationship between culture and the economy, and 'parallax' as an ineluctable gap between the two.[67] It is a gap that has been closed in forms of Marxist analysis that have attempted to reduce one to the other, and which have then resulted in forms of Stalinism (Marxism turned into an ideological belief system that venerates the economy and a bureaucratic caste appointed to manage and guide the population).[68]

Karatani is also witness to and representative of a tradition in Japanese radical politics that links Marxist and anarchist perspectives, and which is open to difference.[69] Karatani endorses the view that Marxism was the only system of thought imported into Japan that 'left a true mark'. Even Christianity failed to make as big an impact, and was quickly incorporated. Against this, Marxism 'permeated the intellectual community in the 1920s and was then oppressed, left an almost religious trauma, in those who had converted. What followed was that Marxism came to bear Existentialism.'[70] In that space of agonizing about the nature of being in the world we might now also place psychoanalysis. Karatani's work draws attention the way that certain 'insiders' to Japanese culture have always maintained some distance from it, and the process of political critique that this distance makes possible is reminiscent of the point Shingu Kazushige makes about the role that an awareness of 'foreignness' of an individual to their culture necessarily plays in psychoanalysis.[71] The 'New Associationist Movement' (NAM) was one attempt by Karatani to develop forms of political intervention that took parallax seriously, and that would constructively engage with the power of consumers as collective agents in contemporary capitalism.[72]

The foregrounding of ethics in NAM has been one expression of attempts by the Japanese political left to connect with the 'prefigurative politics' of the socialist-feminist tradition, the recognition that the means by which radical politics is conducted is intimately connected with the kind of society that will result from it.[73] Such a political link between Marxism and feminism is seen as all the more necessary given the background of violent sectarian conflict between the left groups of the late 1960s, and the way stereotypically masculine forms of organization were reproduced at that time.[74] There has been an attention to the way that personal relationships are 'political' in Japanese feminism, with a focus on gender and sexuality, and upon the reproduction of power in forms of language.[75] Unlike the Western feminist tradition, however, there is little or no engagement with psychoanalysis, which many feminists in the West looked to in order to account for why women seemed to desire their own oppression despite their conscious intentions to change gender power relations.[76] Psychotherapy and counselling that does connect with feminism tends to steer clear of psychoanalysis, and those therapeutic approaches are closer to humanistic or educational models. There are some important exceptions, and Kawano Kiyomi, for example, trained in social work in Boston where the theoretical orientation was guided by ego psychology. Kawano has been one of the leading figures in feminist therapy, but it was only after she set up her first 'Companion' centre for women that she turned to the psychoanalytic ideas of Harry Stack Sullivan because of the emphasis on 'interpersonal' aspects of the analytic relationship.[77] The Japan Psychoanalytic Society has two women among its 23 full members, and feminist debates have yet to impinge upon it.[78]

Among the other axes of difference that give lie to the image of the Japanese as a homogeneous culture are geographical differences. The four main islands each have their own distinctive character, and some of the dialects used in different regions are mutually unintelligible to Japanese from other places. The supposed tendency of Japanese to be group-oriented, but to prefer dealing with psychological problems in individual therapy because it is less challenging – an argument that we heard from group therapists in Tokyo – was rebutted by psychoanalysts in Fukuoka; they claimed that because people were more naturally more comfortable in groups there, it was individual therapy that posed a real, and so genuinely transformative, challenge to their clients. The relationship between the group and individual is thus contradictory, but contradictory in quite different ways across Japan (and perhaps this is one of the minimal similarities between Japan and all other only apparently internally cohesive cultures with which it is often mistakenly contrasted).

There are a number of ethnic constituencies that are becoming more vocal in recent years, and the visibility of racial difference is also throwing the supposed homogeneity of the culture into question. The Ainu people in Hokkaidō – described by Freud in *Totem and Taboo* – have a representative in the Diet, though there are only about 200 members of this ethnic group who can claim full identity through both parents. Some of the early Japanese eugenic research was carried out on the Ainu, and the 'scientific' backing to myths and stereotypes included claims that their strong body odour was evidence of their links to the 'white race'.[79] A traditionally outcast 'lower-caste' group of a few million, the 'Burakumin' – those viewed as 'polluted' in Shintōism and Buddhism by virtue of occupations such as chopping meat or digging graves – have become more active.[80] A Buraku Liberation League fights against exclusion and oppression that for many years was quite intense but most-times invisible, and it is bad form to mention it in polite company.[81]

The question of Korea has also become more visible, not only as an external problem or historical embarrassment, but also – alongside the historical relationship sedimented in the Japanese language that

Karatani describes – inside the body of the culture. Japanese feminists have been active around the question of Korean 'comfort women' used by the military during the war,[82] and academic study of young *Zainichi* – Koreans of first and second generations who comprise about 1% of the total Japanese population – has challenged the definition of Japanese identity defined by law as 'blood inheritance'.[83] Meanwhile, psychoanalysts of different persuasions in Japan have developed strong ties with their colleagues in Korea, where the impact of Confucianism and neo-Confucianism poses its own particular challenges to psychoanalytic theory.[84]

The fracturing of Japanese culture is evident in the representations of immigrant communities and some alarming images of foreigners as a threat to peace and stability. Kirino Natsuo's award-winning feminist crime thriller *Out*, for example, follows the fortunes of women working in a lunch-box factory in a Tokyo industrial estate, and already on page 2 there is speculation that the sexual assaults and murders around which the book revolves are carried out by one of the migrant Brazilian workers.[85] In many cases the migrant workers are returnees from abroad, whose behaviour and use of the language is viewed as 'unnatural' (even more outsiders than *kikokushijo*, children who have been brought up overseas and then return home).[86] The largest Japanese community outside Japan is in Brazil, and Brazil is a culture saturated with psychoanalysis, with thousands of practising psychoanalysts.[87] Now, in addition to the *kikokushijo*, there are over a quarter million Brazilian workers in the country, many of whom do not speak Japanese.[88] Until now, however, the Japanese psychoanalytic scene has remained fairly impervious to the debates happening there (and this may well be indicative of the way psychoanalysis, even in Brazil, is largely confined to the middle classes, and not so popular among unskilled workers seeking work in Japan). It is also worth noting that the 'psycho-thriller' by Murakami Ryu *In the Miso Soup* also has a killer who turns out to be a foreigner, this time a viciously sadistic US American.[89]

Anxiety about the subjugation of the Japanese by the 'white race' that cries out for psychoanalytic interpretation was produced in a science fiction serialization that apparently turns out to have been authored by a Tokyo Superior Court Judge. It ranks with the autobiography of Judge Schreber, an account famously analysed by Freud, for bizarre imagery that discloses something of the dominant fantasies of some of those with power in the culture.[90] The 1960s series, eventually published in two-volumes in the early 1990s, is about the 'Yapoo' who have been classified as sub-human by their new masters in the twenty-first century:

> Surgery is performed, for example, on some Yapoo to elongate the mouth to fit the genitals of the white masters and thus enable them more readily to swallow the urine and eat feces of their white masters without dripping. A white master's urine was considered to be 'divine aqua,' whose taste was unequalled by any other beverage. The Yapoo considered their master's feces the most delectable of foods and thanked God for the privilege of being allowed to partake of that feast. The tongues of some of them were surgically elongated to provide maximum sexual stimulation for their female masters.[91]

Just as an independent self-contained self is a fantasy, so the fantasy of a unified culture free of contradictions always operates to seal over what it is difficult to come to terms with. The question then is not only how psychoanalysis opens up the process by which defences are constructed against threatening 'Others', 'outsiders' and 'insiders', but also how psychoanalysis itself operates as a force from the outside that is still Other to Japan.

Christians

Jung, the son of a Christian pastor, was a controversial choice to be first president of the International Psychoanalytical Association when it was founded in Nuremberg in 1910. It was an understandable choice given the isolation Freud feared for psychoanalysis at the time – that it might be seen only as a 'Jewish science' – but it was something he came to regret. He was very relieved to be rid of 'the brutal holy Jung and his pious parrots',[92] as he put it when Jung resigned to found his own 'analytical psychology' school. Notwithstanding his other dialogues with Christian colleagues,[93] Freud and many of his followers tended to be very suspicious of Christianity, and psychoanalysis has usually been pitted against any form of religious worldview. European anti-Semitism has since given a negative valence to Christianity in psychoanalytic discourse, and this raises a number of questions about the role of psychoanalysis in Japan, where Christianity is very much in the minority.

Christian evangelical organizations complain that 'Japan is largely unresponsive to the gospel', and put this down to cultural pressures to conform as well as to the 'intense work ethic', but despite their claim that 'Japanese Christians have made little impact on the centres of power',

Christianity has had some influence, in fantasy if not in reality.[94] Anti-Christian edicts of the Tokugawa Shogunate during the period of national seclusion (before the 1868 opening of the Meiji era) expelled foreigners and those who had been converted by missionaries, mainly on the island of Kyushu.[95] An Inquisition office 'Kirishitan Shumōn Aratame Yaku' was established in 1640 to eliminate Christianity, but some communities went underground and survived as 'Kakure Kirishitan', and when the prohibition laws were abolished in 1873 some of these communities had drifted so far from Christianity that they have maintained their status as separated Christians.[96] During the period of seclusion Christianity was portrayed in influential texts like Aizawa Seishisai's *New Theses* of 1825 as 'an alien, occult religion' that 'posed a mortal threat to Japan', aiming to destroy Japan's national identity and 'create a single world order'.[97]

The numbers of Christians have remained small and fairly constant in the last 100 years at around 1% of the population, and allegiance today is more to Protestantism than to the Catholic Church.[98] First-wave feminism in Japan included Christian activists, there is still a 'Christian Women's Temperance Union',[99] and a number of influential figures – politicians and intellectuals – have been Christian. The Socialist Party, which had suffered from pre-war bans on leftists, took control of the cabinet in the 1946 elections, and General MacArthur was reported to have been particularly pleased that, despite it being a left-wing party (for the Americans) its leader and new Prime Minister Katayama Tetsu was a Christian.[100] The first psychologist Motora Yujiro was a Christian, and some prominent psychoanalysts have also been Christians. This is all the more significant given the very small number of practising psychoanalysts in the country.

Doi Takeo converted to Protestantism and then to Catholicism, and the International Christian University – where Doi was once professor – has an explicit rule that only Christians could be appointed to full tenured professorial positions. This university is now the base for an internationally recognized group psychotherapy training, for the *International Journal of Counseling and Psychotherapy* and is home of its editor Kotani Hidefumi. The other leading group therapist is Suzuki Junichi, who was Protestant born, and had the same priest – a well-known figure ministering to middle-class Christians in Tokyo – as Doi. Suzuki worked with Nakakuki Masafumi for two years in a therapeutic community before travelling to England and Scotland to meet Maxwell Jones – a key figure in the history of therapeutic communities in Britain – and to study with British analysts in the field of 'group analysis'.[101]

The influence of Christianity has been quite evident in the field of psychoanalysis, and this should be approached not simply by counting heads but by noting a preoccupation with Christian imagery. The 50th anniversary volume of the Japan Psychoanalytic Society, for example, includes a detailed discussion by Kitayama Osamu of Western images of Madonna and Child,[102] and it should be noted that such imagery has been employed for some years in Japanese film and literature.[103] Christian weddings, which account for almost half of weddings in Japan now, do not necessarily express the religious belief of participants but are a 'particularised social fashion'.[104] This might go some way to explaining the liberal use of New Testament Biblical examples in Shingu's *Rakan no Seishin-Bunseki*, and the motif of 'confession'; even the subject 'suffering' language is described by him using the term *junan*, which has resonances with the 'passion' of suffering in the Passion of Christ.[105]

The most explicit Christian recasting of psychoanalysis, however, has been in Doi's work. This is evident in his best-seller *The Anatomy of Dependence* where the lesson of Christ is spelt out at length and in such a way as to chime with the theme of *amae*. Far from showing that individual 'freedom' should be striven for, it is the sense of dependence on and obligation to others that appears as the main message of scripture; 'One might say', Doi argues, that it was because Christ 'was too free that he was killed',[106] and now that the West is 'caught in a morass of despair and nihilism', it is useful, he says, to remember that 'the Japanese experience long ago taught the psychological impossibility of freedom'.[107]

Further conceptual consequences for psychoanalysis are drawn out in Doi's *The Anatomy of Self*, in which there is an intriguing discussion of 'secrecy', and of the way that 'Freud apparently failed to perceive that secrets are indispensable to [the] psyche'.[108] While psychoanalysis has historically been seen as a practice of self-understanding in which secrets are uncovered, Doi argues that it may be healthier to acknowledge the human need to keep some things secret, in their heart, for which he deliberately uses the term *kokoro* ('heart-mind' or 'soul').[109] Reflecting on the Japanese custom of not opening a gift at the moment it is received; Doi comments that while he did once upon a time think that his American colleagues were right to open a present right away, he is now less sure about this apparently 'rational' behaviour:

> The gift of a present is a gift of the heart. The present, the thing itself, is merely a sign. Therefore, just as the heart is wrapped in flesh and cannot be seen from the outside, a gift must also be wrapped. And because this is true, to open a gift on the spot is unfeeling, an act without *kokoro*, and can even give the impression that one has not accepted it as a symbol of the other person's feelings, but simply

> with an eye to the thing itself. This beautiful custom of not opening gifts immediately has been almost completely lost, and I think it can be said that this is a result of the spirit of the age, an age which places no value on anything that is concealed.[110]

In this way Doi implicitly mobilizes an array of Japanese concepts – *omote* as a public façade versus *ura* to mark what lies behind the surface; *tatemae* as the appearances versus *honne* as hidden opinion – and this enables him to rework the difference between public and private spaces of the self in order to also link psychoanalysis to the Christian tradition. If Karatani's analysis of Japanese language and the relation of Japanese to their language is correct, then Christianity may also operate as a grid of knowledge, a set of signifiers that would be overlaid on the primordial 'becoming' of the nation.

Jews

The particular role of Christians in Japan has changed as Japanese images of its Others have mutated. Cultural anxieties about historical influence and competition has shifted in the twentieth century from China to the West, and have entailed processes of condensation, splitting and displacement that also then construct a particular position for psychoanalysis. There are also consequences for images of Jews, for it is as a 'Jewish science' sealed off from the dominant Christian culture in the West that psychoanalysis has often been perceived as a threat to civilization as such.[111] Jung's departure was then not only a betrayal of psychoanalysis but also invited collusion with anti-Semitism.[112] The issue here, however, is not whether Jung was or was not personally anti-Semitic, but how 'analytical psychology' concerned with integrity of the self and unity of culture tends to endorse nationalist fantasies and the attempt to exclude those who disrupt integrity and unity. The particular 'contents' that Jungians claim to find in myths and legends of a culture then risk compounding that first most dangerous conceptual move. It is against that background that the characterization of Freud as a 'non-European' takes on particular meanings in Japan, but the twists and turns of that characterization have to traverse cultural images of Christians and Jews.[113]

First, there appears to be some degree of condensation in the way Christians and Jews have often been equated in the popular imagination, and many Japanese still apparently confuse the two.[114] Nineteenth-century warnings about the conspiratorial ambitions of the Christians were easily applied to the Jews when the Russian anti-Semitic tract *The Protocols of the Elders of Zion* was translated into Japanese following the Russian Revolution and distributed to Japanese troops drafted in to combat the Bolsheviks. It is possible that the *Protocols* became so popular (and still on sale in many bookshops to this day), because the book resonated with the 'occult religious conspiracy' images – images of Christians – already circulating.[115] Many of the images of Jews in Japan were actually already introduced by Christians, and stereotypical images were relayed by such well-known texts as *Merchant of Venice*, which was the first of Shakespeare's plays to be staged in Japan (in 1885) and the one most frequently performed throughout the twentieth century.[116]

However, the image of Jews that took root in Japan, more powerfully than that of them as Christ-killers – an image that would not mark them out as particularly venal in a culture that did not venerate Christ in the first place – was of them as God's 'chosen people'. This image was itself actually one of the staples of European anti-Semitism, and was popular in the tradition of British 'Anglo-Israelism', which also developed the notion that there was a common ancestry between the Jews and the Japanese.[117] The Christian Sakai Katsuisa, who admired the Jews but argued that it was the Japanese that were actually God's true chosen people, wrote in his 1924 book *The Great Jewish Conspiracy* that what Japan should fear most was 'ideological deviation' and international machinations:

> Today the world is a battlefield. Japan is under attack from savage external threats and internal confusion... Like the Jews, I am an advocate of the restoration of Divine Rule and a Zionist. Nevertheless, I do not wish their conspiracy to succeed anywhere in Japan or for it to contaminate our Imperial Land, for I believe that Imperial Japan has no need of their conspiracy and in fact is in a position to enlighten them. However, since the people of Japan have not yet roused themselves from their infatuation with foreign cultures, the black hand of [the Jews'] great conspiracy has already begun to invade their thinking.[118]

One of the best-sellers in the 1970s, winning the Ōya Sōichi prize for non-fiction, was the book *The Japanese and the Jews* pseudonymously written by one Isaiah BenDasan, and by 1989 even the hardcover edition of the book had been reprinted 50 times.[119] The comparison between Japanese and Jews here recycles the 'chosen people' motif, but this popular book argues that when any foreign religion enters Japan it is turned into particular sect of a cover-all religion BenDasan terms *Nihonkyō*. Here we actually have a reversal of the concern often expressed within Jewish communities in the Western world – that Jews might be 'assimilated' and lose their own special religious and cultural identity – and here it is that the Japanese, who are rather like the Jews in this particular narrative, have precisely the kind of culture that is capable of assimilating anything and everything else.[120]

Secondly, alongside condensation, it is possible to identify a process of splitting by which the Jew as such becomes an unthinkably malevolent figure, alien to Japanese culture, so much so that it would not then make sense for psychoanalysts to include Jews as practitioners. We are concerned with representations here, and these speculations about cultural position are focused on the domain of fantasy, though there are then, of course, material consequences of those fantasies. Splitting, psychoanalytically-speaking, does not necessarily mean that objects of hatred are always conceptually distinct from objects of love, and it is precisely the slippage between love and hate that requires splitting as a defence to be perpetually re-enacted. It is possible to see this quite clearly in the way fear of Jews and the Jewish conspiracy is accompanied by some awe and admiration of their supposed power.

Aum Shinrikyō published a special issue of its magazine *Vajrayāna Sacca* entitled 'Manual of Fear' in 1995, two months before its sarin gas attack on the Tokyo subway system. This special issue was devoted to the Jewish enemy and the 'world shadow government' that was eating away at the vital substance of Japan.[121] This is an aspect of Aum that was central to the group's political programme. However, there was another twist in the tale, for while there were lengthy quotes from *The Protocols of the Elders of Zion* in the Aum magazine, it also asserted that even those who call themselves Jews are not really Jews at all. The 'world shadow government' is thus an even deeper threat to Japan than would be posed by a particular ethnic group, and when Aum referred to 'Jews' it included a wide range of individuals and organizations that were in on the conspiracy. The network of 'Jewish Japanese' encompassed the followers of Sun Myung Moon and the Sōka Gakkai Buddhist sect who were actually, Aum claimed, 'Jewish' sects. Anyone in Japan might be a Jew in disguise, and may not even know it themselves.[122]

So, when Japanese psychoanalysts declare that such an attack means that the Japanese are 'killing their mothers', we might also read into such a statement another frisson of horror; the implication could be that Aum's deliberate attempt to wipe out the 'Jewish Japanese' may also include an attempt to wipe out the psychoanalysts because they have some kind of sinister link with the Jews. Conspiracy theories operate as fixed grids that promise to assuage uncertainty and anxiety about self-identity, and the assumption that only those who can see the conspiracy at work, and can therefore define who is a 'Jew', is a classic motif of anti-Semitic conspiracy theories. In this sense, Aum were able to kill two birds with one stone, addressing political-economic anxieties and specific cultural ambiguities and imagining that it was possible to resolve them (and to note that they were killing their mothers has a further uncanny resonance here when one recalls that a 'Jew' is usually defined by lineage through the side of the mother).

Thirdly, there is a displacement in which the anti-Semitic linkage of psychoanalysis and Jews can be dealt with by attributing positive stereotypical characteristics of Jews to Christians. To some limited extent, then, it is possible to treat the Christians of Japan – a small minority once forced underground but now with prominent figures contributing to intellectual debate – as its Jews. It then makes perfect sense that so many of the small number of psychoanalysts should be Christians. On the one hand, there is a risk that the modernizing and secular practice of scientific elaboration and individual enlightenment that psychoanalysis allies itself with could be elided too closely with Western conspiracies to undermine traditional Japanese cultural identity. On the other hand, psychoanalysis is maintained as an avant-garde theoretical system restricted to a small group of highly-educated practitioners very aware of their role as interpreters of the culture.

To employ psychoanalytic theory to make sense of a culture in which psychoanalysis is still quite marginal is, at the very least, to only provide a partial account. Perhaps it is an account that will only pertain to aspects of the culture that have absorbed psychoanalytic ideas, but there is evidence that some notion of the unconscious and the various forms of defence that are used to defend the subject do already circulate in Japan. Versions of Freudian and Jungian ideas are implicitly at work even when those who draw upon them may not consciously be aware of the implications and consequences of the discourse they speak. And because this discourse is still, when it is noticed, marked as being from 'outside' Japan, the position of those who use it to make sense of the culture is necessarily that of a stranger, something akin to what it was to be a Jew in Western Europe where psychoanalysis first appeared.[123]

5

Mirrors of the Other: 'Why are you asking *these* questions?'

Images of Japan that aim to capture what is culturally-specific about its people have a peculiarly reflexive quality, for such images are themselves structured by the attempt of an outsider to focus somewhere else, 'other'. 'Japan' then functions as a marker of the difference between inside and outside 'our' culture, surreptitiously defining and confirming the development and identity of the Western observer. A Western reader therefore needs to reflect on their own position and historically locate their own assumptions about culture and about the Japanese, and also to examine how they – in that 'other' culture – employ images of themselves which supply certain kinds of mirror for the West. The processes of incorporation and juxtaposition of contradictory concepts of self enabled certain kinds of psychoanalytic conceptual framework to appear in Japan which also necessarily attend to contradiction as such. That conceptual framework cues us into narratives of the self that tend to confirm commonsensical representations of subjectivity in the West, and it provides a vantage point from which to question dominant narratives about the nature of the unconscious in global culture. Then we can redraw the map in which Japan appears at the margins of psychoanalysis, to show how the questions it tackles have now come to operate at the centre of reflexive critical practices tackling contemporary subjectivity.

Gaze

A Monday evening group convened by Matsuki Kunihiro, head of the JPS Fukuoka Psychoanalytic Centre on Kyushu island, opened with a short introductory description of the visitors from England who were interested in psychoanalysis in Japan.[1] Questions of culture, etiquette, gender and language were designed to elicit descriptions of what is distinctive about psychoanalytic practice in this place. But the agenda of the meeting started to take a different and more interesting direction when one of the puzzled participants in the group suddenly asked 'why are you asking *these* questions?' It is a typically psychoanalytic move, quite right in these circumstances, to direct attention to the interpretative frame that is being used to examine an object. So here we need to turn for a moment from the object – psychoanalysis in Japan – to the questions about it that structure the gaze of its interested observers (which should now, of course, include many readers of this account).[2]

One of the most powerful conceptual analyses of this gaze has been provided by those describing the way the West positioned its strange, disturbing and exotic others using 'orientalist' imagery.[3] While the term 'orientalism' was initially designed to describe the world of sultans and harems in the near and 'middle' East, near enough to pose a threat to the West, the exact place of the 'orient' was always in shifting sands. The orientalist gaze very quickly mutated to include the 'far' east, and one favourite here for the orientalists has been Japan.[4] The historical period in which Japan appeared to the West is important, for it could be argued that 'modernity' – a cultural era that appears to accompany the rise of capitalism – privileges vision. This, not only in the ambition of scientific discovery which in its early flowering proceeded by way of careful observation, but also in the colonial project of knowing about the natives that would thereby come into the 'empire of the gaze' as the modern world included them as its subjects.[5] Psychoanalysis too is a child of this modernity, and has a strange paradoxical relationship with the earliest images of hysteria, which were at first visual images.[6]

A gaze on the other which appears to give the observer a thrill, enjoyment at seeing something strange which is also kept at a safe distance, forms the basis of psychoanalytic theories of voyeurism, and the analyst expects to find sadistic elements mingled in with such a gaze. Images of picturesque victims in 'underdeveloped' countries fit the bill here, and the role of fantasy becomes evident when these poor people start to act for themselves and break out of the coordinates of the orientalist gaze.[7] Psychoanalytic assumptions then also play a role in our understanding of the way the gaze of the West which sees evil is itself the 'evil', maintaining the conditions of those it holds within it.[8] We are thus able to explore the investments in certain ways of seeing the world and some underlying dynamics in ostensibly neutral scientific descriptions of people different from us.

Japan was one of the testing grounds for Western notions of 'racial' categorization, though its fortunes waxed and waned according to whether it presented a military or commercial threat, or not. While nineteenth-century explorers like Isabella Bird compared the Japanese unfavourably to the Chinese, recording a 'general impression of degeneracy',[9] the tide was even then turning and American visitors saw them as 'far superior to the Chinese'.[10] Japan's victory in the Sino-Japanese war of 1894–1895, for example, was seen as due to 'the supremacy of Western technology and Christian virtue'.[11] However, though the Japanese had been described by Western visitors during the nineteenth-century as having 'skins as white as our own',[12] by the end of the century the consensus was that they were 'almost white',[13] and then they became 'yellow', as can be seen in Kaiser Wilhelm's 1905 comment that 'This is the yellow peril, the greatest danger threatening the white race, Christianity, and our entire culture'.[14]

Orientalism does not only focus on negative characteristics of course, and apart from attributions to the other of strength or intelligence, there are invariably smuggled in speculations about sexual potency which mingle admiration with envy. The Japanese have attracted a good deal of such attention, and an emphasis on the supposedly violently pornographic nature of the culture in some popular Western accounts provides another reason why psychoanalysis is relevant to understanding images of Japan as well as why a study of psychoanalysis in Japan will also at times itself be caught within an orientalist frame.[15] There is a further twist to the story here, for Western fantasies of racial difference and sexual threat were also mobilized to stigmatize and contain the work of Freud as a Jew dabbling in the dark underside of white Christian culture.[16]

Stereotypes of Japan abound in US culture today, and one can find bucket-loads of them in, for example, episodes of the cartoon series 'The Simpsons', where motifs range from the predilection for eating poisonous fish to technologically-advanced toilets to sadistic game shows.[17] More high-brow versions of such stereotypes were provided in the film *Lost in Translation*, which was widely-touted as providing an insightful window on modern Japan and focusing on questions of cultural difference.[18] That film is interesting not only because of the difference between the reception in the West, where it was popular in art-house cinemas, and Japan where it was very much disliked.[19]

The film also draws attention to some typical aspects of orientialism, one being that while sexuality is focused upon, and there is often some obsessive attention given to oriental males as predatory and over-sexed, there is also at the same time a feminization of the Other. This motif – of feminization in orientalist imagery – serves to play up the threat of the Other to white women, providing a frisson of enjoyment at what might befall her, while keeping that threat at bay by rendering it as something ridiculous and less than fully male. A scientific observer with Commodore Perry after Japan was forced to open to the West at the end of the nineteenth century, for example, found the Japanese interpreters to be intelligent and gentlemanly but also noted that 'they are effeminate and run about and act more like delicate females than men'.[20]

In *Lost in Translation* Bill Murray plays 'Bob Harris' who has travelled to Tokyo to shoot a whisky advertisement. As one critical analysis of the film notes, when Bob turns up for the photo shoot 'he is confronted with the images that Japanese culture has projected onto him as a representative of Hollywood masculinity', but then we see orientalist tropes at work in the way the Japanese men who seem to emasculate him are then represented:

> The photographer commands him to assume various iconic poses – a James Bond wink, a Dean Martin swagger – as he reluctantly tips his glass for the camera. The scene is acted and shot for humor at the expense of the Japanese perception of what a desirable American male looks like: how he sits and gestures, what kind of suit he wears, what kind of whiskey he drinks. The more Bob gives the photographer what he wants, the more he is emasculated, both because he is following the orders of a man who cannot correctly pronounce 'Rat Pack,' and because the images he recreates seem antiquated and fey by contemporary American standards. But this emasculation does not stick to Bob. It is returned to sender: attributed to Japanese naïveté rather than to its American source.[21]

Such aspects of the gaze of the West, which treat 'the Orient as primitive, feminized, and eroticized',[22] thus provide an invisible backdrop to questions we ask about psychoanalysis in Japan.

Limit

Japan is often positioned outside the Western world, as if it is beyond the purview of fully developed civilization, but outside the limits of the civilized world it poses a puzzle for those concerned with limits as such. Not only do Buddhist precepts concern 'nothing', but there is a shift of attention away from separate boundaried beings or selves toward something 'in-between'. So the question from the West, when faced with this puzzling, apparently insouciant attitude to the limits and boundaries that define home-grown conceptions of the world and the things in it, is how to incorporate Japan back again within its own – the West's own – understanding of the difference between itself and other. The West fails in this quest, but in the place of this failure it re-inscribes Japan as the limit. Japan thus comes to functions in the social sciences as a 'limit case' by which what is normal in the West can be tested and guaranteed.[23] And one significant research field where this comparative work takes place is, appropriately enough, in developmental psychology. There are then some quite serious consequences for how the West conceptualizes psychoanalysis, and not only psychoanalysis in Japan.

Within US psychology, then, studies of the individual in the group, of guilt and shame, and of styles of attachment have each functioned to mark out what is distinctive about Japan precisely in order to reassure Americans about the normative shape of their own psychology.[24] As is always the case in psychological research, academic studies of different phenomena are intimately linked with the culture in which they take place and the findings are avidly consumed by an audience schooled to believe what psychologists tell them about themselves. And, as is often the case in research on the Japanese, images of Japan are quickly noted and absorbed into culturally-available self-representations in different versions of the popular *nihonjinron* literature in Japan.

The motif of childishness, for example, that has many times been rehearsed in Western psychological research, and in which the Japanese are depicted as failing to develop fully into adulthood, has been taken up and embraced in Japanese modern art. Powerful cultural resources in forms of technological development, for which Japan is known to excel, can then be mobilized to turn a supposed lack of development into something positive, to be affirmed. An interview with Murakami Takashi is a case in point, and following a description of him at his studio in Tokyo as being quite 'childlike',[25] he is quoted as saying;

> ...Japanese society is really similar to the story in the *Matrix* movies... People cannot rise up or wake up because they are sleeping protected in a capsule. We already found out that *that* society is not real. But it is our normality. Perhaps this is why Japanese subculture has been so strong these 20 years. Maybe if we can keep our

> minds really childish we can be free... So think of a computer's OS [operating system] as people's awareness of 'war' and of 'country'... When people from the UK see a violent *manga* they think it's violent and they're shocked. But because Japanese people don't have this OS they need something more shocking, even more extreme to shock them.[26]

As we have seen, admiration of another culture can be just as potent as hostility in orientalist imagery, and every positive attribute can be factored into evidence of shortcomings.

One striking limit case in therapeutic work is that of 'touch', for this motif operates both to define what may be more authentically Japanese and to mark out psychoanalysis in Japan as a conceptual framework that cannot easily fit into such cultural assumptions. Discussions in the field of dance therapy in Japan, for example, claim that for the Japanese, 'touch is considered a natural aspect of interactions learned from birth and essential to a healthy *being-in-the-world*'.[27] Notice here some resonances with the emphasis on the relationship between mother and child in Japan in work by local psychoanalysts,[28] and also the formulation 'being-in-the-world' which is taken from forms of Western phenomenology that also searched for authenticity.[29] Already, then, Japan and what is essential for Japanese development is framed by theoretical systems imported from the outside.

Here, though, a contrast is set up between 'Westernized "touch-starved" nations' and Japan, and there is then a claim that 'there is a portion of the American population that still represses touch based on ethical and/or moral principles'.[30] The observation that this part of the population in the West 'still represses' touch thus serves to turn around the idea that Japan is less civilized in order to imply that it may actually in this respect be more advanced, more developed than the West precisely because it is more in tune with underlying human needs.[31] The relationship between Japanese children and their parents is described as something deeper than that which pertains in the West, an intimate relationship that has been termed 'skinship'.[32]

The ethical code of practice of the Japan Dance Therapy Association recognizes the importance of touch (unlike the code of its American sister organization), and it stipulates that the therapist be 'always conscious' of the importance of touching; 'We must pay attention', the code says, 'to how clients feel about touch in order to help them feel comfortable and maintain their boundaries, so that they don't feel invaded'.[33] There is thus a concern with 'boundaries', a concern that governs most forms of psychotherapy, but also an attempt to formulate the nature of the boundaries in such a way as to work with the need for touch rather than to prohibit it. The psychoanalytic tradition, on the other hand, treats touch as something taboo, and it is viewed at the very least as a form of acting out or unwarranted gratification for analyst or analysand that calls for interpretation.[34] Psychoanalysis is governed by an ethics of speech, of language as the necessary mediation between human subjects and essential medium of contact in therapy. Attempts in the history of psychoanalysis to bypass speech and make direct contact with the body, to touch, have ended in disaster enough times for analysts today to be very wary of experimenting with it.[35] Psychoanalysis in Japan has therefore been obliged to operate in such a way as to observe boundaries and so then to exist on the Western side of such limits that are mobilized to define what is supposed to be authentic about its own culture.[36]

English

'Japan' is necessarily framed in this book, in general terms by the use of the English language to describe it, and specifically by the close cultural relationship between England and Japan. It is not possible simply to sidestep the romanticizing of Japanese culture by imagining it, as Barthes does, to be a 'fictive nation' and thereby to claim that 'the Orient is a matter of indifference'.[37] The issue here is not simply one of transference – the replaying of relationships with idealized or disprized others – but of the historical relationship between images of Japan and England.[38] I could confess how I think I really feel about Japan for the rest of the book, but that would not help you evaluate the account; it is more productive to explore how some of the material used to develop the account has been constructed.[39] Here, in such a construction of Japan from the vantage point of England, some elements of orientalist imagery are derived from US (and Australian) popular stereotypical representations, though some aspects are quite distinctive.

Nineteenth century enchantment with Japan often led visitors to compare it with an idealized version of England, commenting, for example, on the loveliness of the scenery, 'a Devon foreground set in a background of the Alps'.[40] Sir Charles Wentworth Dilke thought Japan to be a 'traveller's paradise', and waxed lyrical about the inhabitants, employing some familiar themes about the nature of childhood to characterize them:

> It is impossible to realise that the Japanese are real men and women. What with the smallness of the people, their incessant laughing chatter, and their funny gestures, one feels one's self in elf-land... All who love children must love the Japanese, the most gracious, the most courteous, and the most smiling of all peoples, whose rural districts form, with Through-the-Looking-Glass-Country and Wonderland, three kingdoms of merry dreams.[41]

Observers of Japan used it as a vantage point from which to bemoan the increasing vulgarity of their own civilization, and the 'New Japan' that they saw appearing in the spread of modern office buildings toward the end of the nineteenth century was in marked contrast to the 'Old Japan' they loved to romanticize; such new buildings suggested, in the words of one writer, 'an irruption of Birmingham into Arcadia'.[42] Journalists of the time often used the motif of 'Japan' in order to express opinions about the state of Britain that would otherwise have been suppressed.[43]

The British press abounds with amusing examples from Japanese culture, a recent one being the popularity of KitKat, 'Britain's biggest-selling chocolate bar', in Japan; this particularly during the exam season because the schoolchild motto during this time is '*kitto katsu*' ('I'll do my best to make sure I succeed').[44] And England figures in 'cute' (*kawaii*) iconography such as 'Hello Kitty', whose name comes from one of the cats in *Alice through the Looking Glass*; her 'real' name is Kitty White, and 'she lives in London, England with her parents and her twin sister'.[45] Perhaps one of the attractions of Ishiguro's *Remains of the Day* (which was mentioned by a number of Japanese psychoanalysts, psychotherapists and psychologists during the course of research for this book) is the description it gives of the butler Stevens struggling to adapt to the more relaxed etiquette of his new US American master.[46] It is tempting to read this account of old English reserved sensibility in the face of a brash new dispensation as also evoking the predicament of Japan opened up to the New World. It is easy to imagine that there is a symmetrical relationship between the two islands, and one can find 'Japan' functioning as a reference point in contemporary attempts to define what makes the English 'English', a genre that is not as widespread in England as *nihonjinron* writing is in Japan but which is nonetheless fairly popular.

A recent best-selling book among the English middle-classes, *Watching the English*, which is a book that seems designed to reassure rather than disturb its readers, makes a number of telling comparisons with Japan. The *Daily Mail* is quoted on the paperback edition with an approving comment that reiterates a theme in the book (that the English have the facility to be ironic about themselves); 'fortunately she doesn't write like an anthropologist but like an English woman – with amusement, not solemnity, able to laugh at herself as well as us'.[47] The deviation from conventional social norms in public drinking places is said to be 'particularly striking in the English case', to take one case in point, but then the author points out that this is only matched by the Japanese who are also noted for their 'reserve, formality and acute sensitivity to status differences'.[48] With respect to gardening, '[o]nly the Japanese – our fellow crowded-small-island-dwellers – can be said to make comparable effort';[49] and, '[a]pparently we read more newspapers than any other nation, except – surprise, surprise – the Japanese'.[50]

The motif of 'irony' is a pervasive motif in this popular anthropological text, and also equally important in more academic literary theory reflections on 'Englishness'. Such reflections on classic irony – 'an indirect means to refer to reality' – have been more critical, treating it almost as a form of ideology, as a way of 'discriminating insiders from outsiders, those party to the irony from those stuck with a literal reading'.[51] So here, 'irony always slides towards static, uncommitted ambivalence', and the insider is caught between liberal 'insight into what lies behind appearance' on the one hand and 'conservative acknowledgement that common sense, the body and reality are forever fixed and ineluctable, so you cannot do anything about it'.[52] Needless to say, irony serves to establish and reinforce the class positions of those who 'get' it and those who do not. This characterization of the English invites a thought experiment about the place of psychoanalysis in the culture.

What would a study of the development of psychoanalysis in English culture as something 'English' look like and what would awareness of the limits of such an exercise be for the study of Japanese psychoanalysis? The marginal status of Jews in anti-Semitic English culture and the 'modernist' tension between surface and depth explored in literary circles like the Bloomsbury group has been explored in studies of psychoanalysis in Britain, as has the role of 'English' empiricism and the consequent attempt to actually observe the traumatic relationship between child and mother, a more horrific interaction in the eyes of Kleinians working in Britain after the Second World War.[53] It would seem to be the *distance* from the dominant culture that is more important to psychoanalysis in the 'British tradition' rather than the definition of itself as being distinctively 'English'. The focus on psychoanalysis as 'English' rather than 'British' here (despite the characterization of it sometimes as being a 'British tradition') seems to be pertinent given the restriction of it to the south of England (apart from a small Kleinian and then 'independent' group in Edinburgh).

As far as the clinical practice of psychoanalysis is concerned, it could be said to call upon reservoirs of irony so that accounts offered by analysands can be heard at a number of different levels, indirectly referring to another reality and engaging in transferential strategies of inclusion and exclusion of the audience (that is, the analyst). For interpretations to be heard, and to work as 'mutative' interpretations in this psychoanalytic tradition, there must be an engagement with different aspects of the relationship simultaneously so that 'resistance' on the part of the analysand can be addressed, during which time – it was once said – 'the analyst temporarily takes over the functions of the patient's super-ego during the treatment'.[54] The play with double-meanings of words and the use of puns to draw attention to a number of different issues at the same time could, at best, be seen as an expression of English classic irony, and at worst an indication that we are being subject to jokes by our elders and betters.[55] In Japan there are similar claims with respect to generational differences of humour and a suspicion now of 'old men's puns' that would seem to bode ill for psychoanalysis.[56] The tradition of punning in complex poetic forms like *haiku* and *waka* – in which the ambiguous relationship between phonetic and semantic readings of *kanji* provide huge resources – is quite different from some of the current derogated 'old men's puns'; 'Even now, the Royal family members must announce a Waka on the first day of the year in order to promulgate peace of the Japanese nation, although they are not asked to make waka with as many puns as they can.'[57] Psychoanalysis has always had to navigate the scorn of those who see it as futile and endless at the very same time as they acknowledge that it is in precisely that respect that a psychoanalytic sensitivity to language chimes with something of the human condition and facilitates a form of 'enlightenment' that must itself necessarily be ironic.

As with psychoanalysis in Britain, to make one last comparison, Japanese psychoanalysis needs to be understood in how it too takes a distance from its own culture and then engages with elements of culture from inside and outside in order to forge itself as a conceptual framework that is both distinctive and distinctively Japanese.

Appropriation

The process by which Japan accumulates cultural practices from the outside – among which we include psychoanalysis as our main concern here, of course – is intimately bound up with how it engages with orientalist images of itself. If the culture is indeed a kind of 'warehouse',[58] then we have to ask how specific self-reflexive theoretical frameworks that have been imported into it can survive. What needs to be emphasized here is how psychoanalysis is positioned against other ostensibly authentic Japanese cultural traditions at the very same time as it attempts to mark itself out as different from the West.

There is tendency for psychoanalysis, perhaps as a necessary characteristic of it, to be marginal, a quality of being 'outside' the very practices that it enters into, and then even works its way into at some depth. It is worth noting here how, while psychoanalysis in Japan may have had some close relationship with psychiatry, this does not at all mean that the psychiatric system was wholly sympathetic to it. Psychoanalysis had to struggle to define itself as a clinical practice (as we saw in Chapter 2), and its alliance with psychiatry after the Second World War has been increasingly uneasy as the years have gone on.[59] And this struggle meant that it also defined itself against literary and cultural traditions, where there was some interest but no real movement in those spheres for supporting or elaborating psychoanalysis as such.[60]

The development of psychology in Japan has also been such that psychoanalysis was never able to find a niche within it, and was never even able to claim historical connections which would then be shut out, as was the case in Western psychology.[61] Nevertheless, it is possible to discover some elements of early Japanese psychology that were more compatible with psychoanalytic perspectives than the Western 'scientific' theories that eventually became dominant in the discipline. There are significant markers of the differentiation of psychoanalysis from psychology, and here, ironically, from 'Japanese psychology'. The first Japanese psychologist, Motora Yujiro, had a view of emotion that was very different from European and American nineteenth-century laboratory-experimental models, and he posited a single dimension of 'pleasure and displeasure' very similar to that proposed by Freud.[62] This view was lost following the eventual success of more mainstream theories of emotion.

Another potential opening to alternative perspectives in psychology was closed down when Fukurai Tomokichi, a student of Motora's, was forced out from his position at Tokyo University in 1913 for conducting experiments on clairvoyance and other parapsychological phenomena.[63] Whilst Freud himself was quite sympathetic to parapsychology, and favoured research into telepathic aspects of transference relationships in the clinic, this interest has never gone down very well with his followers who wished for scientific respectability.[64] A former director of the Fukurai Institute of Psychology in Sendai, Kuroda Masasuke, is now an emeritus member of the Japanese Association for Humanistic Psychology,[65] an organization that has included some discussion of Jungian ideas, though not to the extent that humanistic or 'New Age' movements have linked with Jung in the West. Japanese humanistic psychologists have kept their distance from recent moves toward 'qualitative' approaches in academic psychology, which they view as merely trying to colonize a deeper understanding of human experience.[66] Even the label 'humanistic psychology' is contentious, and members of the Japanese Association for Humanistic Psychology prefer the term *ningen-sei-shinrigaku*, which could be translated as 'the psychology of human nature'.[67]

A further complication is that Jungians have assumed dominance within the field of clinical psychology and educational psychology, and through the Association of Japanese Clinical Psychology have been pushing for a national licensing system which would then reinforce their own position.[68] One of the consequences of the Fukurai affair on clinical psychology in Japan was that no clinical psychologists were appointed as university professors from 1913 until after the Second World War,[69] and so the field of clinical psychology was built up from scratch during the US occupation, and was then ripe for Kawai to move in when he returned from his Jungian training in Zurich. There is now a Jungian training in Kyoto established in the last few years, and there are about 30 fully-fledged Jungian analysts (that is a little more than the membership of the Japan Psychoanalytic Society). Unlike the JPS, about half of these analysts are women, and about half are psychologists.[70] The 'Jungian Club' (which was established in 1980) has 800 members, the Sanno Training Institute has around 100 staff and trainees, and the Association of Japanese Clinical Psychology has now installed its own licensing system which had by 2002 certified over 8,500 psychologists.[71] Four years later, 2006, the Japanese Certification Board for Clinical Psychologists claimed over 15,000 registrants, which is an indication of how fast this process is occurring. The Jungian-led group, 'firmly established as a wing of clinical psychology in Japan', has also had influence on Ministry of Education licensing systems for counsellors in schools following the 1995 Kobe earthquake.[72]

There is therefore a complex terrain of psychological practice that for so few Freudian analysts facilitates psychoanalytic ideas on a cultural level but which is hostile to the practice of psychoanalysis. This tension between cultural incorporation and exclusion gives a particular colouring to psychoanalysis in Japan. When Freudian concepts are brought into the warehouse of ideas they are accepted on certain conditions that then makes the actual practice of psychoanalysis still quite alien to the culture. One way of grasping the way images are taken in from the outside is to see the process as entailing 'auto-orientalism', a 'masochistic' process of 'do-it-yourself Orientalism' by which there is 'acceptance and internalization' of racist definitions given by the 'Orientalizers'.[73] Another way of conceptualizing this process of appropriation has come from within the Japanese feminist movement, and here engagement with images of Japan has been termed 'reverse Orientalism'.[74] In this way, it is said, 'Japanese intellectuals repeatedly take advantage of the cycles of self-criticism within European thought', but with specific attention to definitions of the Other.[75]

The feminist writer Ueno Chizuko describes such reverse orientalism as 'a process of devaluation followed by a process of reevaluation, in which an Orientalist perspective is taken up to define a positive national identity'.[76] The distinctive feminist aspect of this process can be seen in the particular cases Ueno explores, but there are broader consequences for Japanese subjectivity and for the place of psychoanalysis concerned with self-understanding. For example, Takamure Itsue's attempt to reclaim matrilineality, matriarchy and women's power in Japanese heritage was, Ueno argues, a 'counter-modernist' response to the feminization of Japanese men and the devaluation of Japanese women.[77] This search for an affirmation of women's power led Takamure to Japanese creation myths:

> According to those cosmological myths, Japan's first great ancestral goddess was Amaterasu, from whom all creations derived. Takamure proposed the idea of a 'maternal self' as a Japanese cultural ideal, identifying herself and all Japanese women with the first, great goddess. For her, this solution went beyond the Western individualism to which she attributed the destruction of Japan's traditional community structure. Within her concept of a 'maternal self', woman is at the center of everything. There is no conflict between community and individual in this ideal culture, and it is only women who can lead.[78]

One can also recognize once again an appeal to underlying assumptions about the supposed homogeneity of Japanese culture and here it led Takamure to enthusiastic participation in the war and to celebration of fascism as a political ideology that, she thought, 'encourages women to have more children, values womanhood and therefore is liberating for women'.[79] More recent ideological claims for the value of motherhood – claims that chime uncannily with Kawai's Jungian archetypal motifs of Japan as the 'Great Mother'[80] – have pitted themselves explicitly against feminism. Hasegawa Michiko's reference to the emperor as 'mother of the nation', for example, is in line with new images of the imperial system that are quite acceptable to its most conservative supporters. Ueno argues that these changes run 'parallel to the transformation of capitalism – from hard to soft, visible to invisible, industrial to informational and service-oriented, centred to decentred'.[81]

Such a discourse about the emperor is, as Ueno points out, precisely that which was elaborated a while back by Barthes in *Empire of Signs*, and so the postmodern adoration of Japan as the place of emptiness and passivity is now taken up and used to warrant traditional power relations and new economic practices in conditions of globalization that require that capitalism undergoes a process of 'feminization'.[82] Here, in this feminist account, such 'feminization' draws on stereotypical qualities historically associated with women – intuition, sensitivity and care for others – and reifies them so that they can be deployed by men and women working in the service sector, usually to the detriment of women themselves. Hasegawa's opposition to feminism, feminism which is often confused with feminization, might be expected to entail some hostility to the West, but there is another unpleasant turn here, for she actually characterizes feminism as *karagokoro*, or 'Chinese mind'.[83] This characterization thus serves to settle accounts with a historical relationship with China, and to sever those connections with a view to greater Japanese identity.

Such 'reverse orientalism' is thus a response that is also a trap, a response mired in a romantic nationalism that will idealize rather than question prevailing gender relations. Psychoanalysis, on the other hand, is a practice of questioning and self-questioning that has had to take on board certain conceptions of identity but which is at its heart a process of unravelling how a particular individual in analysis may have come to acquire identity as such.

Voice

In some respects the role of therapy in Japan and what is expected of it would appear to be similar to how it operates in other advanced capitalist countries, providing a place for self-questioning and personal enlightenment. A report on the work of the Japanese Union for Survivors of Trauma, for example, includes an account by a woman who tells how her husband expected her to be his slave and how she complied 'because that's what is expected from women'; she continues '[a]fter therapy I realized how stupid I had been'.[84] Such 'women's therapy' as does exist in Japan is directly focussed on the empowerment of women and the development of specific techniques for raising their consciousness,[85] and this means that psychoanalysis as a therapeutic practice is viewed with some suspicion. Psychoanalysis in the clinic does not explicitly take sides in disputes between ideological worldviews, including over the rights and wrongs of the position of women. The standpoint of the psychoanalyst is usually something that is kept out of the analytic relationship, certainly not made visible to the analysand for it would distort the transference, and perhaps it is even rendered invisible to the analyst themselves.[86]

The oft-made accusation levelled against orthodox psychoanalysis would then be that the avoidance of a worldview of any kind actually renders the approach complicit with taken-for-granted assumptions about human relationships that are not explicitly marked out as a particular ideological position.[87] So, from this critical perspective, when we are examining how someone is given voice in psychoanalytic therapy, we need to ask whose 'voice' it is. If it is not specifically the voice of a woman, for example, that may mean that the voice of men and the position of men in society are being privileged. If the voice is not specifically the voice of lesbians or gay men, then this may mean that heterosexuality is privileged because it is being taken for granted as the conceptual frame within which 'healthy' or 'normal' sexual relationships are expected to take place. And, if the voice is not distinctively 'Japanese', it may mean that the default norm is that of an enlightened fully-analysed Westerner. By the same token, if the voice is expected to be distinctively 'Japanese', the question may need to turn around what particular identities within Japanese society are being silenced.[88]

One way of addressing the potentially pernicious role of a default conservative worldview in psychoanalysis is through attention to the 'countertransference', the analyst's conscious and unconscious responses to the material brought to the therapeutic relationship. This kind of attention is particular influential among the JPS analysts, partly through the formative role of the British Psycho-Analytical Society in which discussions of countertransference as a tool in analysis were first developed and elaborated.[89] There is a striking example of the role of 'projective identification' in the transference – how psychic matter is transmitted from analysand to analyst so that the analyst comes to experience it themselves – in a contribution to the JPS anniversary volume.[90] There comes a point in the analysis where the analyst gazes at a photo of his daughter in his consulting room after he had failed to move it into a position where it could not also be seen by the analysand. The analyst then sees an image of his analysand there, and in puzzling over the perplexing and suffocating nature of the experience comes to understand something of the way he is positioned in the transference as his analysand's father.[91]

While it could conceivably be possible to reframe the theoretical discussion of the 'third subject' that is produced in the analytic relationship between these two speaking subjects around themes of nothingness and interdependency, this JPS contribution actually does not require that. There are no references to Japan or things Japanese, conceptual or cultural, in the paper. Furthermore, there are other contributions to the book likewise that do not refer at all to the fact that the analytic material is Japanese: Papers on aggression,[92] on research on 'borderline personality disorder' in Britain,[93] on metaphor in a therapeutic alliance with borderline and schizophrenic adolescents,[94] on work with a depressed boy,[95] on therapeutic communities,[96] on group treatments,[97] and on 'developmental psychopathology',[98] each of these papers do not even refer to Japan. If we were to include papers that make passing references to anxiety on the analysand's part that the analyst will view them as 'Buraku' but which play no part in the theoretical discussion of the case as distinctive cultural issues,[99] and the discussion of narrative therapies and systems theory that simply uses the Ajase story for illustrative purposes, even then half of the contributions to the volume do not claim to be distinctively 'Japanese'.[100] The same applies to the second JPS volume, in which the nine papers by Japanese analysts focus mainly on historical and technical questions in readings of Freud and elaboration of post-Freudian theory (and reflections on the distinctive 'Japanese' nature of their work is handled by the five contributions by 'overseas psychoanalysts.[101]

Apart from discussions of Japanese mythology, the Ajase complex and the role of *amae* – questions concerning the content of relationships that have been of interest to social anthropologists,[102] and that do have profound consequences for the form of relationships in the clinical setting – the other bid for things 'Japanese' in analysis concerns what appears to be a technical question, the number of times a week an analysand comes to see an analyst.[103] Impassioned defence of analysis at least five-times a week has been mobilized by the British Psycho-Analytic Society as a bulwark against the claims of those outside the IPA being able to claim the title 'psychoanalyst', but it is not really seen as a matter of so much consequence outside the English-speaking world. The discussion, which turns around what is referred to in the JPS volume as the 'so-called Japanese method', thus illustrates the particular section of the psychoanalytic world that the JPS analysts hope to address, though it will not make comfortable reading for that audience.

After pointing out that weekly sessions using a chair with the analyst behind the analysand of the kind employed by Kosawa are viewed by the IPA as 'psychoanalytic psychotherapy' (and so merely 'supportive' therapy rather than 'exploratory' psychoanalysis),[104] the author turns to a discussion of weekly 'free association using a couch':

> I do not limit the therapeutic goal of the 'so-called Japanese method' to be in the supportive dimension, which is the main subject of 'psychoanalytic psychotherapy', nor do I focus only on the improvement of symptoms, or on the resolution of current problems. This is because I have seen many cases in which by applying the 'so-called Japanese method', as a result of expressive and exploratory therapy, the character structure changed significantly, the patients were liberated from pathology, and the therapeutic effect could be seen from a psychoanalytical point of view.[105]

The burning 'cultural' questions here are thus framed as institutional prescriptions and to do with the relationship of the 'so-called Japanese method' to methods used outside Japan.

Global

The International Psychoanalytical Association constitution ratified at its 30th Congress in Jerusalem in 1977 defined three main geographical areas of the IPA's world: '[1] America north of the United States – Mexican border; [2] all America south of that border; and [3] the rest of the world.'[106] The current listing of 'IPA Constituent

Organizations' rectifies this problem, to an extent: However, there are again three main geographical areas identified; [1] 'Europe, including Australia, India and Israel', [2] 'Latin America' and [3] 'North America including Japan.'[107] This strange demarcation of parts of the world and of the place of Japan in it is not confined to the IPA. Every 'international' psychoanalytic organization will necessarily express certain cultural assumptions in the way it constitutes different cultures, makes them legible within certain institutional structures. (Shingu Kazushige's Lacanian credentials are marked, for example, by way of him being secretary of the 'Groupe franco-japonais of the Champ freudien'.)

A paradox which is particularly pertinent to the case of Japanese psychoanalysts is that separation of them off as a distinctive cultural group working in a specific part of the world may actually serve to obscure their adherence to psychoanalysis as something 'universal'.[108] In this respect Japanese psychoanalysis is unlike many other varieties of psychoanalysis in different parts of the world that are actually very provincial, even when they do not appear to make great play of their cultural heritage.[109] To overstate the cultural peculiarities of Japanese psychoanalysis, then, would precisely miss what is significant about it and what psychoanalysts around the world can learn from it.

One of the ways this lesson from Japanese psychoanalysis has been missed is in the attempt to discover what is distinctive about 'the Japanese' and the way they engage with psychoanalysis in the West. This approach can end up reifying cultural differences, homogenizing both cultures and aiming to adapt outsiders to a culture: A most balanced liberal and tolerant version of the argument (framed by US ego psychological conceptions of identity) is that:

> The goals of psychodynamic psychotherapy for Japanese living in the US should not be that they either become acculturated to Western traditions or preserve their Japanese identity, but rather that they attain a new stability with an already acculturated Japanese identity blended with Western values... For first- and second-generation immigrants, and those who are temporarily in the US, reintegration of their identity, accommodating an outer layer of Western personality constructs to the core of their original identity, will be a goal. For those who have been in the US for more than two generations but still carry Japanese cultural influences in psychological issues, collaboratively exploring these influences is useful.[110]

There is a more nuanced discussion by other US writers, who discuss the role of *amae* in the analysis, for example, and attend to issues like 'empathic sensing' (*omoiyari*) which is assumed to play a greater role than verbal expression with certain clients; 'The Japanese saying that nothing important is ever to be communicated verbally goes directly against a cardinal value of American psychoanalysis and culture to express all kinds of feelings and thoughts verbally'.[111] This account continues with the observation that 'an American analyst working with a Japanese patient should be attuned to the possibility that a great deal may be going on by innuendo, more so at an earlier stage than with an American'.[112] This might throw light on the popularity among Japanese analysts of themes from English psychoanalysis in recent years, in which countertransference reactions are explored in such a way that almost presumes telepathic communication. Kitayama discusses exactly these issues in the opening section of his paper on 'metaphorization', but then proceeds to discuss linguistic processes, as befits an orthodox psychoanalyst.[113]

Kawai's discussion of forms of narrative in the West and in Japan could be used to question whether the psychoanalytic process would differ in these two parts of the world. Kawai argues that whereas in a typical Brothers Grimm tale there is a process of 'ego establishment' that fits with cultural assumptions in the West 'where the patriarchal principle is dominant', in Japan the hero does not go through such ego-building adventures, the story does not culminate in anything spectacular, and instead one could say '*nothing has happened*'.[114] This '*nothing has happened*', which is illustrated by way of a Japanese tale about a bird in a plum tree 'The bush warbler's home', can also be interpreted as a 'Nothingness' that has happened, Kawai says, and he then folds this 'Nothingness' into a more conventional (and non-psychoanalytic) Jungian sense of '*The Whole*'. In this way, the 'global' context is mirrored in a little global whole, which Kawai refers to here as the 'Japanese community'.[115]

Different traditions in psychoanalysis that we have examined in the earlier chapters of this book have elaborated quite different ideas for what the 'end' of analysis might look like. For Freud, analysis was 'interminable', and there was no happy end that would avoid the 'bedrock' of castration, the limitation of power that is a necessary condition for someone to exist in a culture composed of other human beings.[116] A more upbeat ending was envisaged by the ego psychologists (discussed in Chapter 1), and identification with the ego of the analyst could then also facilitate healthy adaptation to culture. Kleinians (described in

Chapter 2) are less sanguine, and the resolution of bloody battles that raged in the infant's mind with its objects of love and hate could only take place through accomplishment of a 'depressive' position in which the analysand came to terms with the coordinates of the war they themselves waged against others. Lacanians (we met in Chapter 3) have usually taken an equally gloomy view of the end of analysis, and if it is indeed possible that much suffering disappears when we work through the causal relationships that define who we are, the 'passion' of language still includes a suffering that defines us as human.

Jungians have tended to promise 'individuation' that will accomplish a harmonious resolution of the relationship between a unitary self and wholesome culture, but this 'analytical psychology' that broke away from the psychoanalytic movement and defined itself against it still keeps alive some surprising conceptual resources in Japan. This does not mean that analytical psychology is compatible with psychoanalysis, but it does draw attention to the fact that psychoanalysis can only flower in the context of certain cultural conditions in which there is some conception of the unconscious and an attention to the importance of sexuality embedded within that unconscious domain. In this case, it is the connection with analysis of patriarchy – even if it is not 'feminist' as such, and even if it risks essentializing the qualities of 'male' and 'female' – that connects feminization of the subject with a conception of 'nothingness' that unravels any substantial sense of identity. In this case Kawai is actually close to psychoanalysis, much closer than popular images of it in the West that have it culminating in a dramatic interpretation and transformation of the analysand's life,[117] and the narrative of a psychoanalysis will quite possibly be one in which nothing appears to happen.[118]

Psychoanalysis is, by definition, concerned with what cannot be said, and if there is 'culture' at work inside it, it must be a culture of the unconscious, with its influences operating through processes that are not amenable to being summed up, to being articulated clearly in any language. Psychoanalysis appeared at a certain point in history alongside the consolidation of capitalism in Western Europe, as a form of intense self-reflection upon conditions of life in which it appeared that the new world had displaced an old one in which there was more authentic connection with who one was and where one was from.

The sense of disconnection and rootlessness which afflicted the middle-classes, and which provided a counterpoint to the alienation experienced by the growing industrial working class, incited romantic yearning for full wholesome social relationships – personal identity, economic solidarity, and community – that had never actually existed as such in the first place. As we saw in Chapter 1, the process of industrialization in Japan and the formation of a workforce schooled in the alienating practices of factory labour were accompanied by just such ideological practices to encourage workers to pull together for the benefit of their employers. At a key point in this industrial development, however, the US occupation encouraged romantic yearning for life before capitalist exploitation to be linked to what then appeared to be 'authentic' Japanese culture.

The isolation of small groups of people, separated from each other by virtue of their membership of a particular nuclear family, and with their personal life intensely privatized, turned subjective experience into a puzzle, divided into what was expected and what was prohibited. Sexuality at the heart of this divided intimacy was transformed into something that became a mystery to each individual as they negotiated the transition from childhood to adulthood and were expected to leave the security of their family in order to create another one of their own. Kitayama's discussion of the motif of the 'wounded caretaker' traces the way the position of women as martyrs to the cause of their children induces a 'false guilt' in those they care for. He picks up his earlier analysis of the 'don't look' prohibition – sometimes expressed in Japanese folk tales through the image of an injured animal who sacrifices her body to meet the hero's endless demands after he rescues her and 'hides her painful sacrifice with the prohibition' – to claim that this forms the background for 'masochistic altruism which we take as our cultural feminine ideal'.[119] This account, which should be read alongside Doi's descriptions of *amae* as love and Nakakuki's defence of 'normal masochism',[120] not only offers a perspective on clinical practice in Japan but also illuminates the conditions under which psychoanalysis has come to develop in the West.

At the same time, and as a necessary ideological accompaniment to the economic imperative to sell one's own labour power to survive, experience was increasingly individualized as industrialization proceeded apace. The search for authenticity and identity – an apparent solution to the political-economic conditions of insecurity and meaninglessness – was directed inward, deep inward to be equated with sexuality in something Freud discovered a name for, the unconscious. The invention of the unconscious in psychoanalysis, then, was made in certain cultural conditions, but with the development of capitalism those conditions now pertain to a global economic system which is, for sure, segmented and unequal in its distribution.

As has been noted in the field of cultural studies in Japan, discussions of the 'dark side of globalization' inevitably raise questions about colonialism and postcolonialism,[121] and this present-day 'postcolonial' condition merely serves to facilitate transformations in global capitalism, transformations that Ueno describes as its 'feminization'.[122] Just as appeals to something genuinely feminine would become trapped in a counter-modernist 'reverse orientalism' that essentialized experiences of gender and sexuality, so an appeal to the 'dark side' as authentically Japanese would be to be trapped in the idea that psychoanalysis must be different because it grows from different national soil. Instead, it is the very universal nature of psychoanalysis that permits difference to be articulated, but for each subject, against assumptions in their culture rather than through being reduced to it.

When Freud puzzled about the persistent and problematic 'repudiation of femininity' in analysis and the nature of the 'dark continent' of feminine sexuality, it was to draw attention to something mysterious at the heart of psychoanalytic practice for analysands of whatever sex.[123] Nascent capitalism confined to particular geographical locations invited a view of personal life that confined 'femininity' to women, but now globalizing late capitalism entails the feminization of the economy, culture and the experience of women and men making sense of who and where they are. In this sense, Japan and its psychoanalytic discourse is ahead of the game, and now provides diverse – ego-psychological, object-relations, Kleinian, Lacanian – 'cultural' reflections on global phenomena.

All psychoanalysis is 'cultural', and the lesson from psychoanalysis in Japan is that globalization has facilitated forms of subjectivity that have now been both rendered interpretable, understandable to individuals in different parts of the world and at the same time distinctive, specific to their points of origin. Japan in analysis is a culture that refracts elements of the unconscious, has become a culture of the unconscious, in such a way as to show everyone else outside it what psychoanalysis really is.

Notes

Chapter 1 Dependency in Development: 'Where id was, there ego shall be'

1. Freud (1913), pp. 44–45.
2. Ibid., p. 80. Freud refers to the Ainu as the 'Aino' people, a rather antiquated and now disrespectful term.
3. Ibid., p. 139.
4. Okonogi (1995), reprinted as Okonogi (2004a).
5. This startling announcement was for the Arususha edition (the publisher of the rival edition was Shunyodo), Sato (2002), p. 11.
6. Ibid.
7. Freud (1920).
8. Blowers and Yang (1997), p. 123, highlight this translation, but *'geist'* rarely appears in Freud's writing (and only a few times in *Jenseits des Lustprinzips*). Shingu Kazushige (personal communication, May 2007) also points out, in addition to these niceties of translation from the German, that the Japanese sound 'shinteki' can be equivocal for it can mean 'of heart-mind' and also 'of god' (and the Kanji for these are different, and this is just one example of a crucial difference between speech and writing in the Japanese language that we will return to in Chapters 3 and 4).
9. Blowers and Yang (2001).
10. Oyama et al. (2001).
11. The translation in some English-Japanese dictionaries is misleading; for example, Brannen (1991, p. 240) translates 'psychiatry' as *'seishin byōri' gaku'*. The Japanese term *'seishin-byo-igaku'* might be translated back into English something like 'medicine for mental illnesses', but it is *'seishin-igaku'* that is now the preferred translation for psychiatry (and means 'medicine for the mind').
12. Freud's (1926) missive against the medics, 'The Question of Lay Analysis', was originally translated into English as 'The Problem of Lay Analysis' which rather took the sting out of the tail of Freud's argument. See Bettelheim (1986) for a discussion of this and other problematic translations into an English-language tradition that aimed to turn psychoanalysis into a natural science. In the English translation the German word *Ich* (the 'I') is turned into the 'ego'.
13. See, for example, Jacoby (1983) on the way émigré psychoanalysts from Europe adapted to US culture when they arrived just before and during the Second World War and then developed psychoanalysis as a technique to enable adaptation.
14. Blowers and Yang (2001).
15. Freud (1933), pp. 79–80.
16. Freud (1930), p. 24.

17 Elsewhere Freud provides some other culturally-potent images of the super-ego as a policing agency when he compares the lax and corruptible Russian police with the preferably firm but fair Swiss police.

18 The Ryūkyū islands in the south were held by the Americans to be trustees for an indefinite period, only eventually being given over in 1972, and there is still a good deal of opposition locally to the American bases that remain (Henshall, 2004, p. 155).

19 See Henshall (2004), p. 135. Although the occupation was supposed to be an Allied exercise, in practice it was 'almost entirely an American affair, and MacArthur was very much master of ceremonies' (Ibid., p. 140). In his role as SCAP, MacArthur relied on Hirohito to keep order, and Hirohito was able to amend the text of the broadcast on 1 January 1946 so that he would not also have to renounce his divine descent.

20 Such designations of significant time segments – 'Edo period' and 'Meiji period' – do not correspond to the Western Christian 'centuries', which provide a new way of defining the 'discursive space' of Japan and which signify its incorporation into the West (Karatani, 1991).

21 For a discussion of this two-way cultural traffic, see Yokoyama (1987).

22 Sōseki (whose comment on the West is cited in Henshall, 2004, p. 101) wrote amusing descriptions of changing life in the Meiji period that were read by many generations of Japanese schoolchildren in *I Am a Cat* (Sōseki, 2002). His novel *Kokoro* (Sōseki, 1957) is discussed in the writings of the psychoanalyst Doi Takeo (see, for example, Doi, 1986). There is also a discussion by Matsuki (2004) with reference to the phenomenon of 'unconscious guilt', and by Karatani (2005) who highlights the influence of the English literary tradition on Sōseki's writing.

23 Benedict (1967).

24 Ibid., p. 1.

25 See Okano (1994).

26 Benedict (1967), p. 222.

27 Ibid., p. 203. See also, for examples of analysis by outsiders that dwell on this aspect of Japanese relationships, Buruma (1995). Despite collections of lurid stories from the Japanese popular press still being marketed as offering an insight into a particularly depraved and sex-obsessed culture, all such collections seem to demonstrate is that tabloid journalism in Japan has just about managed to keep abreast of such offerings in the West (for an example, see Botting et al., 2005).

28 Ibid., pp. 203–204.

29 Befu (2001), p. 51.

30 See, for example, Igarashi (2006).

31 Sato et al. (2004).

32 See, for example, Oyama et al. (2001). There are discussions of the influence of US psychology before the War by Nishikawa (2005); Mizoguchi (2005) argues that Pavlov's ideas (from Russia) did not take in Japan also because of the influence of German psychology.

33 Tsutsui (2004) notes that '...Japan must always fight its monstrous invaders alone, with the tens of thousands of American troops stationed in the country permanently on the side-lines and the foreign powers offering just diplomatic lip service, if even that.' (p. 83). He peppers his account of

the Godzilla films with pop-psychoanalytic comments such as 'The Japanese have an old proverb, *jishin kaminari kaji oyaji*, which lists the four most fearsome things in the world as earthquake, thunder, fire, and father.' (p. 16).

34 One psychologist we met even styled himself as a 'peace psychologist', and he was the only person we met who mentioned Hiroshima; perhaps 'peace psychology' is a reclaiming of the 'peace' that was imposed during the occupation and a turning back of this term against the US (a process we will see operating in work at the International Christian University later in this chapter).

35 The Prime Minister was Yoshida. For a description of the impact of the June 1950 invasion by North Korea on the Japanese economy, see Henshall (2004).

36 This was part of the logic of 'peaceful coexistence' which encouraged many parties in the Comintern to side with the 'progressive bourgeoisie' and, where necessary, to stop strikes which would disrupt good diplomatic relations between a regime and the Soviet Union. The JCP, like many other communist parties, was torn between this policy directive from the Kremlin and the struggles of their members and comrades in trades unions, and eventually the centrifugal forces that alliances with governments set in play led the so-called 'Eurocommunist' parties to transfer their allegiance from the Soviet Union to politicians in their own country. Then the JCP effectively became one of the main 'Eurocommunist' parties. For a discussion of this logic, see Mandel (1978).

37 One of the reasons MacArthur allied himself with Hirohito was that this would be the most effective safeguard against the Left; 'they [MacArthur and Hirohito] shared a hatred for communism' (Henshall, 2004, p. 144). The JCP suffered big losses in the 2003 lower house elections, losing nearly half of its votes in the previous five years after adopting a turn to the right in which it promised to work in a coalition government committed to a Japan-US military pact.

38 Van Wolferen (1990), p. 284. Van Wolferen sees Buddhism, Christianity and Marxism as disrupting Japanese societal norms, but as then being contained by it as oppositional forces are harnessed and channelled into the 'system'. This 'system' that underpins 'Japanese power' is machinery in which educational institutions play a prime role. In the final pages Van Wolferen turns to consider what might be done in an ideal situation, and argues that 'For a start, one would have to abolish Tokyo University' (p. 432).

39 On the hope that US workers might also be tamed in the same way as their Japanese counterparts see, for example, Kahn (1970).

40 Ichiyo (1987), p. 35.

41 See Befu (1980) for a critique of the 'group' model of Japanese society, and Takano and Osaka (1999) for a social-psychological critique of the image of the Japanese as 'collectivist'.

42 Nakane (1970), in a classic US study of 'Japanese society' that has also been a best-seller in Japan and one of the key texts in *nihonjinron* speculations about 'groupism', argues that it is defined by a frame that provides a boundary, vertical relationships, exclusivity of membership and hostility towards outsiders.

43 Moloney (1953), p. 291.

44 Moloney's source here, one which he refers to at many points in his paper is King Hall's 1949 edited volume *Kokutai No Hongi (Cardinal Principles of the National Entity of Japan).*

45 Moloney (1953), p. 302.

46 Ibid.

47 Kotani (2003), p. 15. This is an article in the first issue of the *International Journal of Counseling and Psychotherapy* he edits (based at the International Christian University in Tokyo). See also for another example from the same journal, Nishikawa (2003).

48 The reference point for Kotani here is Erikson (1959) in psychoanalysis and Rogers (1951) in the person-centred tradition.

49 Kotani (2005), p. 46. There are a number of theoretical and therapeutic developments of 'Psychoanalytic Systems Theory' at ICU, which include interventions in the field of school counselling (Nishimura, 2007) and exploration of 'jokes as a technique of creating a psychological safe space for schizophrenics' (Ishikawa and Kotani, 2005, p. 94).

50 James (2004); 'Phallic activeness is conceptualized as a force which exceeds the Oedipus complex, and it is considered to be a key function for taming the drive energy in the personality development of a woman' (p. 78). See also, for work on the construction of 'safe space' for women in therapy at the ICU, Nishikawa (2007).

51 International Christian University (2004), p. xxiv. (Kotani's first response to the draft of this book was to tell me that his barber, upon hearing about the book, suggested that Kotani should now write a book about psychoanalysis in Britain, and that these projects might together assist progress toward understanding between nations and toward world peace).

52 For example, Agazarian (1989). There is a discussion of the work of group analysis by Aida (2004) who is a JPS training analyst. One of the group analysts who introduced the work of US-American group therapists to Japan still identified himself with the British tradition in analysis, and referred to his US-trained group-psychotherapy colleague (for we heard him say it *sotto voce* to his wife) as 'the American'.

53 Moloney (1953), p. 303. On the production of the 'individual' as a group fantasy in Western culture, see Wolfenstein (1990).

54 This distancing was something we noticed in our conversations not only with those trained in the US American tradition, but also those analysts allied with British and French psychoanalytic institutions. They enjoyed telling us about the strange practices of Morita and Naikan therapists (and we enjoyed it too). Nevertheless, the JPS did also include a glowing account of Naikan therapy in volume 2 of *Japanese Contributions to Psychoanalysis* (Matsuki, 2007a) by a Dutch IPA analyst (Van Waning, 2007). For a brief description of these approaches as background to a comparison of Buddhist and psychoanalytic ideas, see Shingu and Funaki (2008).

55 For an account of psychotherapies 'originating in Japan', see Sakuta et al. (1996), and for a Western take on these approaches, see, for example, the website of the ToDo Institute (2004). There are also home-grown cognitive-behavioural techniques in 'Dosa therapy' that were first used for children

with epilepsy and later used to treat trauma, but such techniques do not entail a complete worldview that claims to be 'Japanese'; for an account of Dosa therapy, see Muramoto (2001).

56 Popular representations in modern Japanese literature make the link between spiritual retreat and psychiatric care explicit; see, for example, Murakami's (2003a) description (in the 1987 Japanese best-seller *Norwegian Wood*) of Toru's visit to see Naoko at the isolated 'Ami Hostel' in the hills north of Kyoto.

57 There are around 30 Naikan medical centres in Japan, as well as three in Austria, two in Germany and one in the US (Kawahara, 2004).

58 Kitanishi and Azuma (2005). The approach is sometimes known as 'Personal Experience Therapy' (Morita Therapy Center, 2004).

59 Morita Therapy Center (2004).

60 The editor's introduction to Morita's book notes that the US American psychoanalyst Karen Horney visited Japan in 1950 after becoming interested in connections between psychoanalysis and Zen Buddhism (Le Vine, 1998, p. xxiv). On Horney's interest in Zen Buddhism see M. E. Miller (2002). Other analysts who were also (like Horney) critical of mainstream US American psychoanalysis, also dabbled with Zen at various points (e.g., Erich Fromm, 1959).

61 Morita (1998), p. xv. The editor of the English edition helpfully translates the different categories of disorder Morita discusses into categories used by the American Psychiatric Association's Diagnostic and Statistical Manual of Mental Disorders.

62 Morita (1998), p. 96. Kitanishi and Azuma (2005) point out that many papers introducing Morita therapy for audiences outside Japan make a link between Morita and religion, and this tends to obscure the way Morita actually emphasized an engagement with Western mental health practices rather than Zen. (Kitanishi and Azuma's paper also has a useful discussion of the development of Morita therapy in China, and this development also serves to show how the approach departs from Morita's own work to connect with spiritual perspectives and what is taken to be 'traditional' Chinese culture.)

63 See Freud's (1915) essay on the unconscious for an outline of this distinction.

64 Ibid., p. 24.

65 Kitanishi and Azuma (2005) then argue for the applicability of this updated version of Morita therapy to 'multicultural counseling', 'crime victim counseling', 'career counseling' and 'Morita-based therapy for people with incurable cancer'.

66 See, for example, Sugamura and Warren (2006) and Sugamura et al. (2006); these attempts to build upon 'social constructionist' approaches in therapy complement some of the recent links in Western psychiatry between 'mindfulness' and cognitive-behavioural therapy. On the history of 'Buddhist psychology' in Japan, see Onda (2002).

67 For a discussion of notions of the 'ego' in Japanese psychology, see Suzuki (2005).

68 Doi (1973).

69 See Befu (2001). Doi modestly and rather implausibly claimed, when we asked whether analysands might expect to have *amae* interpreted in their sessions with him, that it was rare to meet patients who read his books.

70 'The meaning [of "please help yourself"] is simply "please take what you want without hesitation," but literally translated it has somehow a flavor of "nobody else will help you," and I could not see how it came to be an expression of good will. The Japanese sensibility would demand that, in entertaining, a host should show sensitivity in detecting what was required and should himself "help" his guests' (Doi, 1973, p. 13).

71 Doi (1973), p. 95.

72 For one exception, see the study by Johnson (1993). Enns and Kasai (2003) describe Doi as a 'psychiatrist' rather than a psychoanalyst, a convenient rhetorical move in their narrative about the importance of connections between Buddhism and Jungian analysis.

73 For an example of this, see Morsbach and Tyler's (1986) evocation of the way *amae* signifies in a range of popular cultural texts in Japanese.

74 Miike (2003), p. 107.

75 See Burman (2007a) for an analysis of the way Japan figures in developmental-psychological research (see also Gjerde, 2004, and, for an earlier published account, Gjerde and Onishi, 2000); for examples of this kind of research, see Rothbaum et al. (2000), Behrens (2004) and Yamaguchi (2004). The Japan Psychoanalytic Society endorse this developmental research in the second volume of *Japanese Contributions to Psychoanalysis* (Matsuki, 2007a) by inclusion of two invited papers by 'overseas psychoanalysts' describing what can be learnt about attachment in Japanese infants (Freeman, 2007; Okimoto et al., 2007).

76 Doi (1986).

77 The Japanese analysts we met seemed to want to impress on us how we would need help, without accepting that we should be dependent on others rather than self-sufficient. It is not easy for a Westerner to find their way around Japan, but our hosts seemed to take great delight in telling us how difficult it would be for us to cope on our own, from driving a car on Japanese roads to finding an address (quite complicated because city districts, *ku*, and blocks, *cho*, are usually indicated instead of house numbers and street-names); Doi, who is now in his 80s, sent us a little map to locate his office in the buildings of the PHP Research Institute – PHP stands for 'Peace, Happiness through Prosperity' (and note, again, the importance given to 'peace' here in the title of the institute as a home for Doi following his earlier appointment at ICU). For an analysis of other encounters in which *amae* was evoked as both topic and resource to make sense of our helplessness as visitors, see Parker (2006).

78 See, for example, Doi (1990). For a discussion of these questions in relation to psychotherapy with Japanese clients, see Roland (1996).

79 See, for example, Doi (1993).

80 Doi (2004), p. 35.

81 Michael Balint was part of the independent tradition in British psychoanalysis, influential in setting up groups (now known as 'Balint groups') for medical doctors to discuss psychodynamic factors in relations with

patients (see Balint, 1968); Heinz Kohut developed 'self psychology' in the US as a version object relations theory (and his work has been influential in psychoanalysis in the English-speaking world also in South Africa) (for a classic case study, which later transpired to be of his own analysis, see Kohut, 1979).

82 Doi (1973), p. 75.

83 Ibid., p. 77.

84 Kotani Hidefumi told us with delight, for example that he now occupies Doi's old academic post at the International Christian University, and has Doi's office, desk and hat-stand.

85 Nakakuki is responsible for 'Japanese Liaisons' on the Board of Directors of the IMHPJ (where he is listed as 'Matt Nakakuki'); see http://www.imhpj.org (accessed 8 May 2007). Nakakuki has his office in nearby Roppongi, which is where we interviewed him, and these two districts were where we saw the highest concentrations of Westerners (in Aoyama the wealthiest, and in Roppongi the loudest). Nakakuki also, like Doi, gave us a little map for us to find him for an interview.

86 Nakakuki (1997a), p. 11 of unpublished ms. There is a discussion of the tendency of Doi to 'overgeneralize the psychodynamics of Japanese neurosis as Amae frustration' in an account of a case of the culture-bound disorder '*Taijin Kyofu*' (in which the patient 'develops a specific fear that his gaze bother and hurts others and is afraid of looking at others') by Nakakuki (1997b). For a Lacanian take on this disorder, see Suzuki (2002).

87 Nakakuki (1994).

88 See the account by Kitayama (1991), p. 232. A psychiatrist working with the JPS group in Fukuoka told us that he diagnoses children with 'developmental disorders' and then brings the mother into therapy (to help them address the guilt they suffer, and the suffering they have been enmeshed in that may have created the conditions by which such disorders came about). There is now a an emerging tradition of 'child analysis' in Japan, but this has appeared after the consolidation of Kleinian and object relations theories (rather than, as in Britain, with child analysis itself as provoking the development of new theories and practices).

89 See Freud (1924). Nakakuki cites a number of US-based clinicians, including Erich Fromm, Karen Horney and Rudolph Loewenstein, in his review of sources on 'normal masochism' in psychoanalysis.

90 Nakakuki (1994), p. 251.

91 See Bettelheim (1986) for an argument about the necessary ambiguity of content in the Oedipus story.

92 This version of the story of Ajase is condensed from the account given in Okonogi (2004b), p. 78. It should be emphasized that the received version of Kosawa's (1931) paper is actually very different from the original account, which does not (to take just one instance) include discussion of the mother's attempt to kill her son Ajase. The original paper is reproduced in the second volume of *Japanese Contributions to Psychoanalysis* (Matsuki, 2007a); then even the commentary by an Indian IPA analyst (Basak, 2007) which is included in that volume is evidently upon the version relayed to the Japanese and wider psychoanalytic world by Okonogi.

93 I am grateful to Shingu Kazushige for this extract from Kosawa's account.
94 These three themes are outlined by Okonogi (2004b), pp. 79–80.
95 We will return to the interpretation of this Indian story relayed to Japan via China and Korea – with specific attention to Ajase's attempt to kill his father as well as his mother – in the following chapter and in Chapter 5.
96 Nakakuki (1994), p. 247.
97 Ibid., p. 253.
98 Ibid., p. 255.
99 Ibid., pp. 244–245.
100 See Lasch (1978) for an analysis of what he sees as a contemporary Western 'culture of narcissism' (an analysis Nakakuki refers to and appears to endorse).
101 For essays by Maruyama Masao, see Maruyama (1969).
102 See, for example, Karatani (1991) and Karatani (1998).
103 See Ehara Yumiko (2005a) for arguments directed specifically at Maruyama's work and the way his assumptions about Japanese culture are reproduced in the writings of 'postmodern' feminist' writers; Ueno Chizuko extends this critique to the work of Karatani, complaining that he 'essentializes the feminine attributes of Japaneseness' (Ueno, 2005, p. 237).

Chapter 2 Institutional Politics and Cultural Intervention: 'They were killing their mothers'

1 The reference to Kosawa as the 'the father of Japanese psychoanalysis' is in Okonogi Keigo's (2004a, p. 11) account included in the JPS 50th anniversary showcase volume *Japanese Contributions to Psychoanalysis* (Kitayama, 2004a). It was originally published as the entry on Japan (Okonogi, 1995) for the second volume on psychoanalysis around the world (Kutter, 1995).
2 See Blowers and Yang (1997), p. 121. Sato (2002, p. 11) notes that a back-translation of the Japanese title of Freud's text is the evocative *The Other Shore of Enjoyment*.
3 See Blowers and Yang (2001) on Ohtsuki Kenji and the role of lay analysis. The official JPS version of the history now has it that Yabe and Ohtsuki's Tokyo branch of the IPA 'promoted psychoanalytic theory to the general public only, as a system of thought, without inviting the participation of psychiatrists. It thus never developed as an association of clinical psychoanalytic psychotherapists, and was finally disbanded after the Second World War' (Okonogi, 2004a, p. 10).
4 See Blowers and Yang (1997), p. 124.
5 The German system entailed observation of abnormalities that were then grouped into categories in a classification system, whereas psychoanalysis works through the elaboration of hypotheses about underlying clinical structures, hypotheses that are revised as the treatment progresses. On the influence of the US diagnostic systems in Japanese psychiatry, see Iwasaki (2004).
6 See Blowers and Yang (1997), p. 122.
7 Sato (2002), p. 9.
8 Kosawa Heisaku's meeting with Freud was most probably on the evening of Thursday 11 February 1932 (though Kosawa later noted it as being the

following Thursday 18 February). Detail about the date and Kosawa's account are from Blowers and Yang (1997), pp. 117–118. (I must admit that I was disconcerted when Kitayama Osamu left his umbrella in the café near the university in Fukuoka when he left after our discussion, but will refrain from making interpretations about how much he must have loved his English visitors.)

9 A student of Kosawa's (Takeda Makoto) interpreted the slip in this way after Kosawa told him what had happened during his visit. Blowers and Yang (1997) mention this in their history (p. 118), but give the name of Kosawa's student (who is still, at time of writing this, still alive and running his own psychiatric hospital) as 'Mokoto Takeda'.

10 Freud's brief note simply said 'I have received and read your essay. I'll keep it with me since it seems as if you have no intention to use it otherwise' (in Blowers and Yang, 1997, p. 119). For a version of this 'essay', which makes a plea for Buddhism not be seen as a pathological religion in the way Christianity is viewed in psychoanalysis, see Kosawa (1931).

11 Okonogi (2004a), p. 12.

12 Sato (2002), p. 16.

13 Ibid., p. 31.

14 In Blower and Yang (2001), p. 38. The argument that there be 'acceptance of divided nature rather than the eradication of one impulse in favour of another' is not actually incompatible with psychoanalysis, and (as we will see in Chapter 3) still provides a potential meeting point between the two approaches.

15 Shinran (1173–1262) and Nichiren (1222–1282) were two of the key founders who distinguished Buddhism in Japan from its Chinese variants.

16 Okonogi (2004b), p. 95. Abortion has historically been the main method of birth control in Japan, as Okonogi notes (Ibid., p. 96). The contraceptive pill was only legalized in Japan in 1999. For a discussion of the way Buddhist institutions play on women's guilt over abortion see Miya (1997).

17 Freud (1912–1913). The argument is summed up in the extrapolation from embryological research that the development of each individual repeats or 'recapitulates' the development of species; ontogeny recapitulates phylogeny. This view of anthropological research – the supposition that anthropologists are able to study other 'primitive' cultures that are in some sense the past of 'civilized' societies – is now rejected by most anthropologists.

18 Kitayama (1991, p. 237). Note here that Kitayama is adopting a fairly orthodox Oedipal-centred account of mediation that will then operate as an assumed background to his elaboration of the motif of 'don't look' (that we deal with later in this chapter). There is an interesting Kleinian discussion by Kitayama's colleague Matsuki (2007b) of the way this mediation operates in analysis, in which Matsuki resolves the paradox that the 'neutrality' of the analyst cannot itself be 'neutral' by showing how the 'stable inner structure' of the analyst must be permitted to 'sway' as a kind of mast in the storms of transference and counter-transference.

19 Okonogi (2004b), p. 80.

20 A psychoanalyst might easily say that 'He wanted to kill his mother' is a euphemism of 'He felt sexually seduced by his mother', and the Ajase story might easily be interpreted in classic Freudian theory as another variant of the Oedipus triangle (Shingu, 2007).

21 Shingu Kazushige comments that we can see two postulates in Kosawa's account – that Ajase represents an oral-sadistic and most primitive sin, and that we can rely on Buddha for his forgiveness – and so 'the concept of Ajase complex is half Kleinian and half Buddhist' (Shingu, 2007).
22 Ibid., p. 96.
23 Ibid., p. 81.
24 Ibid.
25 This notion of 'deferred action' in psychoanalysis is outlined by Freud in the early case studies and then underpins his later clinical work (Breuer and Freud, 1895). There is an explicit discussion of this notion in relation to life narratives by Kano (2004) in the JPS anniversary book.
26 Ibid., p. 95.
27 Kitayama (1985), p. 180.
28 Breuer and Freud (1895), p. 305.
29 Nishizono (2004a), p. 234 (citing another Japanese writer, Soeda), describes four kinds of *on*: to parents, to the public, to the king, and to three treasures (Buddha, Law, and the Priest).
30 Benedict (1967), p. 225.
31 Kitayama (1985), p. 173.
32 The 1943–1944 'controversial discussions' were followed by a 'gentleman's agreement' to resolve the conflicts between the warring women in the British society. See Kohon (1986) for an account of the emergence of the independents.
33 Klein is sometimes referred to as an 'object relations' analyst, but she is concerned with internal representations of 'objects' (see Klein, 1986). The 'object relations' did actually take seriously what went on between child and mother, between the child and the 'objects' around it. Michael Balint (an independent in the object relations tradition who developed the notion of the 'basic fault'; Balint, 1968) is often associated with the phrase 'two body' psychoanalysis (in which the relation between analyst and analysand reproduces the relation between mother and child). For a discussion of the way an attention to 'two-body' relationships have served to obscure the original arguments made by John Rickman, see Hanly and Nichols (2001).
34 The positions are not only developmental 'stages' for Klein, and adults will often shift from the depressive position to the paranoid-schizoid position at times of crisis, disappointment and loss. The aim of Kleinian psychoanalysis will enable the analysand to attain a depressive position that approximates the 'common unhappiness' that Freud saw as the most that could be hoped for.
35 Winnicott (1947), p. 201. For representative theoretical statements of his work, see Winnicott (1974). His 1947 paper on 'Hate in the countertransference' also builds upon the work of Kleinian analysts on the unconscious responses that a psychoanalyst has to their analysands (the 'countertransference' that complements the 'transference' the analysand undergoes as they relive past significant relationships with the figure of the analyst in the place of those once loved or loathed).
36 Phillips (1988) p. 100.
37 Okonogi (2004b), pp. 92–93, notes that Kosawa's argument dates from 1932, before Klein's ideas became well-known, but hints that Kosawa may have known of her ideas.

38 Kitayama (1985). p. 180.
39 See, for example, Doi's (2004) chapter in the JPS volume which links with Balint's work.
40 See, for example, Kinugasa's (2004) chapter on borderline research in Britain. In volume II (Matsuki, 2007a), Fukumoto's (2007) study (which makes the only passing reference to Lacan in the JPS volumes) was also supervised from the Tavistock Clinic, and Takahashi's (2007) study of the sexuality of 'paranoid schizophrenics' in object relations group psychotherapy was supervised at the Menninger Clinic (where Doi trained).
41 For example, Matsuki Kunihiro has published an introduction to the work of Klein and has translated work by Patrick Casement; see also Matsuki's (2004) discussion of different forms of guilt.
42 See, for example, one of the contributions by the then president of the JPS, Nishizono (2004a), p. 228.
43 Takano (2004) does not explicitly reference British Kleinian or object relations theories, and this, indeed, is precisely why her very interesting clinical case study is an apparent exception which turns out to prove the rule (that British perspectives have become important to psychoanalysis in the JPS in recent years).
44 Ibid., pp. 179–180.
45 Radich (2004a), p. 173. This translator's note to Shingu's (2004) book on Lacan makes the Buddhist provenance of the term more explicit than it is in Takano's (2004) account.
46 The case is described as 'psychoanalytic psychotherapy', and so the term 'patient' (rather than analysand) is more appropriate here, particularly as the meetings were in a hospital after she had been admitted to an emergency care unit. (The author of the chapter was, at the time of publication, one of the 'psychotherapist' members of JPS.)
47 Ibid., pp. 193–194.
48 This self-representation of Japan as safe and the outside world as dangerous uncannily mirrors Chinese self-representations of themselves as peaceful but as having suffered from the violence of outsiders, often explicitly associated with the Japanese. These Chinese self-representations, with Japan as a site of cruel violence (and with strikingly similar motifs to highlight the cruelty), range from historical novels (e.g., Yan, 2003) to contemporary political satire (e.g., Shuo, 2000).
49 Kitayama (2004b), p. xii. As we will see later in this chapter, Kitayama is well known for his peace activities in the past (and he knew that we knew this). Kitayama became secretary of the JPS in 2003 succeeding Okonogi, who was secretary from 1968: the first secretary, from 1955 to 1968 was Yamamura Michio (Nishizono, 2004b, p. 2).
50 Nishizono was JPS President from 1992 succeeding Doi, who held the post from 1985: Yamamura was president from 1968, taking over from Kosawa who first president from 1955 until he died (Nishizono, 2004b, p. 2).
51 Nishizono (2004a), p. 233.
52 Nishizono (2004a), p. 230. 'The view that the other party is not an independent individual in the Western sense is also found in child rearing. A Japanese proverb says "Children belong to God until they are seven years old". A child is taken as a gift from God to ensure the succession of

the "ie". Accordingly, in the process of the growth of the child, a festival is observed to report the growth of a child to God in a Shinto shrine' (Ibid., pp. 230–231).

53 In her article 'Are the Japanese feminine?' Ueno Chizuko argues that this characterization of the nation as feminized and feminism as something imported from the outside world faces feminists in Japan with a dilemma: 'on the one hand, if feminists ask for equal rights, they are accused of being anti-Japanese; on the other hand, if they stress feminine values, man think it over and say, "Look, in contrast to Western men we are already feminine enough. Why do we have to become more feminine?"' (Ueno, 1997, p. 297). This then enables Ueno to conceptualize why some feminists like Takamure Itsue would have embraced a 'maternalist feminist' position that led her also then to embrace Japanese nationalism (and we will return to this issue in Chapter 5). For a brief history of feminism in Japan see Ehara (2000), and for a detailed analysis of strategies deployed in the media and everyday life to undermine feminist arguments see Ehara (2005b).

54 For a brief account, see Henshall (2004), p. 164.

55 One analyst, referring to the activities of *Sekigun* at Lod Airport, told us with appalled horror that Japan had here produced the world's first 'suicide bombers'. See Murakami's allusions to the student protests and the reluctance of protagonists to be involved in radical politics in *Norwegian Wood* (2003a).

56 McCargo (2004), p. 176.

57 This comment is from an earlier published essay 'The psychology of today's rebellious youth' quoted by him in full in Doi (1973). The comment is on p. 144.

58 Ibid., p. 152.

59 Ibid., p. 150. Doi notes that the slogan on the placard refers to the gingko trees that proliferate on the Tokyo University campus.

60 Lifton (1999), p. 266. Lifton is a US psychiatrist who specialized in the rather dubious discovery of what came to be known as 'brainwashing' that is supposed to facilitate 'cult psychology' (Lifton, 1989); here he seems to be detecting the germs of these dangers in Japanese culture, much in the way as he earlier found them to be present in China and Korea.

61 Murakami (2003b), p. 198. The history he is reminding readers of here concerns Japan in China, something he explores in *The Wind-up Bird Chronicle* (Murakami, 2003c).

62 This was Kitayama's comment on the 1995 events during our conversation with him in Fukuoka.

63 On occasion Kleinian theories of the instinctual wired-in knowledge the infant has of sexual differences and bodily attributes (that the infant already fantasizes about the father's penis inside the stomach of the mother, for example) do function in this way, and Jungian theory outside and inside Japan does appeal to cosmic archetypal principles (as we shall see in Chapter 4). However, Jungian collective psychology is not psychoanalysis, and Japanese psychoanalysts clearly have a more nuanced interpretation of Klein.

64 Ōe's (1996) novel was first published in Japan in 1958. Golding's (1997) *Lord of Flies* was originally published in 1954. See also, on the changing

role of women after the war, the 1940s novel by Dazai (1981) in which Naoji's testament meditates on the predicament of 'victims of a transitional period of morality' (p. 173).

65 The notion of 'joint attention' is Bruner's (1975) from developmental psychology, and Kitayama (2004c, p. 206) connects this with 'viewing together' or 'parallel looking' in a more psychoanalytic conception of the relationship.

66 In the next paragraph he suggests that the difference of emphasis in Japanese and Western child-rearing practices (encouraging the child to focus inward rather than outward), may be down to how 'Westerners, perhaps as hunting people, put value on independence, and Japanese people, perhaps as agricultural people, value interdependence' (Kitayama, 2004c, p. 211).

67 Ibid., p. 217. Kitayama says that the woman was referred to see him and 'looked happy to see me, a psychotherapist', though she may have been happy to see him for other reasons than that he was a psychotherapist, of course (Ibid., 216).

68 Ibid., 218.

69 Ibid., 224. It should be said that Kitayama also claims here that 'It is human nature to peer into a hole for whatever reason'. Against this universalist claim, it is worth noting that one of the 'culture-bound' disorders in Japan, *Taijin Kyofu* is a form of neurosis in which the sufferer imagines that their gaze hurts others, and is then afraid of looking at them (see Nakakuki, 1997b).

70 Writings by Westerners resident in Japan also reveal this preoccupation. Mishima figures in the diaries of the journalist Donald Richie, for example, and there are descriptions of him working hard at the gym (Richie, 2004). Richie has also been fascinated by eroticized masculinity in Japan, and buys unashamedly into orientalist images of the culture, and this in a series of reflections on life in Japan that does not include one mention of psychoanalysis.

71 Ushijima's (2004) paper was originally published in the *Japanese Journal of Psychiatry and Neurology* in 1987. The diagnosis Ushijima arrives at for Mishima is 'severe personality disorder' (p. 260). Although Ushijima notes that 'Mishima Yukio' was not his real name – it was Hiraoka Kimitake – he does not explore what those refused and chosen signifiers of identity might have meant to the boy (as other traditions in psychoanalysis would do).

72 Mishima (1990); the book was first published in 1949. There is an interpretation of Mishima's preoccupations with 'sex, blood and death' as having 'paved the way to his homosexual world' (p. 257). Psychoanalysis in Japan is not particularly gay-friendly (and this may be partly because it operates most of the time as a sub-branch of psychiatry), and some analysts responded to our questions about lesbian and gay psychoanalysts with incredulous amusement. This is very different from claims by other therapists that Japan is an easier context for 'transgender' and 'genderqueer' folk (Wachs, 2007).

73 Ushijima (2004), pp. 254–255.

74 Some of those on the Left were deeply shocked by Mishima's suicide, concluding that it was 'ironic' (Karatani, 1991, p. 217).

75 The book, which has sold over a million copies in Japan, won the Akutagawa prize. It was apparently compiled from emails she sent to her father, who edited them for publication.

76 Kanehara (2005), p. 81.

77 Akasaka (2005). Akasaka was winner of the Noma literature prize for best new writer. The title *Vibrator* is rather misleading, and the blurb on the back cover of the English translation plays up a feminist message that is not so apparent in the main text: 'If you live in a world that's controlled overwhelmingly by men, and if you don't want people making remarks about things that are really none of their business, you've either got to be totally indifferent to how you look or else go around looking beautiful all the time. I attempted to look beautiful all the time. But there are limits to how much you can do...' Contrast this with women's writing of the previous generation that tends to focus on the infidelity of men but with no dramatic rebellion by the heroines (e.g., Mukoda, 1994).

78 Ibid., p. 109.

79 Ibid., pp. 123–124.

80 Japan Psychoanalytic Society (2006).

81 Actually, there is only one full member (a psychologist) who is not also a MD (medical doctor), and all the training analysts are MDs. This makes the Japanese branch of the IPA one of the most medically-oriented (and this is in striking contrast to the British society, which historically had a high proportion of non-medical members even when there was a formal requirement that a candidate be a doctor or see patients under medical supervision).

82 The second volume of *Japanese Contributions to Psychoanalysis* claims that there are '23 active members and 14 associate members' (Nishizono, 2007a, p. ix).

83 'This is because the more a patient is treated, the better the results are' (Japan Psychoanalytic Society, 2006). This draws attention to an uncomfortable story about the accreditation of Japanese analysts which is recounted in the JPS anniversary volume; there was 'international criticism over the application of a 1991 regulation about training at the JPA, which surfaced at the IPA Amsterdam Congress (1993)' (Nishizono, 2004b, p. 5). Most analysts were being trained at less than four times a week (rumour has it that could have been once a week in some cases), 'due to a dearth of training analysts who were actually available' (Ibid., p. 6). The JPS anniversary volume is thus very much a public rehabilitation document, signalling that standards will be strictly maintained, that no less than four times a week will is acceptable in Japan (though this is at a time when some other IPA organizations are acknowledging three times a week analysis, partly as a response to the worldwide 'crisis of psychoanalysis' to which the JPS volume also refers). Nishizono (2007b) is much more upbeat about this 'crisis' in the second JPS volume, pointing also the increasing interest in psychoanalysis in South Korea and Taiwan.

84 Kitayama (2004c), p. 216.

85 The reunion concert CD, which was recorded in 2002, includes well-known international classic folk tracks that include 'Guantanamera' and 'Where have all the flowers gone?'

86 Kitayama told us that one of the tracks on the reunion concert CD was withdrawn as a single from shops because the Korean lyrics, which the band thought were simply a call for peace actually extolled the glories of the Kim Il-Sung regime in North Korea. About a third of the Korean minority population in Japan are from North Korea, and the pachinko parlours – noisy places in which money is gambled by way of little metal balls cascading through slots – are mainly owned by North Koreans who then send the profits back home (Carey, 2005). On the lives of young Koreans in Japan, see Fukuoka (2000).

87 Doi, for example, argues that if Freud was still alive he would be updating his text *Future of an Illusion* (which was an argument against religion, mainly directed against Christianity) to warn against 'the present age's psychoanalytic-socialistic illusions' (Doi, 1973, p. 155). Doi's redemptive message is actually quite Christian (and we will see more of the resonance of this in Chapter 4), but he is quite right to claim that Freud would have been suspicious of messianic brands of socialist thought.

88 See, for example, the quite weird encounter with the characters in Hokkaidō in *Wild Sheep Chase* (Murakami, 2003d) and again in *Dance, Dance, Dance* (Murakami, 2003e). In Murakami's books there is a repetitive theme of delving down into the underworld, and of the protagonist spending time in a well, which is, at least, a possible archetypal image of the unconscious if not an immediately psychoanalytic one; the image recurs, for example, in *Sputnik Sweetheart* (Murakami, 2002) when there are fears that Miu might have fallen down a hole in the ground on a Greek island.

89 Murakami, H. (2005, p. 217).

90 Yoshimoto includes material on ghosts that seem more suited to the secular world, and so closer to a psychoanalytic conception in both *Kitchen* (Yoshimoto, 1993) and *Asleep* (Yoshimoto, 2002). Her *Goodbye Tsugumi* has plenty about the process of separation in relationships between young women, but no ghosts (Yoshimoto, 2003).

91 Japan Psychoanalytic Society (2006).

92 Murakami (1987), p. 25.

93 He refers here specifically to *Hard-boiled Wonderland and the End of the World* (Murakami, 2003f). In *Kafka on the Shore* (Murakami H., 2005), the main character goes into the underworld encountering archetypal figures from Shintō mythology and Western advertising.

94 The club was called 'Peter Cat'. The first best-selling novel was *Norwegian Wood* (2000), which was published in Japan in 1987. One of Murakami's protagonists owns a jazz club in a later novel *South of the Border, West of the Sun* (1998).

95 The Jungian analyst Kawai Hayao works with this version of the story, even though he is more interested in the relation with the mother – and Japan as the 'Great Mother' – than with standard psychoanalytic oedipal relationships (Kawai, 1996). Kawai thus still contrasts the Oedipus and Ajase myths; see also the review by Spradlin (1998) for a sympathetic review of his work by a fellow Jungian.

96 Kitayama (1991), p. 230.

97 This pertinent question also chimes with recent critical analysis by the Palestinian writer Edward Said (2004) on *Freud and the Non-European*, but has some particular resonances with images of Jews in Japan (as we shall see in Chapter 4).

Chapter 3 Civilization and its Contents: 'Buddhistic cyberspace in Kyoto'

1 Freud (1921).
2 Lacan similarly argues in an early seminar that 'The super-ego is constraining and the ego-ideal is exalting', but adds a twist, to insist that the super-ego exerts its hold on the subject is not only through prohibition but also through the imperative to enjoy, 'speech derived of all its meaning', as something that simply tells us '*you must*' (Lacan, 1988, p. 102).
3 See, for example, Chasseguet-Smirgel (1985). Doi cites the notorious Grunberger and Chasseguet-Smirgel book (*L'Univers Contestationnnair ou les Nouveaux Chrétiens – Etude Psychanalytique*), one reaction to the 1960s student riots in Paris in which they accuse the students of regressing to a narcissistic state in which there is an attempt to fuse with an ego-ideal (a factor they also use to diagnose an implicit anti-Semitism in the movement). For Doi (who ironically here, unlike Grunberger and Chasseguet-Smirgel, wants to endorse rather than condemn Christian morality as a response to social ills), the 'French analysts' showed how the student revolt was 'a magical act'; 'an attempt to avoid the Oedipus situation by denying the father without clashing with him in actuality' (Doi, 1973, p. 158).
4 This history is discussed in detail by Shingu (2004). The 'excommunication' is Lacan's term to describe the IPA prohibition on him training analysts.
5 Lacan (1979, p. 276) argues that the analyst's desire is 'not a pure desire', but 'a desire to obtain absolute difference'.
6 That is, 'Lacan's Psychoanalysis'.
7 Shingu (2004), p. 4.
8 Shingu (2007) notes, for example, with respect to the anecdote about my barber in the introduction to this book that this figure 'is threatening because it reminds us of the real: How many analysts in Japan?'
9 Ibid., p. 70.
10 See Parker (2004a) for a review of Shingu's book.
11 Lacan (2001). Lacan's visits were in 1963 and 1971 (Nobus, 2005), during which he gave a lecture in Tokyo that has recently been published (Lacan, 2005).
12 Barthes (1982).
13 Freud (1915). Strictly speaking, consciousness consists of 'word presentations' combined with 'thing presentations', and it is the 'word presentations' that seem to be absent in the unconscious. In Lacan's reading of Freud, however, even the 'thing presentations' are connected to language as signifiers and it is in this sense that it makes sense to say that the unconscious is structured like a language (Lacan, 1979).

14 Freud (1925, p. 273) argued that 'there are three impossible professions – educating, healing and governing', and here he put psychoanalysis in the second, healing, domain.
15 Endo (2002). This account, which focuses on the way that Lacan's work on the Japanese language is used to explore its relationship with China, is discussed again in Chapter 4.
16 I have made use of formulations provided by the translator, Michael Radich, of Shingu's (2004) book during a brief correspondence about my review of it (Parker, 2004a). Radich (2004b) made it clear in this correspondence that he disagreed with the account of language offered by Endo, by Lacan, and indeed by Freud.
17 Shingu (2005a), p. 53.
18 Ibid.
19 The term 'aphanisis' was used by Ernest Jones to describe the 'fading' of desire, but is used by Lacan and his followers to refer to a more drastic 'fading' of the subject.
20 Shingu (2005a), p. 53.
21 Endo (2002). Psychotic clinical structure (according to Lacanians) is produced by a radical 'defence' that does not only 'repress' contents into the unconscious (which is what happens in neuroses), but refuses – 'forecloses' – the possibility that certain key signifiers exist at all and so 'psychotics' could be said not to have an unconscious composed of repressed material (Lacan, 1993).
22 Lacan (1971), session on 12 May 1971.
23 Nobus (2002), p. 35.
24 Lacan writes, 'c'est pourquoi personne qui habite cette langue, n'a besoin d'être psychanalysé, sinon pour régulariser ses relations avec les machines-à-sous' (Lacan, 2001, p. 498).
25 Ibid.
26 'The several features which compose an ideographic character are drawn in a certain order, arbitrary but regular; the line, beginning with a full brush, ends with a brief point, inflected, turned away at the last moment of its direction. It is this same tracing of a pressure which we rediscover in the Japanese eye' (Barthes, 1982, p. 99). Shingu includes this quote in his account, with the difference that the first words of Barthes' article 'The several features' are more conveniently (for Shingu's argument) rendered as 'The several traits' (Shingu, 2005a, p. 57).
27 Shingu (2005a), p. 58.
28 Shingu (2005a), p. 52. Lacan (1962–1963) discusses this in *Seminar X* (on anxiety) in sessions given after his first visit to Japan.
29 Shingu (2005a), p. 52.
30 As Shingu pointed out to an audience in Dublin, Lacan used the opportunity of analysing the work of James Joyce (and of using James Joyce to question psychoanalysis) to state that Catholics are '*unanalyzable*'. Shingu made the point during discussion after his Dublin lecture in 2006 – published later the same year (Shingu, 2006) – repeating the point he had made in the course of a paper published a year before in the same journal (Shingu, 2005a). The discussion of a Japanese Lacanian in Ireland at the end of this section and the beginning of the next is not intended to imply

any correspondence or symmetry between the two island nations (and it could be argued that it is actually Korea that stands in relation to Japan as Ireland stands to Britain).

31 Hoshina (2005) uses this differentiation – and the motif of the absence the shape of the vase encloses – to describe Kleinian and Lacanian notions of sublimation in which an object is raised to the status of a sublime 'Thing' that is, in itself, nothing.

32 This is what Freud (1937) referred to as 'the rock of castration'; that which we are stupidly attached to (the phallus as fantasy representation of potency and a relation to our objects of desire) that we are able to drop for a moment but which then clicks back in place as we speak a language and communicate within relationships that are organized around 'things'.

33 Abe (1997), p. 49.

34 Barthes (1982), p. 63.

35 Ibid., p. 68.

36 Ibid., pp. 46–47. Moloney (1953) included lengthy descriptions of the bits of cloth, *furoshiki*, in which Japanese carried things around, but was not able to draw any particular conclusions about the 'character traits' of the Japanese people more than the implication that they were a bit childish.

37 Barthes was one of the iconic figures within structuralist theory in literature, and Lacan did in 1960 also declare that he was a structuralist, though there is also some use of phenomenology, as the example of the vase enclosing an empty space shows, an example which comes from Martin Heidegger, as Hoshina (2005) points out. One of the key figures responsible for importing structuralist and 'post-structuralist' theory into Japan uses the motif of 'nothingness' to diagnose the predicament of the Japanese Left (Asada, 2000).

38 Guattari discussed architecture with Takamatsu Shin (see Genosko, 2002).

39 Karatani (1991, p. 201). See Derrida's (1995) commentary on Karatani's reading of his (Derrida's) analysis of the nature of writing in the West (and, by implication, in Japan), during which Derrida comments that 'everything taking place in Japan nowadays is a world-wide phenomenon'.

40 William Gibson (2001), author of a string of science fiction novels about 'cyberspace' (and credited with inventing the term) argues that 'Japan is the global imagination's default setting for the future'; Carey's (2005) book *Wrong about Japan* actually circulates around this motif to confirm that the culture is necessarily opaque to the West and presents an account that could more accurately be entitled '*Right about Japan*'.

41 See, for example, Shingu and Funaki (2008).

42 Shingu (2006), pp. 98–99. In this respect it is possible to see how Shingu also remains faithful to his Kleinian beginnings in psychoanalysis, something also evident in the clinical interpretations that he describes in his book on Lacan (Shingu, 2004).

43 Abe (1997), p. 52.

44 The difference between the 'subject of the statement' and 'subject of the enunciation', and also the reduction of the signifiers to nonsense, is discussed in *Four Fundamental Concepts of Psycho-Analysis* (Lacan, 1979). We find this motif also put to work in Leftist interpretations of political events, such as the suicide of Mishima; 'What he attempted to realize was

the destruction of the very thought that aims at realizing something. It is not that the Japanese culture he aimed to defend had nothing in it, but, rather, it was this very nothingness in the culture that he aimed to defend' (Karatani, 1991, p. 217).

45 Takano (2004) – a clinical case employing this concept is discussed in Chapter 2.

46 Shingu (2007).

47 Shingu and Funaki (2008).

48 Shingu (2004), p. 140.

49 J.-A. Miller (2002), p. 155.

50 Ibid., p. 149. Jacques-Alain Miller also emphasizes the way psychoanalysis opposes a view of knowledge that 'sings indefinitely the imaginary wedding of the male and the female principles' (Ibid.).

51 Ibid., p. 56. There is a discussion by the translator of the use of the term 'I', and the apparent objectification of the 'I' in the English translation serves both to convey more accurately the way the pronoun operates in Japanese and, very conveniently, the way Lacanians conceptualize the 'I' as a position reified by language.

52 Ibid., p. 128.

53 Lacan (1998), p. 49.

54 Shingu (2004), p. 98.

55 Ibid., p. 119.

56 Ibid., p. 55. Shingu also employs this device to describe suffering and the suffering of Christ suffering with the Christian believer; 'By realizing the odd fact that we are a whole, despite our bodies being comprised of various parts, we can feel the presence of Christ (again as a formula for the golden mean)' (p. 99).

57 Shingu (2005b), p. 68.

58 Shingu (2007). Strictly speaking, we should say 'kana scripts', for now there are different systems of writing – hiragana with the claim to be the most authentic Japanese 'kana', and katakana that is used to transliterate foreign loan words – that accompany kanji script (in addition to romaji which is roman script used for an increasing number of imported words).

59 Ide (1997, p. 58) notes that 'Women aspiring to upward mobility' are those who are now most likely to use these honorifics; the other group using such archaic terms in hyper-correct or excessive manner would be salesmen.

60 A Jungian analyst discussing the multiple forms of self-reference in Japanese as 'persona' argued that the form '*seisha*' was an archaic form used by samurai, and it would nowadays characterize 'psychotic' speech (Adachi, 2007).

61 Lacan (1998), p. 12.

62 Shingu (2004), p. 176.

63 Ibid.

64 Lacan (2007), session of 20 May 1970.

65 Ibid.

66 Shingu (2004), p. 119.

67 Saito (2004a), p. 38.

68 For a collection devoted to 'cyberpsychology' in the West, see Gordo López and Parker (1999) and for the argument that changes in subjectivity at different points in history have always relied on technological changes, see Gordo López and Cleminson (2004). On the implications of this new anthropological space for psychoanalysis see Parker (2007a).
69 Suzuki Junichi, a group analyst in Tokyo who also trained in Britain, commented on this matter.
70 Seon (2004).
71 Morikawa (2004), p. 18.
72 Ibid., p. 28.
73 Yonezawa (2004), p. 46.
74 Saito (2004a), p. 40.
75 Morikawa (2004), p. 28.
76 Quoted in Carey (2005), p. 112.
77 Ibid.
78 Morikawa (2004), p. 28.
79 Ooshima (2004), p. 36.
80 Quoted in Rees (2002). Saito then goes on to point out that many of these young men then re-enter society. In the same article (linked to a BBC documentary on the subject), a US psychologist complains about the 'softly softly' approach used in Japan: 'If my child was inside that door and I didn't see him, I'd knock the door down and walk in. Simple. But in Japan, everybody says give it time, it's a phase or he'll grow out of it', and so not only are the young men pathologized in Western representations of *hikikomori*, but also the rest of Japanese society.
81 The comment about a 'bit of personality that clashes with Japanese society' is by Futagami Noki, the founder of New Start charity for 'recovering' *hikikomori*; his view and that of Saito about wealthy parents is in McNicol (2003).
82 Kitayama (1991), p. 236.
83 Saito Saturo quoted in a New Zealand magazine article that bemoans the anti-Christian values being transmitted through manga (Wishart, 2003).
84 Freud (1926, p. 212).
85 It was Ernest Jones that threw up his hands in horror at the debates in psychoanalysis that seemed to be leading to what would now be seen as a 'social constructionist' position; see Grigg et al. (1999).
86 For a discussion of these issues, see Parker (2007b).
87 Saito (2004b), p. 4 (of English manuscript of spoken conference paper).
88 Freud (1920). Lacan discusses 'sexuation', in which the distribution of 'male' and 'female' operates. in Seminar XX *Encore* (Lacan, 1998).
89 As Nobus and Quinn (2005) put it in their outline of Lacanian epistemology, Lacan outlines 'an epistemological position in which the phallus need never refer to a penis' (p. 115).
90 Saito (2004b), p. 4 (of English manuscript of spoken conference paper).
91 Ibid., p. 6.
92 Saito (2004b) refers to this genre of 'slash fiction'. There is a detailed account of the slashzine genre by Penley (1997). See also, Herbert (2004).

93 Ibid.
94 Ooshima , p. 37.
95 There is also a backlash among some young women, mobilized online as 'Anti-Yaoi Fans', who aim to support 'singles and couples' and who insist that they are not anti-gay, but simply against 'out of context' yaoi (Anti-Yaoi Fans, 2004).
96 Lacan (1998).
97 Murata (2007), p. 7 (of English manuscript of spoken conference paper). Murata uses Freud's (1919) text 'A child is being beaten' which focuses on the daydream in which a girl may fantasize about being a boy who is being beaten; she also discusses what we might understand to be backlash against the women who produce yaoi in manga representations of young women compelled to draw these things as a result of past trauma (in which, of course, psychoanalytic explanation about childhood abuse and the compulsion to repeat is being deployed in popular culture).
98 Saito (2004b), p. 5 (of English manuscript of spoken conference paper).
99 Wachs (2007) interviews a psychotherapist working with transsexual clients in Japan who makes this claim.
100 Miya (1997). The importance of abortion in psychoanalytic discourse is evident in the number of clinical case examples that include this as a crucial motif in Shingu's (2004) introduction to Lacan.
101 See also Ehara (2005c) on the way that traditionalist and liberal strategies for limiting women are reinforced by contemporary globalization.
102 Parker (1997) argues that Lacanian discourse already circulates in cyberspace to construct forms of individual subject for whom this form of psychoanalysis functions to speak the 'truth' of that condition of being virtual.
103 Ueno (1997) makes this argument, already flagged in Chapter 2.

Chapter 4 Religion, Cohesion and Personal Life: 'A homogeneous culture'

1 To say that the unconscious was 'invented' by Freud rather than 'discovered' by him does already, of course, historically locate the truth claims of psychoanalysis. While some psychoanalysts would like to see their preferred model of the mind as something universal that was revealed to us all by Freud, others have insisted that even modern science constructs its objects within theoretical research paradigms; if the subject of psychoanalysis is indeed the subject of science, then we must be alive to the transformations in knowledge that give rise to different kinds of subject (Lacan, 1989). Within psychoanalysis, both recent US American narrative traditions (e.g., Spence, 1982) and French structuralist approaches (e.g., Lacan, 2006) emphasize the way we reinvent ourselves within a theory that is itself an invention.
2 See, for example, Samuels (1985). It is worth noting that Kitayama (1991) takes care to differentiate his discussion of the motif of the 'wounded caretaker' in Japanese culture from Jungian archetypal forms.

3 Arima (1991) sets out a series of traits that are entailed by what she sees as the preference for rule-governed creativity in Japan, which include a 'covert' level of uniformity. This is what a commentator on her argument glosses as 'homogeneity' (Hoff, 1991).

4 Kawai was also chair of the Commission on Japan's Goals in the 21st Century, which was a private advisory panel set up the former Prime Minister of Japan, and he has been designated a 'Person of Cultural Merit' by the Japanese Government (United Nations, 2004).

5 Befu (2001), p. 53.

6 Kawai (2002a).

7 At time of writing Kawai Hayao was in a coma; *The Daily Yomiuri* of 28 March 2007 reported that the new head of the Cultural Affairs Agency would be Aoki Tamotsu, a cultural anthropologist. Kawai's son Toshio was apparently once interested in Lacan before returning to the fold.

8 Murakami's responses to the Kobe earthquake, in which over 6,000 people died, are available in English in the short stories collected in *After the Quake* (Murakami, 2003g). The stories touch obliquely on the earthquake and its effects on people and their relationships, and we were told by those who had worked in the Kobe area in the aftermath that this muted approach was appreciated by people who had actually lived through it for it contrasted with the 'noisy' chatter of those in other parts of Japan who had lots to say about something they actually knew little about. The earthquake was a turning point for work on 'trauma' in Japan, and it was after 1995 that the diagnosis was applied to those suffering during major disasters with large loss of life (Muramoto, 2001).

9 Murakami was in the States from 1991 to 1995, during which time Kawai was a visiting scholar there. The dialogues were not included in the English translation of *Underground,* which combined victim and Aum follower accounts (Murakami, 2003b). There is a discussion of the responses of Murakami and Ōe Kenzaburo to Aum by Okuyama (2001).

10 See, for example, Okuyama (2001, p. 36); and Welch (2005, p. 58), who includes a series of questions from *Underground* that could actually have come from a Lacanian as well as a Jungian: 'Haven't you offered some part of your Self to someone (or something) and taken on a "narrative" in return?'; 'Haven't we entrusted some part of our personality to some greater system or Order?', and 'Is the narrative you possess now really and truly your own?' The difference between the two traditions is that a Lacanian would not see any happy resolution to the idea that for all of us the system has, as Murakami puts it, 'at some stage demanded of us some kind of "insanity"' (Ibid.).

11 See, for example, Holthaus's (2000) review of two books by Kawai read alongside Murakami's (2003c) *The Wind-Up Bird Chronicle.*

12 Cassegard (2001), p. 85.

13 Ibid., p. 86.

14 Against this, there are also Lacanian readings of Murakami that emphasize the split character of his protagonists and the obscene underside of authorities, the injunction to 'enjoy!' that is said to line the prohibitions of the superego (e.g., Flutsch, 2006).

15 Kawai (1996). See also a clear statement of Kawai's Jungian argument for a creative multiplicity of self-reference in Kawai (2002b). A favourable review of the book in the Jungian *Journal of Analytical Psychology* saw him as drawing contrasts between 'the Western and Japanese psyches' and aiming for 'a synthesis of Buddhist wisdom and Jungian analysis' (Spradlin, 1998, p. 414). There is a discussion of Kawai's study of individuation of a Buddhist priest which also emphasizes the impetus toward a wholeness of existence as part of the unification of the self in Nagatomo (1994). On the intersection between Jungian and Buddhist ideas see Kirsch (1959) and Muramoto (2002). The 1958 dialogue between Jung and Hisamatsu was finally published in a new translation (Hisamatsu and Jung, 2002); Jung had originally refused to allow it to be published, probably because the translation was so bad.

16 Kawai (1991), pp. 179–180. See also Kawai's (1995) lengthier exploration of the Japanese psyche.

17 Shingu Kazushige (2004, p. 119) uses the notion of the 'golden mean' in quite a different way in his introduction to Lacanian psychoanalysis, and is concerned with the way this 'ratio' – which might also include the relationship between male and female – operates in fantasy.

18 This harmonious relationship is necessary, according to Kawai, if the Japanese 'mother-complex' is not always to remain pathological. The title of one of Kawai's books in Japanese was *The Pathology of Japan, a Mother-Complex Society* (Befu, 2001, p. 155).

19 Kawai (1998).

20 On the connections between Jungian analysis and psychology see Sato (2002).

21 This, of course, was the case in the US, and Freud's arguments for 'lay analysis' were directed against medical control of psychoanalytic bodies. In the British section of the IPA there has historically been a high proportion of non-medics (many of whom were women, and neither Anna Freud nor Melanie Klein were doctors), even though training candidates were obliged to have their practice overseen by a medical practitioner (Frosh, 2003). In France, while Lacan and many of his colleagues were trained first as psychiatrists, the formation of Lacan's school outside the IPA saw the influx of many psychologists, which did not prevent Lacan often railing against the malign influence of psychology in psychoanalysis (Roudinesco, 1990).

22 For an account of sandplay therapy in Japan, see Enns and Kasai (2003).

23 All forms of psychoanalysis proceed through interpretation, though Lacanians are very cautious about interpreting transference and only do so in exceptional circumstances (Lacan, 1952; Cottet, 1993). For a discussion of the differences between Lacanians and Kleinians over transference interpretation see Burgoyne (1997).

24 See, for example, Igarashi (2006) for a discussion of qualitative approaches and more recent 'critical' psychology. Igarashi points to the role of US psychology in shaping the discipline in Japan and to 1972, when the 20th International Congress of Psychology was held in Tokyo, as marking 'recognition of Japanese psychology by "advanced" western psychologists' (p. 3). Some of the research in qualitative psychology cited by Igarashi is

interpretive, though clearly not at all psychoanalytic; one example being an article in *Qualitative Psychology Research* (a journal founded in 2002) entitled 'Why people mention the brightness of the sky and weather at the critical boundary of life and death'. There is also an emerging strand of social constructionist research based in Kyoto that connects with both sociological theory and collaborative community inquiry (see, for example, Sugiman, 2006, 2007).

25 See Sato (2005) for key dates and resources on the history of psychology in Japan.

26 Oyama et al. (2001). For a discussion of Motora's doctoral research, and for his comments on the 'unity of society', see Suzuki (2005).

27 Oyama et al. (2001). The first Japanese-language book on psychology, *Shin-ri-gaku* was published in 1875, a translation of J. Haven's 1857 *Mental Philosophy Including Intellect, Sensibilities, and Will* (see Igarashi, 2006).

28 Ibid. See also Sato and Fumino (2005) and, for a more detailed account, Sato and Sato (2005).

29 Motora (1905). As Oyama et al. (2001, p. 399) point out, Motora was actually a Christian. On the relationship between Zen and academic psychology, and a discussion of Motora's research in the Buddhist temple, see Kato (2005). There is a trend now in US American cognitive-behavioural psychology to incorporate Buddhist perspectives as a form of 'mindfulness' that might be good for mental health (e.g., Wallace and Shapiro, 2006).

30 Sato et al. (2004), p. 306.

31 Oyama et al. (2001), p. 401.

32 Sato et al. (2004), p. 312.

33 Ibid.

34 Sato et al. (2004), pp. 317–321. This chapter on 'Japanese Conception of and Research on Human Intelligence' in Sternberg's (2004) *International Handbook of Intelligence* is followed by a chapter on Chinese perspectives entitled 'Diligence makes people smart' (Shi, 2004).

35 Sato et al. (2004), p. 322.

36 See Igarashi (2005), who points out that a journal *Education and Medicine* was already founded in Japan as early as 1953; new journals include *Japanese Journal of Health Psychology* (founded in 1988) and *Japanese Health Psychology* (founded in 1992).

37 For background on Crayon House, see Ochiai (1997). There are some individual attempts to connect Jungian analysis with feminism in work by Muramoto Kuniko, see for example Muramoto (2001).

38 Befu (2001), p. 112.

39 Ibid., p. 84.

40 Varley (2000).

41 Kitayama (1985); his account is discussed in Chapter 2 of this book.

42 This is one reason why the US occupation enforced a separation of Shintō from the Japanese state (Henshall, 2004).

43 Shintō imagery then operates as a fertile source of Japanese version of magical realism in the writing of Murakami, appearing, for example, in the postmodern archetypal images of Johnnie Walker and Colonel Sanders in *Kafka on the Shore* (Murakami H., 2005).

44 For discussions of the distinctive structure of Chinese, Korean and Japanese Buddhism, see Lusthaus (2000), Cho (2000) and Maraldo (2000), respectively. A more detailed examination of Japanese Zen Buddhism is provided by Abe (1997).
45 Sato (1997), p. 118.
46 Ibid., p. 127. The suggestion was made by language professors at Tokyo Imperial University.
47 Karatani (1998), p. 10. With respect to comparisons between Japan and England, he argues that '...the most significant difference between England and Japan is that, while England is facing the European continent directly across the channel, Japan has Korea between itself and the continent.' (ibid.).
48 This characterization of current Korean research, not the argument as such, is made by Befu (2001), p. 43.
49 Karatani draws upon the work of the political theorist Maruyama Masao (1969), and we can also see here a Heideggerian problematic being deployed (in the notion of 'becoming' as overlaid by a technological 'made' world). Karatani is quite clear that we need to avoid romanticizing that 'becoming' as Heidegger did, romanticism attached to national identity which led Heidegger to look to Nazism as the true ground of 'Being' of the German nation (Endo, 2002). For a feminist consideration of Maruyama's work (discussed briefly in Chapter 1) see Ehara (2005a).
50 One might argue, in similar vein (and Karatani is again paraphrasing Maruyama here, who borrows an argument from other writers), that 'in ancient Greece, "becoming" was the dominant view of the world, while the Platonic idea that "the world was made" was secondary', and so after Christianity was introduced 'becoming was oppressed' (Karatani, 1998, p. 3).
51 Ibid.
52 Ibid., p. 1.
53 'One way to approach the difference between Korea and Japan is to analyze the writing system (*écriture*) that exists materially, rather than imaginary constructs such as *Volksgeist* or national mentality' (Karatani, 1998, p. 3). The suspicion of 'imaginary constructs' should alert us to the way Karatani will draw upon Lacanian psychoanalysis, which prioritizes the 'symbolic' dimension (which exists materially) over the 'imaginary'. A psychoanalytic sensibility is also evident in Karatani's scathing account of the way Japanese colonial domination of Korea was seen by some nationalists 'not as a Western-style colonization but rather as an attempt to transform Koreans through "love"', an indictment of Taisho era 'humanism' (Karatani, 1991, p. 205).
54 Korean *hangeul* consists of 24 letters which form syllables that do have some resemblance to the clusters that form Chinese characters, but though most Korean vocabulary has come from China, the Chinese *kanji* characters (*hanja*) are now falling out of use (following policy decisions by the South Korean government).
55 Karatani (1998), p. 6.
56 Ibid., pp. 6–7.

57 Ibid., p. 8. Karatani is here explicitly drawing on Lacan's argument as to why psychoanalysis is neither possible nor necessary for the Japanese.

58 Castration installs a relationship to others in which it is possible to accept relations of dependence and obligation and it enables the subject to develop a relation to the 'phallus' as something which operates as a fantasy of power to which an individual cannot ever have complete access, to fully have it or be it (Parker, 2007b).

59 Lacan (1993) outlines this argument in his seminar on psychosis.

60 Maruyama (1969); and this is an argument which poses a question about where women fit into such chains of power, the implication is that they are outside the public sphere altogether perhaps (Ehara, 2005a).

61 Karatani (1998) explores the political consequences of this non-oedipal power, and there is a discussion of his diagnosis of a threat of a return to Japanese nationalism of the 1930s by Endo (2002).

62 Karatani (1998), p. 4.

63 Ibid., p. 8. It should be pointed out that Korean Lacanians, who should really be quite happy with being 'castrated' by the signifier (for it is a condition of being able to enter the symbolic and acceptance of this castration indicates that they are not psychotic) were not so happy with Karatani's account; those we spoke to told us that Karatani (whose writings have been translated into Korean) tends to romanticize the Koreans and the Chinese (who he describes in one of his books as being more creative and closer to a childlike state of being because they inhabit a world structured by pictographic script). There is a long tradition of romantic discussion of the peculiarities of Chinese written characters; Ezra Pound, for example, was very taken with *kanji* as the key to understanding and appreciating Confucius, and detected profound similarities between his work and that of Mussolini and Hitler (see Longenbach and Litz, 1991).

64 Ibid.

65 On the impact of modernity on women in Japan and feminist responses, see Numazaki (2003). For an account of the emergence of the 'new family' in Japan (one based on the Western nuclear family) and the position of women which is linked to an analysis of Murakami's (2003h) *South of the Border, West of the Sun*, see Handa (2005).

66 See, for example, the report by Lindow (1994). For a grim account of conditions in Japanese private mental hospitals see Cohen (1988). In 2006, under pressure from psychiatric system user groups, the Japanese Society of Psychiatry and Neurology abandoned the concept of 'schizophrenia'; 'The old term "Seishin Bunretsu Byo" [*Seishin Bunretsu Byō*] (mind split disease) has been formally replaced with "Togo Shitco Sho" [*Tōgō Shitchō Shō*] (Integration disorder)' (Hammersley, 2006, p. 6). (Corrected notations for the Japanese terms are in square brackets.)

67 Karatani's (2003) *Transcritique* is a meditation on the progressive role of Kant in Marxism which we could see as an attempt to bring about an Enlightenment (of which Kant was a key figure in the Western tradition) in Marxist thought.

68 The notion of 'parallax' has been taken up by the psychoanalytic social theorist Slavoj Žižek (2006), who does acknowledge his theoretical debt to

Karatani in this respect but who then tends to merely use the notion to repeat arguments he had previously made about 'looking awry' in a new key (Žižek, 1991). See Žižek (2004) for an appreciation of Karatani's work, and Flutsch (2006) for an analysis of Murakami Haruki's work using Žižek's work. For a critical account of Žižek's reading of Lacan and Marx (and Hegel), see Parker (2004b).

69 On the early influence of anarchism in Japan, see Garcia (2000).

70 'According to Maruyama, the only imported thought that left a true mark was Marxism. Christianity, for instance, had attracted many intellectuals in the Meiji era, but the mass conversion barely left a ripple' (Karatani, 1998, pp. 1–2). See also Karatani's (1991) published account of the 'discursive space' of modern Japan for a restatement of this argument.

71 Shingu (2005a), p. 58.

72 See Karatani (2000). For a description of the New Associationist Movement (NAM), see Harootunian (2001), and for a political response to Karatani's (2003) theoretical underpinning of NAM, see Harootunian (2004).

73 See, for examples, the contributions in Buckley (1997).

74 For a discussion of the history of feminism in Japan, see Saitō (1997).

75 On the writing and reception of a Japanese version of the US feminist text *Our Bodies, Ourselves*, see Nakanishi (1997), and on the reproduction of sexism in Japanese, see Endo (1995). On feminism, identity and cultural politics, see Inoue (2003).

76 This is a controversial issue in Western feminism; some feminists (including those who have later trained as psychoanalysts) argue that Freud must be taken seriously if women want to change gender relations (e.g., Mitchell, 1974), while others (including those who have suffered at the hands of psychiatry) insist that feminism should steer clear of Freud as one of the single most reactionary forces in patriarchal culture (e.g., Millett, 1977).

77 See, for example, Kawano (1990, 2004). Sullivan was influential to a generation of radicals working psychoanalytically in the US who looked for descriptions of distress that would be more 'relational' than classical psychoanalysis (see, e.g., Sullivan, 1962). Muramoto Kuniko also set up women's advice and therapy centres, in an orientation more closely linked to Jungian perspectives (though this is not stipulated as an orientation for all women who work in the three centres). It is significant that these traditions of women's therapy, even though they draw on psychoanalytic ideas, were not known by the JPS analysts we spoke to.

78 Kobayashi Kazu, who writes on the weekly sessions of free association on the couch in the JPS anniversary volume (Kobayashi, 2004), is one. A colleague member of the JPS, Sato Noriko, died in 2006, and a new woman analyst, Suzuki Tomomi, was awarded membership the same year.

79 Siddle (1997), p. 144. Siddle claims that 'the Ainu, in the guise of the primitive Other, served also as a yardstick against which the civilization and progress of Japan could be measured' (p. 138). For an account of the lives of Ainu women in past centuries, see Katsuichi (2000).

80 See, for example, the report in *The Japan Times* by Yamaguchi (2004). Impurity considered as pollution, *kegare*, in Shintōism, also meant that menstruating women were banned from sacred places, and women are still not permitted on some mountains (Henshall, 2004, p. 207).

81 See the website of the Buraku Liberation League (2001).

82 See, for example, the discussions in Ueno (2004).

83 Fukuoka (2000) points out the Japanese government argued as late as 1980 that 'minorities' as defined by the United Nations covenants on Human Rights 'did not exist', and his study starts with a challenge to the popularly-held assumption that Japan is 'a homogeneous society'. Ōe's 1958 classic novel includes descriptions of the encounter between the boys and a boy they immediately identify as Korean (Ōe, 1996).

84 See, for example, work by Kim (2005). On the other end of the spectrum ranging from ancient culture to high technology, some of the most impassioned debates over the role of psychoanalysis over the telephone inside the IPA have been prompted by concern that Korean members have been using this approach (International Psychoanalytical Association, 2002).

85 Kuniko reports to Masako that 'Everybody's saying that the pervert is probably a Brazilian' (Kirino, 2003, p. 2).

86 See Yoshino (1997) on the impact this has on the discourse on identity in Japan.

87 For a description of the current state of psychoanalysis in Brazil, see Dunker (2008).

88 For a non-psychoanalytic review of 'panic disorder' cases among Japanese-Brazilians in Japan see Tsuji et al. (2001).

89 Murakami, R. (2005).

90 For the discussion of Schreber's fantasies that he was being penetrated by 'the rays of God' and turned into a woman so that he may redeem mankind, see Freud (1911). For a psychoanalytic reading of Schreber's fantasies to disclose something about the nature of German culture at the time, see Santner (1996). For Santner, Schreber's 'Jewish transvestism' condenses the feminization he feared and enjoyed as well as the feminization in German culture of the Jews he identified with. Shingu's (2007) take on this is that '[t]he destiny of Schreber who wanted to be a patriotic father to find himself in the position of the woman of the God, is also the one of the Japanese subject'.

91 *Kurata Takuji's account Kachikujin Yapū* was published under the pseudonym Numa Shōzō in 1991; this paraphrase (and identification of the author) is from Befu (2001), pp. 138–139. It would be possible for Japanese as well as native English-speakers to notice here a condensation of 'Japan' and 'Yahoo', those subordinate to the Houyhnhnms in Swift's (1967) *Gulliver's Travels*.

92 Freud quoted in Gay (1988), p. 241. On the relationship between Buddhist and Christian motifs in Jung's work see Heisig (2002).

93 Freud's (1927) critique of religion *Future of an Illusion* was followed by psychoanalyst Oscar Pfister's *The Illusion of the Future* as a defence of Christianity, which Freud encouraged his colleague to write (Isbister, 1985, p. 213).

94 See the website of OMF International (2006).

95 In the Shimabara massacre of 1638 around 35,000 people, many of whom were Christians, died, and there are memorials to such events now around Nagasaki (Henshall, 2004, p. 58)

96 They are now known as 'Hanare Kirishitan'; see the Kodansha Encyclopedia of Japan (2006) entry on Kakure Kirishitan. Henshall (2004, pp. 86–87) points out that the ban on Christianity was affirmed in 1868 at the beginning of the Meiji era, but lifted in 1873 following protests by foreign powers (and there were even suggestions at this time that Japan might officially adopt Christianity since it was the religion of the Western powers with which Japan was now starting to trade).
97 This characterization of Aizawa's arguments is in Goodman (1997), p. 179.
98 Henshall (2004), p. 87.
99 Buckley (1997).
100 Henshall (2004), p. 150.
101 The Japanese group-analytic session Agazarian (1989) describes was conducted by Suzuki (for Agazarian did not speak Japanese, and it was necessary to have a translator who was effectively also a group conductor). Suzuki commented that Doi's conversion to Catholicism had initially caused him some consternation. There is a discussion of group analysis in the tradition of Michael Foulkes (who developed the approach in Britain after the Second World War) in the JPS anniversary volume (Aida, 2004).
102 Kitayama (2004c).
103 See, for example, the discussion of Mizoguchi's 1948 film *Women of the Night* by Buruma (1995), p. 34. Dazai's (1981) *The Setting Sun* likens both Kazuko and her mother as the Virgin Mary.
104 Henshall (2004), p. 213. Karatani Kōjin's wife, a scholar in theology, explained that the cross she was wearing was a fashion item, not because she was Christian.
105 Shingu (2004), p. 69. In France Lacan has been accused of 'christianizing' psychoanalysis (Green, 1995–1996), so perhaps the imagery is appropriate here.
106 Doi (1973), p. 92.
107 Ibid., p. 95.
108 Doi (1986), p. 113.
109 Befu (2001, p. 32) points out that the motif of *kokoro* is a favourite in *nihonjnron* writing, and should be read as evoking the 'heart' of Japan.
110 Doi (1986), p. 112.
111 See Frosh (2005) for a discussion of psychoanalysis in Germany with the rise of Nazism.
112 For Jungian attempts to address Jung's anti-Semitism, see Samuels (1992).
113 On some differences between Japanese stereotypes of Jews – that they do not often smile and are very bitter – and Chinese stereotypes, in which Jews are friendly and industrious people, see Xun (1997).
114 There is a small long-standing Jewish community in Kobe (the community in Nagasaki was decimated by the US bombing), though the synagogue was burned down in a US air raid during the Second World War and rebuilt later (Engel, 1995).
115 Goodman (1997, p. 181) makes this suggestion.
116 The *Merchant* has also been a classic school text for many years (Goodman, 1997).
117 Goodman (1997), p. 181.
118 Cited in Goodman (1997), p. 182.

119 Befu (2001), p. 105. Befu argues that the real identity of Isaiah BenDasan is Yamamoto Shichihei, who owned the publishing house (Yamamoto Shoten) that put out the book.

120 Naoji's testament in Dazai's (1981) *The Setting Sun* likens the abased position of the aristocracy after the Second World War to the humiliation suffered by Jews (p. 158).

121 Goodman (1997), p. 177.

122 Goodman (1997), p. 197.

123 Jacques-Alain Miller (1986, p. 77) draws upon Lacan's notion of 'extimacy' to capture the way psychoanalytic phenomena operate in such a way as to be external to the subject at the same time as being so intimate, and he comments that perhaps '*it is this position of the psychoanalyst's extimacy that makes so distinct and constant the role of the Jew in the history of psychoanalysis*'.

Chapter 5 Mirrors of the Other: 'Why are you asking *these* questions?'

1 The introduction was in Japanese, but we could tell that Matsuki was dwelling on particular aspects of the detailed research that had preceded the visit, which included visiting the pretty little town of Tsuwano on the drive over to Fukuoka and reading books by Murakami Haruki and Yoshimoto Banana. The group was suitably amused by the nature of this project, and I realized how ill-equipped I was to undertake it. The same questions went down better, needless to say, at the mainly US-expatriate IMHPJ-Kanto Chapter psychotherapy group in Tokyo.

2 I have been concerned throughout this book with the interplay of representations of psychoanalysis and of culture in Japan, and have not pretended to offer an account of what Japanese relationships 'really' are like; for ethnographic studies of Japanese life see Hendry (1986a) and for a situated study of Japanese schooling see Hendry (1986b).

3 The key figure here, author of the key text on 'orientalism', is the Palestinian writer Edward Said (1985).

4 For a discussion of Japan within the orientalist gaze see Kang (2005).

5 Martin Jay (1993).

6 Psychoanalysis, however, came to privilege speech, as we shall see later in this chapter, and the role of the gaze assumes a different role in psychoanalytic theory. Psychoanalysis has also been accused of participating in a male 'gaze', which renders women into hysterical objects who then complain (and are further pathologized when they complain) about men observing them (Kaplan, 1984).

7 For discussions of the intersection of different senses of 'development', see Burman (2007b).

8 The notion of the gaze which sees evil as itself being evil is present in the work of Hegel, one of the pre-eminent philosophers of the Western Enlightenment, became influential in the work of Lacan, and has then been elaborated in Hegelian-Lacanian psychoanalytic theory to describe Western representations of others (e.g., Žižek, 1991).

9 Isabella Bird cited in Kowner (2000), p. 116.
10 James Lawrence cited in Kowner (2000), p. 115.
11 Kowner (2000), p. 126.
12 Marquis Alfred de Mages, cited in Kowner (2000), p. 115.
13 Joseph Denier cited in Kowner (2000), p. 128.
14 Kaiser Wilhelm II cited in Kowner (2000), p. 129.
15 Buruma's (1995) study is an example of this genre.
16 Kowner (2000, p. 105) cites the work of Sander Gilman as drawing attention to the way signs of difference are used to construct 'a representational system for the Other', and this kind of study has been elaborated in detail by Gilman (e.g., 1993) with respect to Freud.
17 In a tiny backstreet of Marrakech recently I came across a cinema showing *Battle Royale* (Fujiwara, 2001), the Japanese film devoted to one-by-one massacres of teenage school-children (though I do not know what the viewers will have made of 'Japan' in such a film).
18 Coppola (2003).
19 '…the film's Japanese distributor, Tohokushinsha Co., opted for a delayed opening at a single Tokyo movie theatre, with a website trailer as its sole advertisement', and Asian Media Watch (based in Los Angeles) campaigned against its four Academy Award nominations (King, 2005, p. 45).
20 James Morrow cited in Kowner (2000), p. 106.
21 King (2005), p. 46.
22 King (2005), p. 46.
23 For this notion of Japan as 'limit case' I draw on the work of my companion on travels and discussions with analysts in Japan, Erica Burman (2007a).
24 Key examples in the US experimental-paradigm research concern questions of attachment which often revolve around descriptions of '*amae*' abstracted from psychoanalytic context (e.g., Rothbaum et al., 2000). These areas of work are reviewed by Burman (2007a, p. 194), who concludes that research into these differences should not be 'a matter of discovering some authentic form of cultural specificity that is as yet untainted by Western psychological practices, but rather of attending to close and missed encounters structured by the history of colonialism, which is also the history of psychology'.
25 'Murakami [Takashi] is a friendly well-fed man in his 40s with round glasses and a pony-tail' (Lee, 2005, p. 7).
26 Murakami Takashi quoted in Lee (2005), p. 7.
27 Sakiyama and Koch (2003), p. 92.
28 In, for example, the discussions of mother-child imagery by Kitayama (2004c).
29 We have already noted the way Heidegger, who used this term, eventually found an authentic mode of being in the German 'Volk' under Nazism (Endo, 2002).
30 Sakiyama and Koch (2003), p. 86.
31 This again is very much in line with a Heideggerian view of apparently 'advanced' technological society as drawing us away from the ground of being.
32 Field cited in Sakiyama and Koch (2003), p. 84.

33 Sakiyama and Koch (2003), p. 89. The Japan Dance Therapy Association, which was founded in 1992, developed its ethical code of practice in 1998.

34 For a review and response to debates around touch in the Western psychoanalytic tradition see Casement (2000). Sakiyama and Koch (2003, p. 87) do cite research by one Haraguchi that they understand as taking place within the field of psychoanalytic practice in Japan and which apparently includes 'mental touching as another form of therapeutic communication'. (Haraguchi is not listed as a member of the JPS.)

35 For Freud's responses to Ferenczi's experiments in 'active technique' see Gay (1988).

36 For an analysis of the way each 'civilization' develops in such a way as to produce its own forms of 'barbarism', see Achcar (2006); this kind of account is a useful corrective to racist representations of the West as the 'civilized' parts of the world that then need to educate those parts that are less developed.

37 Barthes (1982, p. 3) also claims that 'I am not lovingly gazing toward an Oriental essence', but then presents an incredibly sentimental set of essays that idealize the place precisely because it is where the structuralist fantasy of signs – defined by way of their difference from each other rather than being positive terms – appears to have been realized.

38 In Lacanian terms, if there is transference at work here it is through the way signifiers represent a subject to another signifier (e.g., Lacan, 2007); here signifiers of 'the Japanese' produce certain subject positions for us to read it by way of their relationship to signifiers of 'the English'.

39 Compare this with the attempt to reassure the reader in the Davies and Kasama (2004) study of gender; 'Bronwyn came to the study with no negative feelings towards the overt subjection that takes place in Japanese preschools' (p. 139), which begs questions about why she did not (as someone from Australia who clearly positions herself elsewhere in the text as a feminist) and what led her to view it as 'overt subjection' in the first place.

40 Sir Cyprian Bridge cited in Yokoyama (1987), p. 156.

41 Sir Charles Wentworth Dilke cited in Yokoyama (1987), pp. 158–159.

42 Sir Cyprian Bridge cited in Yokoyama (1987), p. 162.

43 Yokoyama (1987), p. 175.

44 The item also alarms British readers with reports that KitKat, originally launched in 1935, is available in Japan in 'banana, lemon cheesecake, passion fruit and green tea flavours' (Guardian, 2005, p. 3. How like 'us' they are, the reader is invited to think, and yet at the same time so different.

45 http://www.sanrio.com/main/gallery/characters/kt.html (accessed 8 January 2007). She was born on 1 November 1974 (blood type A), her height is that of five apples, her weight is that of three apples, her favourite word is 'friendship' and she likes to collect small cute things. On the Hello Kitty phenomenon, see Belson and Bremner (2003).

46 Ishiguro (1990).

47 Fox (2004).

48 And 'perhaps significantly, a society inhabiting a small, overcrowded island' (Fox, 2004, p. 107).

49 And 'perhaps it is no coincidence that the more trendy, design-conscious English gardeners are often influenced by Japanese styles' (Fox, 2004, p. 129).

50 'What *is* it about small, overcrowded, islands?' (Fox, 2004, p. 122).

51 Easthope (1999), p. 97. It is unclear how a Paris demonstration on 31 December 2006 would fit here: Hundreds of marchers, apparently celebrating the French readiness to say 'Non', waved placards saying 'No to 2007!' and 'Now is better!', and they 'called on the UN and international leaders to stop "time's mad race'; 'when the clock announced the arrival of 2007, the protesters simply changed their chant to "No to 2008!"' (*The Week*, 2007, p. 11). (This report appeared in an English magazine, reporting English tabloid newspapers, and so there are other levels of class-inflected irony at work here.)

52 Easthope (1999), p. 168.

53 See Frosh (2003) on the impact of modernism, and Parker (1997) for a discussion of empiricism and the impact of the Second World War on the development of Kleinian approaches. See also Hinshelwood (1995) and Richards (2000) who both, in different ways, draw attention to psychoanalysis as a concern of fractions of the English middle and upper classes.

54 Strachey (1934), p. 135. This key text lays the ground for a focus on transference interpretations in all three main strands of the British tradition (Kleinian, object-relations 'independent' analysts and 'contemporary Freudian' followers of Anna Freud). There are also Lacanian and Jungian varieties of psychoanalysis in Britain, thought it is beyond the scope of this book to describe them in detail here; see, on the relationship between Lacanian and Kleinian psychoanalysis, Burgoyne and Sullivan (1997), and, on Jungians and 'post-Jungians', Samuels (1985).

55 'Generally speaking, a tendentious joke calls for three people: in addition to the one who makes the joke, there must be second who is taken as the object of the hostile or sexual aggressiveness, and a third in whom the joke's aim of producing pleasure is fulfilled.' (Freud, 1905, 100). Then we can identify with those who told the joke as we retell it to others.

56 Enomoto (2004), p. 99.

57 Shingu (2007).

58 Maruyama (1969). The elaboration of Maruyama's argument by Karatani (1998) was discussed in the previous chapter.

59 See Kitanaka (2003).

60 The emergence of cultural studies in Japan has not been much affected by psychoanalytic debates (for a review, see Tamari, 2006), and neither was women's studies (Watanabe, 1994). However, Asada Akira's influential introduction to French philosophical thought *Structure and Power* did include discussion of Lacan's ideas (see Asada, 2000), and some of Žižek's books have now been translated into Japanese. Karatani's (2003) work has been influenced by these ideas, but has steered a different path around them and back to classic European Enlightenment texts.

61 Burman (2007c) refers to psychoanalysis as the 'repressed other' of psychology, and here she is alluding to the way early connections – Piaget as a member of the IPA, for example – are excised from contemporary textbooks.

62 Arakawa (2005), p. 108. Freud elaborated a homeostatic model of excitation in the mental apparatus that was then complicated by excessive pleasurable excitations that then became too painful to bear (Freud, 1920). See also the discussion in Suzuki (2005), which does nonetheless refer favourably to the work of Erikson (a psychoanalyst who has traditionally been more acceptable to US psychologists).

63 Arakawa (2005, p. 108) says Fukurai 'resigned' and 'then his name faded away together with this theory [of many emotions]', but Muramoto and Hoffman (2005, p. 468) claim he was suspended and then discharged.

64 For a discussion of Freud's correspondence with Ferenczi on these matters, see Gay (1988).

65 Muramoto and Hoffman (2005), p. 468.

66 'Growing interest in qualitative research methods in the broad field of psychology may pose a threat to the identity and raison d'être of humanistic psychology in Japan because these methods offer the impression that its mission is over' (Muramoto and Hoffman, 2005, p. 479).

67 Muramoto and Hoffman (2005), p. 478. Followers of Rogers in Japan, organized in a tight-knit group of about 40 people, are apparently suspicious of Jungian ideas (possibly because of the role of Jungians in the fields of clinical, counselling and educational psychology).

68 Kitanaka (2003), p. 242.

69 See Sato (2007). Clinical psychology now outstrips educational psychology in popularity and in numbers of tenured academic staff devoted to teaching it in universities (Fumino, 2005).

70 It is a requirement of training in Jungian analysis in Kyoto that the candidate spends a year in Europe or the US.

71 From 1988, when it was established, the licensing system included 8,799 certified clinical psychologists including 318 medical doctors (Kitanaka, 2003, p. 244).

72 Kitanaka (2003), p. 244. On Certification Board, see Igarashi (2007).

73 Befu (2001), p. 127.

74 Ueno (1997).

75 Ueno (1997), p. 295.

76 Ueno (1997), p. 295.

77 Ueno (1997) points out that Takamure 'mistook matrilineality for matriarchy', and it is not certain that reclaiming this kind of anthropological tradition makes scientific or political sense; there have been heated debates in the Marxist and feminist movement over Engels' (1972) claim that early matriarchal culture was a form of primitive communism.

78 Ueno (1997), pp. 295–296. See also Mackie (1988) for a detailed review of the history of the women's movement in Japan, including its 'maternalist' aspects, and Watanabe (1994) for an account of the development of 'women's studies' in Japan.

79 Takamure Itsue cited in Ueno (1997), p. 296.

80 Kawai (1995).

81 Ueno (1997), p. 299.

82 Ueno (1997, p. 300) refers to the 'soft, invisible empire' posited by Barthes (1982).

83 Hasegawa Michiko cited in Ueno (1997), p. 299. Ueno claims that Hasegawa 'is a Japanese equivalent of Jean Bethke Elshtain, the American political scientist who, rather confusingly, claims to be feminist'; Elshtain, who has support among some psychoanalytic writers in the US and England who define themselves as being to the left, uses psychoanalytic theory to reinforce gender stereotypes (see, e.g., Elshtain, 1984). For further discussion of the context for this conception of feminism as 'Chinese mind', see Ueno (2005).
84 Kakuchi (2003).
85 See, for example, Kawano (1990, 2004) and Matsuyuki (1988).
86 In discussions about the relationship between psychoanalysis and feminism in the English-speaking world, for example, there is still often an insistence on the part of founders of the 'women's therapy' movement that therapeutic work and feminist activity are separate, even if one may inform the other (see, for example, Orbach, 2003).
87 Freud (1933, p. 181) argued that 'Psycho-analysis, in my opinion, is incapable of creating a *Weltanshauung* [worldview]. It does not need one: it is a part of science and can adhere to the scientific *Weltanshauung*.'
88 If Befu (2001) is right, then the 'hegemony of homogeneity' would pose exactly these kinds of problems for minorities in the culture when they go into therapy of any kind.
89 See, for example, discussions from within the Kleinian tradition by Heimann (1950); in the 'independent' tradition there were influential contributions by Winnicott (e.g., 1947).
90 Fujiyama (2004).
91 The theoretical discussion draws on Winnicott and the US analyst Thomas Ogden on the 'analytic third' (Fujiyama, 2004).
92 Kikuchi (2004).
93 Kinugasa (2004). In this case the analysand is described as a 'Japanese bachelor', though nothing is made of this cultural identity in the paper.
94 Minakawa (2004).
95 Ogura (2004).
96 Aida (2004). This paper is about 'group analysis' in the Foulkesian tradition, and includes references to one of the few Japanese group analysts Suzuki Junichi (who is not a member of the JPS) as well as the US group psychotherapist Agazarian (see, e.g., Agazarian, 1989). A paper in the second JPS volume also refers to Suzuki and the therapeutic community tradition in group psychotherapy applied in psychiatric settings (Aida, 2007).
97 Takahashi's (2004) paper is about US-based work.
98 Tsutsumi (2004).
99 'Buraku', we are told, is a 'derogatory and discriminatory term in Japan', and the anxiety was voiced by an analysand who had a 'concrete figure of the crucified Christ in his mind-chest' (Matsuki, 2004, p. 61). The reference to 'mind-chest' here is presumably a translation and allusion to the complexity of the word *kokoro*.
100 Some of the papers are not actually concerned primarily with psychoanalysis either. Tsutsumi's (2004) paper on 'developmental psychopathology' presents quantitative date interpreted within a strictly psychiatry

frame, and Iwasaki's (2004) is on the influence of German and then US diagnostic systems on Japanese psychiatry.

101 For example, Kitayama (2007) and Kinugasa (2007) discuss Freud's own cases, and the Argentinean IPA analyst Bianchedi (2007) discusses the 'caesura' between East and West drawing on the work of Bion (in a paper originally given in Tokyo in 1992).

102 For a brief review of three cultural trends in Japanese psychoanalysis from the perspective of social anthropology, see Alvis (2003).

103 Kobayashi (2004). Kobayashi Kazu is one of the few women members of the JPS.

104 In discussions over possible categories of practitioner to be regulated through the United Kingdom Council for Psychotherapy (UKCP), the British Psycho-Analytical Society (BP-AS) at one point (when it was still involved in the UKCP, and before it split away to set up its own registration body), agreed that counselling took place once a week, psychodynamic counselling twice, psychotherapy three times, psychoanalytic psychotherapy four times, and psychoanalysis five times a week. This tidy but unworkable category system was quickly abandoned, and many psychoanalysts learnt that other IPA analysts in sister organizations of the BP-AS were being trained on a basis of as little as three-times week (Parker, 2003). For discussion of the progress and lack of progress in the regulation of psychoanalytic practitioners, see Parker and Revelli (2008). For an account of the way these questions pertain to Japan, see Shingu (2008).

105 Kobayashi (2004), pp. 149–150. It is against this background that accounts of the work of a 'part-timer psychoanalyst' (who is actually also a JPS training analyst) in the second JPS volume should be read (Aida, 2007), and the explicit references to four times a week analysis in two of the other case studies included in this volume (Fukumoto, 2007; Suzuki, 2007).

106 This is noted in Derrida's (1988, p. 75) exploration of '...the IPA's geographical schematism, apoliticism, and even apsychoanalyticism in the name of a certain conception of human rights.' This conference was itself a culturally and politically significant event, because of the state of Israeli-Arab relations at the time and because of heated debates over proposals that the next conference take place in Berlin (Moses, 1992). Psychoanalysis, wherever it is, is implicated in the culture in which it operates.

107 International Psychoanalytical Association (2006).

108 Michael Radich (2004b), the translator of Shingu's (2004) book on Lacan, makes an interesting point in this respect: 'Despite what even many Japanese intellectuals themselves think – and *pace* Buruma? [a reference to Buruma's (1995) book] – Japanese intellectual life, I believe, is on the whole *less* bound by parochial facts of culture than the intellectual life of the Anglophone world, or Europe'. Radich goes on to say that he believes that psychoanalysis gets to 'underlying realities of the human condition', to which I would say that I think it gets to the underlying historically-constructed 'realities' because it has been constructed as a reflexive practice within those 'realities', one of which is contemporary Japan.

109 For collections that review the development of psychoanalysis in different countries, see Kutter (1991, and 1995, which includes Okonogi's contribution on Japan).

110 Kozuki and Kennedy (2004), p. 37.

111 Roland (1996), p. 80. Alan Roland's work was recommended to me as a key text on 'the Japanese' by quite a few psychoanalysts and psychoanalytic psychotherapists in Japan.

112 Roland (1996), p. 80.

113 Kitayama's (1987, p. 504) discussion of transference interpretations proceeding by way of metaphor (in examples of work with 'schizophrenic patients') includes the observation in a footnote that 'Japanese do not distinguish between similes and metaphors and such a distinction is not workable for the analysis of schizophrenic language', and it is perhaps this particular aspect of language that would enable an analyst suspicious of psychiatric categories to reflect on the value of the diagnostic label 'schizophrenic' in psychoanalytic discourse.

114 Kawai (1991, p. 173).

115 Ibid., p. 174.

116 Freud (1937, p. 252) points out that the refusal of such limitation of power – the fantasy of power – is to be found in the 'repudiation of femininity'.

117 Sensationalized images of psychoanalysis have been popular in Hollywood representations of it, and in recent ostensibly-Lacanian readings of popular culture that often focus on film to claim that the end of analysis involves a dramatic 'act' (see, for example, Žižek, 1991; for a critical assessment of such claims see Parker, 2004b).

118 Kano's (2004) emphasis on the phenomenon of 'Nachträglichkeit' – a form of 'deferred action' in which precipitating causes are activated after the event – in narrative, is here genuinely psychoanalytic and provides a conceptual challenge to the 'narrative therapies' he describes.

119 Kitayama (1991), p. 232.

120 Doi (2004); Nakakuki (1994).

121 Tamari (2006), p. 295.

122 Ueno (1997).

123 On the 'repudiation of femininity' in analysis, see Freud (1937, p. 252). Freud (1926, p. 212) says 'the sexual life of adult women is a "dark continent" for psychology'; the phrase 'dark continent' in the German original was in English.

References

Abe, M. (1997) *Zen and Comparative Studies: Part Two of a Two-Volume Sequel to* Zen and Western Thought. London: Palgrave.

Achcar, G. (2006) *The Clash of Barbarisms: The Making of the New World Disorder*. London: Saqi Books.

Adachi, M. (2007) 'A Jungian practice in Japan', Japan in Analysis Video Conferencing Symposium, Institute for Advanced Studies of Clinical Psychology, International Christian University, Tokyo, Japan, April.

Agazarian, Y. M. (1989) 'The invisible group: An integrational theory of group-as-a-whole', *Group Analysis*, 22, pp. 355–369.

Aida, N. (2004) 'Leadership in community meetings: Toward a therapeutic community approach', in O. Kitayama (ed.) *Japanese Contributions to Psychoanalysis*. Tokyo: Japan Psychoanalytic Society.

Aida, N. (2007) 'The existence of groups in the psychiatric hospital: Benefits and cautions', in K. Matsuki (ed.) *Japanese Contributions to Psychoanalysis, Volume 2*. Tokyo: Japan Psychoanalytic Society.

Akasaka, M. (2005) *Vibrator* (translated by M. Emmerich, originally published 1999). London: Faber & Faber.

Alvis, A. (2003) 'Psychoanalysis in Japan', *International Institute for Asian Studies Newsletter*, 30, p. 9.

Anti-Yaoi Fans (2004) 'Anti-Yaoi Fans: a site for people who are against out of context yaoi', http://www.myrrhlynn.net/antiyaoi/(accessed 7 January 2008).

Arakawa, A. (2005) 'Psychology of feelings and emotions: Its history in Japan', *Japanese Psychological Research*, 47 (2), pp. 106–114.

Arima, M. (1991) 'Creative interpretation of the text and the Japanese mentality', in Ikegami, Y. (ed.) *The Empire of Signs: Semiotic Essays on Japanese Culture*. Amsterdam: John Benjamins Publishing Co.

Asada, A. (2000) 'A left within the place of nothingness', *New Left Review II*, 5, pp. 15–40.

Balint, M. (1968) *The Basic Fault*. London: Tavistock.

Barthes, R. (1982) *Empire of Signs* (translated by R. Howard, originally published 1970). New York: Hill & Wang.

Basak, J. (2007) 'Reflections on "The Prohibition of Don't look" and repression as an impact: Japan and India', in K. Matsuki (ed.) *Japanese Contributions to Psychoanalysis, Volume 2*. Tokyo: Japan Psychoanalytic Society.

Befu, H. (1980) 'A critique of the group model of Japanese society', *Social Analysis*, 5/6, pp. 29–43.

Befu, H. (2001) *Hegemony of Homogeneity: An Anthropological Analysis of* Nihonjinron. Melbourne: Trans Pacific Press.

Behrens, K. Y. (2004) 'A multifaceted view of the concept of *amae*: Reconsidering the indigenous Japanese concept of relatedness', *Human Development*, 47, pp. 1–27.

Belson, K. and Bremner, B. (2003) *Hello Kitty: The Remarkable Story of Sanrio and the Billion Dollar Feline Phenomenon*. Chichester: John Wiley & Sons Inc.

Benedict, R. (1967) *The Chrysanthemum and the Sword: Patterns of Japanese Culture* (originally published 1946). London: Routledge & Kegan Paul.

Bettelheim, B. (1986) *Freud and Man's Soul*. Harmondsworth: Pelican.

Bianchedi, E. T. de (2007) 'Transcending the caesura between East and West through Bion's psychoanalytic ideas' in K. Matsuki (ed.) *Japanese Contributions to Psychoanalysis, Volume 2*. Tokyo: Japan Psychoanalytic Society.

Blowers, G. H. and Yang, S. H. (1997) 'Freud's *Deshi*: The coming of psychoanalysis to Japan', *Journal of the History of the Behavioral Sciences*, 32 (2), pp. 115–126.

Blowers, G. H. and Yang, S. H. (2001) 'Ohtsuki Kenji and the beginnings of lay analysis in Japan', *International Journal of Psychoanalysis*, 82 (27), pp. 27–42.

Botting, G., Connell, R., Hoffman, M. and Schreiber, M. (2005) *Tabloid Tokyo: 101 Tales of Sex, Crime and the Bizarre from Japan's Wild Weeklies*. Tokyo: Kodansha International.

Brannen, N. (1991) *The Practical English-Japanese Dictionary*. New York and Tokyo: Weatherill Inc.

Breuer, J. and Freud, S. (1895) 'Studies on Hysteria', in J. Strachey (ed.) *The Standard Edition of the Complete Psychological Works of Sigmund Freud*, Vol. 2, London: Vintage, The Hogarth Press and the Institute of Psycho-Analysis.

Bruner, J. (1975) 'The capacity for joint visual attention in the infant', *Nature*, 253, pp. 265–266.

Buckley, S. (ed.) (1997) *Broken Silence: Voices of Japanese Feminism*. Berkeley: University of California Press.

Buraku Liberation League (2001) 'What is Buraku discrimination?', http://www.bll.gr.jp/eng.html (accessed 7 January 2008).

Burgoyne, B. (1997) 'Interpretation', in B. Burgoyne and M. Sullivan (eds) *The Klein-Lacan Dialogues*. London: Rebus Press.

Burgoyne, B. and Sullivan, M. (1997) (eds) *The Klein-Lacan Dialogues*. London: Rebus Press.

Burman, E. (2007a) 'Between orientalism and normalisation: Cross-cultural lessons from Japan for a critical history of psychology', *History of Psychology*, 16 (2), pp. 179–198.

Burman, E. (2007b) *Developments: Child, Image, Nation*. London: Routledge.

Burman, E. (2007c) *Deconstructing Developmental Psychology (Second Edition)*. London: Routledge.

Buruma, I. (1995) *A Japanese Mirror: Heroes and Villains of Japanese Culture*. London: Vintage.

Carey, P. (2005) *Wrong About Japan: A Father's Journey with his Son*. London: Faber & Faber.

Casement, P. (2000) 'The issue of touch: A retrospective overview', *Psychoanalytic Inquiry*, 20 (1), pp. 160–184.

Cassegard, C. (2001) 'Murakami Haruki and the naturalization of modernity', *International Journal of Japanese Sociology*, 10, pp. 80–92.

Chasseguet-Smirgel, J. (1985) *The Ego Ideal: A Psychoanalytic Essay on the Malady of the Ideal*. London: Free Association Books.

Cho, S. (2000) 'Buddhist philosophy, Korean', in *Concise Routledge Encyclopedia of Philosophy*. London and New York: Routledge, pp. 111–112.

Cohen, D. (1988) *Forgotten Millions: The Treatment of the Mentally Ill – A Global Perspective*. London: Paladin.

Coppola, S. (dir.) (2003) *Lost in Translation*. Los Angeles, CA.: Universal.
Cottet, S. (1993) 'Should we analyse the transference?', *Journal of the Centre for Freudian Analysis and Research*, 2, pp. 3–10.
Davies, B. and Kasama, H. (2004) *Gender in Japanese Preschools: Frogs and Snails and Feminist Tales in Japan*. Cresskill, NJ: Hampton Press Inc.
Dazai, O. (1981) *The Setting Sun* (translated by D. Keene, originally published 1947). Tokyo: Tuttle Publishing.
Derrida, J. (1988) 'Geopsychoanalysis: "...and the rest of the world"', in C. Lane (ed.) *The Psychoanalysis of Race*. New York: Columbia University Press.
Derrida, J. (1995) 'Introduction to Kojin Karatani's "Nationalism and Ecriture"', *Surfaces*, 5, http://www.pum.umontreal.ca/revues/surfaces/vol5/derrida.html (accessed 7 January 2008).
Doi, T. (1973) *The Anatomy of Dependence* (translated by J. Bester, originally published 1971). Tokyo: Kodansha International.
Doi, T. (1986) *The Anatomy of Self: The Individual Versus Society* (translated by J. A. Harbison, originally published 1985). Tokyo: Kodansha International.
Doi, T. (1990) 'The cultural assumptions of psychoanalysis', in J. W. Stigler, R. A. Shweder and G. Herdt (eds) *Cultural Psychology: Essays on Comparative Human Development*, Cambridge: Cambridge University Press.
Doi, T. (1993) 'Psychoanalysis in a cross-cultural context: A Japanese view', presented at International Psychoanalytical Association Congress, Amsterdam (forthcoming in Doi, T. *Collected Papers*, Tokyo: Global Oriental Ltd.)
Doi, T. (2004) '*Amae* and the western concept of love', in O. Kitayama (ed.) *Japanese Contributions to Psychoanalysis*. Tokyo: Japan Psychoanalytic Society.
Dunker, C. (2008) 'Psychology and psychoanalysis in Brazil: From cultural syncretism to the collapse of liberal individualism', *Theory & Psychology*, 18 (2), pp. 223–236.
Easthope, A. (1999) *Englishness and National Culture*. London: Routledge.
Ehara, Y. (2000) 'Feminism's growing pains', *Japan Quarterly*, 47, pp. 41–48.
Ehara, Y. (2005a) 'A feminist view of Maruyama Masao's modernity', in R. F. Calichman (ed.) *Contemporary Japanese Thought*. New York: Columbia University Press.
Ehara, Y. (2005b) 'The politics of teasing', in R. F. Calichman (ed.) *Contemporary Japanese Thought*. New York: Columbia University Press.
Ehara, Y. (2005c) 'Feminism in the grips of a pincer attack: Traditionalism, liberalism, and globalism', *International Journal of Japanese Sociology*, 14,pp. 6–14.
Elshtain, J. B. (1984) 'Symmetry and soporifics: A critique of feminist accounts of gender development', in B. Richards (ed.) *Capitalism and Infancy: Essays on Psychoanalysis and Politics*. London: Free Association Books.
Endo, F. (2002) 'Kojin Karatani and the return of the thirties: Psychoanalysis in/of Japan', *Semiotic Review of Books*, 13 (1), www.chass.utoronto.ca/epc/srb/srb/kojin.pdf (accessed 7 January 2008).
Endo, O. (1995) 'Aspects of sexism in language', in K. Fugimura-Fanselow and A. Kaneda (eds) *Japanese Women: New Feminist Perspectives on the Past, Present and Future*. New York: The Feminist Press.
Engel, T. (1995) 'The Jews of Kobe', http://www-cs-students.stanford.edu/~tamar/Kobe/Kobe.html (accessed 7 January 2008).
Engels, F. (1972) *The Origin of the Family, Private Property and the State* (originally published 1884). New York: Pathfinder Press.

Enns, C. Z. and Kasai, M. (2003) 'Hakoniwa: Japanese sandplay therapy', *The Counseling Psychologist*, 31 (1), pp. 93–112.

Enomoto, T. (2004) *Japan: Point and Speak Phrasebook*. Tokyo: Joho Center Publishing Co. Ltd.

Erikson, E. H. (1959) *Identity and the Life Cycle*. New York: W. W. Norton and Co.

Flutsch, M. (2006) 'Murakami Haruki's teenage murderer: A Žižekian view', 16th Biennial Conference of the Asian Studies Association of Australia, Wollongong, June. http://coombs.anu.edu.au/SpecialProj/ASAA/biennial-conference/2006/Flutsch-Maria-ASAA2006.pdf (accessed 7 January 2008).

Fox, K. (2004) *Watching the English: The Hidden Rules of English Behaviour*. London: Hodder.

Freeman, D. (2007) 'Learning from each other: What Western psychoanalysts can learn from the Japanese', in K. Matsuki (ed.) *Japanese Contributions to Psychoanalysis, Volume 2*. Tokyo: Japan Psychoanalytic Society.

Freud, S. (1905) 'Jokes and their relation to the unconscious', in J. Strachey (ed.) *The Standard Edition of the Complete Psychological Works of Sigmund Freud*, Vol. 8, London: Vintage, The Hogarth Press and the Institute of Psycho-Analysis.

Freud, S. (1911) 'Psycho-analytic notes on an autobiographical account of a case of paranoia (dementia paranoides)', in J. Strachey (ed.) *The Standard Edition of the Complete Psychological Works of Sigmund Freud*, Vol. 12, London: Vintage, The Hogarth Press and the Institute of Psycho-Analysis.

Freud, S. (1915) 'The unconscious', in J. Strachey (ed.) *The Standard Edition of the Complete Psychological Works of Sigmund Freud*, Vol. 14, London: Vintage, The Hogarth Press and the Institute of Psycho-Analysis.

Freud, S. (1913 [1912–1913]) 'Totem and Taboo', in J. Strachey (ed.) *The Standard Edition of the Complete Psychological Works of Sigmund Freud*, Vol. 13. London: The Hogarth Press and the Institute of Psycho-Analysis.

Freud, S. (1919) '"A child is being beaten": A contribution to the study of the origin of sexual perversions', in J. Strachey (ed.) *The Standard Edition of the Complete Psychological Works of Sigmund Freud*, Vol. 17, London: Vintage, The Hogarth Press and the Institute of Psycho-Analysis.

Freud, S. (1920) 'Beyond the pleasure principle', in J. Strachey (ed.) *The Standard Edition of the Complete Psychological Works of Sigmund Freud*, Vol. 18, London: Vintage, The Hogarth Press and the Institute of Psycho-Analysis.

Freud, S. (1921) 'Group psychology and the analysis of the ego', in J. Strachey (ed.) *The Standard Edition of the Complete Psychological Works of Sigmund Freud*, Vol. 18, London: Vintage, The Hogarth Press and the Institute of Psycho-Analysis.

Freud, S. (1924) 'The economic problem of masochism', in J. Strachey (ed.) *The Standard Edition of the Complete Psychological Works of Sigmund Freud*, Vol. 19, London: Vintage, The Hogarth Press and the Institute of Psycho-Analysis.

Freud, S. (1925) 'Preface to Aichorn's *Wayward Youth*', in J. Strachey (ed.) *The Standard Edition of the Complete Psychological Works of Sigmund Freud*, Vol. 19, London: Vintage, The Hogarth Press and the Institute of Psycho-Analysis.

Freud, S. (1926) 'The question of lay analysis: Conversations with an impartial person', in J. Strachey (ed.) *The Standard Edition of the Complete Psychological Works of Sigmund Freud*, Vol. 20, London: Vintage, The Hogarth Press and the Institute of Psycho-Analysis.

Freud, S. (1927) 'The future of an illusion', in J. Strachey (ed.) *The Standard Edition of the Complete Psychological Works of Sigmund Freud*, Vol. 21, London: Vintage, The Hogarth Press and the Institute of Psycho-Analysis.

Freud, S. (1930[1929]) 'Civilization and its discontents', in J. Strachey (ed.) *The Standard Edition of the Complete Psychological Works of Sigmund Freud*, Vol. 21, London: Vintage, The Hogarth Press and the Institute of Psycho-Analysis.

Freud, S. (1933) 'New introductory lectures on psycho-analysis', in J. Strachey (ed.) *The Standard Edition of the Complete Psychological Works of Sigmund Freud*, Vol. 22, London: Vintage, The Hogarth Press and the Institute of Psycho-Analysis.

Freud, S. (1937) 'Analysis terminable and interminable', in J. Strachey (ed.) *The Standard Edition of the Complete Psychological Works of Sigmund Freud*, Vol. 23, London: Vintage, The Hogarth Press and the Institute of Psycho-Analysis.

Fromm, E. (1959) 'Psychoanalysis and Zen Buddhism', *Psychologia: An International Journal of Psychology in the Orient*, 2 (2), pp. 79–99.

Frosh, S. (2003) 'Psychoanalysis in Britain', in D. Bradshaw (ed.) *A Concise Companion to Modernism*. Oxford: Blackwell.

Frosh, S. (2005) *Hate and the 'Jewish science': Anti-Semitism, Nazism, and Psychoanalysis*. London: Palgrave.

Fujiwara, T. (dir.) (2001) *Battle Royale*. London: Tartan Videos.

Fujiyama, N. (2004) 'An object no longer being just an object – the art of not knowing, being alive, and becoming open', in O. Kitayama (ed.) *Japanese Contributions to Psychoanalysis*. Tokyo: Japan Psychoanalytic Society.

Fukumoto, O. (2007) 'Did the bird take off?: The inner world and external reality of an eating disorder patient with a borderline personality psychic functioning', in K. Matsuki (ed.) *Japanese Contributions to Psychoanalysis, Volume 2*. Tokyo: Japan Psychoanalytic Society.

Fukuoka, Y. (2000) *Lives of Young Koreans in Japan* (translated by T. Gill). Melbourne: Trans Pacific Press.

Fumino, Y. (2005) 'Establishment of new universities and the growth of psychology in postwar Japan', *Japanese Psychological Research*, 47 (2), pp. 144–150.

Garcia, V. (2000) *Three Japanese Anarchists: Kotoku, Osugi and Yamaga*. London and Berkeley: Kate Sharpley Library.

Gay, P. (1988) *Freud: A Life for Our Time*. New York: W.W. Norton.

Genosko, G. (2002) *Félix Guattari: An Aberrant Introduction*. London: Continuum.

Gibson, W. (2001) 'Modern boys and mobile girls', *The Observer*, 1 April.

Gilman, S. L. (1993) *Freud, Race, and Gender*. New York: Princeton University Press.

Gjerde, P. F. (2004) 'Amae and attachment: Some conceptual clarifications', International Congress of Psychology, Beijing, China, August.

Gjerde, P. F. and Onishi, M. (2000) 'Selves, cultures and nations: The psychological imagination of 'the Japanese' in the era of globalization', *Human Development*, 43, pp. 216–226.

Golding, W. (1997) *Lord of the Flies*. London: Faber & Faber.

Goodman, D. (1997) 'Anti-Semitism in Japan: Its history and current implications', in F. Dikötter (ed.) *The Construction of Racial Identities in China and Japan: Historical and Contemporary Perspectives*. London: Hurst & Company.

Gordo López, Á. J. and Cleminson, R. (2004) *Techno-Sexual Landscapes: Changing Relations between Technology and Sexuality*. London: Free Association Books.

Gordo López, Á. J. and Parker, I. (eds) (1999) *Cyberpsychology*. London: Macmillan.

Green, A. (1995–1996) 'Against Lacanism: A Conversation of André Green with Sergio Benvenuto', *Journal of European Psychoanalysis*, 2, http://www.psychomedia.it/jep/number2/greenbenv.htm (accessed 7 January 2008).

Grigg, R., Hecq, D. and Smith, C. (eds) (1999) *Female Sexuality: The Early Psychoanalytic Controversies*. London: Rebus Press.

Guardian (2005) 'Pass notes, No. 2,564: KitKat', *G2*, 3 February, p. 3.

Hammersley, P. (2006) 'Stop press [on the Japanese Society of Psychiatry and Neurology decision on the label schizophrenia]', *Asylum*, 15 (2), p. 6.

Handa, A. (2005) 'The myth of the Japanese 'New Family' in the 1980s: Murakami Haruki's *South of the Border, West of the Sun*', *Bulletin of the Tokyo Gakugei University, Section II*, 56, pp. 67–79.

Hanly, C. and Nichols, C. (2001) 'A disturbance of psychoanalytic memory: The case of John Rickman's three-person psychology', *Philosophy of the Social Sciences*, 31 (3), pp. 279–301.

Harootunian, H. (2001) 'Out of Japan: The New Associationist Movement', *Radical Philosophy*, 108, pp. 2–6.

Harootunian, H. (2004) 'Karatani's Marxian parallax', *Radical Philosophy*, 127, pp. 29–34.

Heimann, P. (1950) 'On countertransference', *International Journal of Psycho-Analysis*, 31, pp. 81–84.

Heisig, J. W. (2002) 'Jung, Christianity, and Buddhism', in P. Young-Eisendrath and S. Muramoto (eds) *Awakening and Insight: Zen Buddhism and Psychotherapy*. East Sussex, UK: Brunner-Routledge.

Hendry, J. (ed.) (1986a) *Interpreting Japanese Society: Anthropological Approaches (Second Edition)*. London: Routledge.

Hendry, J. (1986b) *Becoming Japanese: The World of the Pre-School Child*. Honolulu: University of Hawaii Press.

Henshall, K. (2004) *A History of Japan: From Stone Age to Superpower (Second Edition)*. London: Palgrave.

Herbert, J. (2004) 'Japan for the uninvited: Yaoi', http://ballz.ababa.net/uninvited/yaoi.htm (accessed 14 December 2004).

Hinshelwood, R. D. (1995) 'Psychoanalysis in Britain: Points of cultural access, 1893–1918', *International Journal of Psycho-Analysis*, 76, pp. 135–151.

Hisamatsu, S. and Jung, C. (2002) 'The Jung-Hisamatsu Conversation', in P. Young-Eisendrath and S. Muramoto (eds) *Awakening and Insight: Zen Buddhism and Psychotherapy*. East Sussex, UK: Brunner-Routledge.

Hoff, F. (1991) 'Signs of Japan', *Semiotic Review of Books*, 2 (3), www.chass.utoronto.ca/epc/srb/srb/japan.html (accessed 7 January 2008).

Holthaus, M. A. (2000) 'Novelist and analyst search the Japanese psyche', *San Francisco Jung Institute Library Journal*, 75 (19), pp. 35–48.

Hoshina, M. (2005) 'On sublimation', *The Letter: Lacanian Perspectives on Psychoanalysis*, 34, pp. 108–113.

Ichiyo, M. (1987) *Class Struggle and Technological Innovation in Japan since 1945*. Amsterdam: IIRE.

Ide, S. (1997) 'Women's language, men's language', in S. Buckley (ed.) *Broken Silence: Voices of Japanese Feminism*. Berkeley: University of California Press.

Igarashi, Y. (2005) 'Health psychology in Japan: Collective construction of a discipline', *European Health Psychology Society Electronic Newsletter*, 2, pp. 12–13.

Igarashi, Y. (2006) 'The role of critical psychology in Japan: Protest against positivistic psychology and the search for new knowledge of the mind', *Annual Review of Critical Psychology*, 5, www.discourseunit.com/arcp/5

Igarashi, Y. (2007) 'Clinical psychology as a technology of subjectivity: A Japanese case', International Society for Theoretical Psychology Conference, Toronto, June.

Inoue, T. (2003) 'Constructing male aesthetics in rock and makeup: Gender strategies by musicians and fans of visual rock in Japan', in Y. Hayami, A. Tanabe and Y. Tokita-Tanabe (eds) *Gender and Modernity: Perspectives from Asia and the Pacific*. Kyoto and Melbourne: Kyoto University Press and Trans Pacific Press.

International Christian University (2004) *The 21st Century Center of Excellence Program: Research and Education for Peace, Security and Conviviality*. Tokyo: ICU.

International Psychoanalytical Association (2002) 'Report of the IPA Exploratory Committee to Korea', *International Psychoanalysis*, 11 (2), p. 42.

International Psychoanalytical Association (2006) 'Constituent and Other Organisations', http://www.ipa.org.uk/site/cms/contentViewArticle.asp?article 1054 (accessed 7 January 2008).

Isbister, J. N. (1985) *Freud: An Introduction to his Life and Work*. Cambridge: Polity.

Ishiguro, K. (1990) *The Remains of the Day*. London: Faber & Faber.

Ishikawa, Y. and Kotani, H. (2005) 'On jokes: A technique of creating psychological safe space for schizophrenic patients', *International Journal of Counseling and Psychotherapy*, 3, pp. 93–97.

Iwasaki, T. (2004) 'Current status of psychoanalytic contributions to Japanese psychiatry', in O. Kitayama (ed.) *Japanese Contributions to Psychoanalysis*. Tokyo: Japan Psychoanalytic Society.

Jacoby, R. (1983) *The Repression of Psychoanalysis*. New York: Basic Books.

James, T. (2004) 'The key psychodynamics of female personality development: Phallic activeness and safe space', *International Journal of Counseling and Psychotherapy*, 2, pp. 77–85.

Japan Psychoanalytic Society (2006) Japan Psychoanalytic Society, http://jpas.jp (accessed 7 January 2008).

Jay, M. (1993) *Downcast Eyes: The Denigration of Vision in Twentieth-Century French Thought*. Berkeley: University of California Press.

Johnson, F. A. (1993) *Dependency and Japanese Socialization: Psychoanalytic and Anthropological Investigations into Amae*. New York: IUP.

Kahn, H. (1970) *The Emerging Japanese Superstate: Challenge and Response*. Englewood, NJ: Prentice-Hall.

Kakuchi, S. (2003) 'Japan's battler's of sex abuse confront, culture, law', *Women's News*, 17 April, http://www.feminist.com/news/news187html (accessed 30 July 2004).

Kanehara, H. (2005) *Snakes and Earrings* (translated by D. J. Karashima, originally published 2004). London: Vintage.

Kang, S. (2005) 'The discovery of the 'Orient' and orientalism', in R. F. Calichman (ed.) *Contemporary Japanese Thought*. New York: Columbia University Press.

Kano, R. (2004) 'Life phenomena and narrative: Psychoanalysis, psychotherapy and the systems theory', in O. Kitayama (ed.) *Japanese Contributions to Psychoanalysis*. Tokyo: Japan Psychoanalytic Society.

Kaplan, E. A. (1984) 'Is the gaze male?', in A. Snitow, C. Stansell and Thompson, S. (eds) *Desire: The Politics of Sexuality*. London: Virago.

Karatani, K. (1991) 'The discursive space of modern Japan', *boundary 2*, 18 (3), pp. 191–219.

Karatani, K. (1998) 'A geopolitics of literation – Toward a psychoanalysis of Japan', unpublished ms. (published version appeared as 'The new historicism and Japanese literary studies', Proceedings of the Midwest Association for Japanese Literary Studies 4).

Karatani, K. (2000) 'The Principles of the New Associationist Movement (NAM)', http://www.clas.ufl.edu/users/jmurphy/Karatani01file/NAM.Principles.html (accessed 7 January 2008).

Karatani, K. (2003) *Transcritique: On Kant and Marx*. Cambridge, MA: MIT Press.

Karatani, K. (2005) 'Sōseki's diversity: On *Kokoro*', in R. F. Calichman (ed.) *Contemporary Japanese Thought*. New York: Columbia University Press.

Kato, H. (2005) 'Zen and psychology', *Japanese Psychological Research*, 47 (2), pp. 125–136.

Katsuichi, H. (2000) *Harukor: An Ainu Woman's Tale* (translated by K. Selden, originally published 1993). Berkeley: University of California Press.

Kawahara, R. (2004) 'The current situation of the internationalization of the Naikan therapy' (in Japanese), *Seishin Shinkeigaku Zasshi*, 105 (8), pp. 988–993, abstract via http://www.ncbi.nlm.nih.gov (accessed 9 January 2008).

Kawai, H. (1991) '"The forbidden chamber" motif in a Japanese fairy tale', in Ikegami, Y. (ed.) *The Empire of Signs: Semiotic Essays on Japanese Culture*. Amsterdam: John Benjamins Publishing Co.

Kawai, H. (1995) *The Japanese Psyche: Major Motifs in the Fairy Tales of Japan*. Putnam, CT: Spring Publications.

Kawai, H. (1996) *Buddhism and the Art of Psychotherapy*. College Station, TX: Texas A&M University Press.

Kawai, H. (1998) 'A Buddhist remedy', *UNESCO Courier*, 51 (2), pp. 12–15.

Kawai, H. (2002a) 'Foreword', Agency for Cultural Affairs Brochure, http://www.bunka.go.jp/english/pdf/04_foreword.pdf (accessed 29 December 2006).

Kawai, H. (2002b) 'What is I? Reflections from Buddhism and psychotherapy', in P. Young-Eisendrath and S. Muramoto (eds) *Awakening and Insight: Zen Buddhism and Psychotherapy*. East Sussex, UK: Brunner-Routledge.

Kawano, K. (1990) 'Feminist therapy with Japanese women', *Journal of Social Work Practice*, 4 (3/4), pp. 44–55.

Kawano, K. (2004) 'Feminist counselling within the Japanese women's movement', International Council of Psychologists, Jinan, China, August.

Kikuchi, T. (2004) 'Aggression: The two directions it takes', in O. Kitayama (ed.) *Japanese Contributions to Psychoanalysis*. Tokyo: Japan Psychoanalytic Society.

Kim, J. (2005) 'Depression and neo-Confucian ethics', *The Letter: Lacanian Perspectives on Psychoanalysis*, 34, pp. 91–107.

King, H. (2005) 'Lost in Translation', *Film Quarterly*, 59 (1), pp. 45–48.

Kinugasa, T. (2004) 'Borderline research in Britain and a case report', in O. Kitayama (ed.) *Japanese Contributions to Psychoanalysis*. Tokyo: Japan Psychoanalytic Society.

Kinugasa, T. (2007) 'Transference in the Wolf Man's dream', in K. Matsuki (ed.) *Japanese Contributions to Psychoanalysis, Volume 2*. Tokyo: Japan Psychoanalytic Society.

Kirino, N. (2003) *Out* (translated by S. Snyder, originally published 1997). Tokyo: Kodansha International.

Kirsch, J. (1959) 'Affinities between Zen and analytical psychology', *Psychologia: An International Journal of Psychology in the Orient*, 2 (2), pp. 85–92.

Kitanaka, J. (2003) 'Jungians and the rise of psychotherapy in Japan: A brief historical note', *Transcultural Psychiatry*, 40 (2), pp. 239–247.

Kitanishi, K. and Azuma, N. (2005) 'Morita therapy in modern times: Review from 1995 to 2004', *International Journal of Counseling and Psychotherapy*, 3, pp. 67–85.

Kitayama, O. (1985) 'Pre-Oedipal "taboo" in Japanese folk tragedies', *International Review of Psycho-Analysis*, 12, pp. 173–186.

Kitayama, O. (1987) 'Metaphorization: Making terms', *International Journal of Psycho-Analysis*, 68, pp. 499–509.

Kitayama, O. (1991) 'The wounded caretaker and guilt', *International Review of Psycho-Analysis*, 18, pp. 229–240.

Kitayama, O. (ed.) (2004a) *Japanese Contributions to Psychoanalysis*. Tokyo: Japan Psychoanalytic Society.

Kitayama, O. (2004b) 'Preface', in O. Kitayama (ed.) (2004a) *Japanese Contributions to Psychoanalysis*. Tokyo: Japan Psychoanalytic Society.

Kitayama, O. (2004c) 'Descending love from a "Great Mother": Towards Henry Moore from Japan with a clinical insight', in O. Kitayama (ed.) *Japanese Contributions to Psychoanalysis*. Tokyo: Japan Psychoanalytic Society.

Kitayama, O. (2007) 'A study of the "Rat Man" from a technical perspective', in K. Matsuki (ed.) *Japanese Contributions to Psychoanalysis, Volume 2*. Tokyo: Japan Psychoanalytic Society.

Klein, M. (1986) *The Selected Works of Melanie Klein*. Harmondsworth: Pelican.

Kobayashi, K. (2004) 'Weekly session of free association using a couch: A discussion on frequency', in O. Kitayama (ed.) *Japanese Contributions to Psychoanalysis*. Tokyo: Japan Psychoanalytic Society.

Kodansha Encyclopedia of Japan (2006) 'Kakure Kirishitan', http://www.baobab.or.jp/~stranger/mypage/kakure.htm (accessed 27 December 2006).

Kohon, G. (1986) *The British School of Psychoanalysis: The Independent Tradition*. London: Free Association Books.

Kohut, H. (1979) 'The two analyses of Mr Z', *International Journal of Psycho-Analysis*, 60 (3), pp. 3–27.

Kosawa, H. (1931) 'Two kinds of guilt feelings: The Ajase Complex', in K. Matsuki (ed.) (2007) *Japanese Contributions to Psychoanalysis, Volume 2*. Tokyo: Japan Psychoanalytic Society.

Kotani, H. (2003) 'Counseling and Psychotherapy – To make them more effective for difficult adolescents', *International Journal of Counseling and Psychotherapy*, 1, pp. 5–16.

Kotani, H. (2005) 'Contemporary meanings of psychological space for dynamic psychotherapy', *International Journal of Counseling and Psychotherapy*, 3, pp. 31–47.

Kowner, R. (2000) '"Lighter than yellow, but not enough": Western discourse on the Japanese "race", 1854–1904', *The Historical Journal*, 43 (1), pp. 103–131.

Kozuki, Y. and Kennedy, M. G. (2004) 'Cultural incommensurability in psychodynamic psychotherapy in Western and Japanese traditions', *Journal of Nursing Scholarship*, 36 (1), pp. 30–38.

Kutter, P. (ed.) (1991) *Psychoanalysis International: A Guide to Psychoanalysis Throughout the World, Volume 1.* Stuttgart-Bad-Canstatt: Fromman-Holzboorg.

Kutter, P. (ed.) (1995) *Psychoanalysis International: A Guide to Psychoanalysis Throughout the World, Volume 2.* Stuttgart-Bad-Canstatt: Fromman-Holzboorg.

Lacan, J. (1952) 'Intervention on transference', in J. Mitchell and J. Rose (eds) (1982) *Feminine Sexuality: Jacques Lacan and the école freudienne*. London: Macmillan.

Lacan, J. (1971) *The Seminar. Book XVIII: On a discourse that might not be a semblance* (translated from unedited French manuscripts by C. Gallagher), unpublished.

Lacan, J. (1979) *Four Fundamental Concepts of Psycho-Analysis* (translated by A. Sheridan, originally published 1973). Harmondsworth: Penguin.

Lacan, J. (1988) *The Seminar of Jacques Lacan Book I: Freud's Papers on Technique 1953–1954* (translated with notes by John Forrester, originally published 1975). London & New York NY: W.W. Norton & Company.

Lacan, J. (1989) 'Science and truth', *Newsletter of the Freudian Field*, 3, pp. 4–29.

Lacan, J. (1993) *The Psychoses: The Seminar of Jacques Lacan, Book III 1955–1956* (translated with notes by R. Grigg, originally published 1981). London: Routledge.

Lacan, J. (1998) *The Seminar. Book XX: On the Limits of Love and Knowledge (Encore)*, J.-A. Miller (ed.) (translated by B. Fink, originally published 1975). London & New York NY: W.W. Norton & Company.

Lacan, J. (2001) 'Avis au lecteur japonais', in *Autres Écrits*, J.-A. Miller (ed.). Paris: du Seuil.

Lacan, J. (2005) 'The Tokyo discourse', *Journal for Lacanian Studies*, 3 (1), pp. 129–144.

Lacan, J. (2006) *Écrits: The First Complete Edition in English* (translated with notes by Bruce Fink in collaboration with Héloïse Fink and Russell Grigg). New York: W. W. Norton & Co.

Lacan, J. (2007) *The Other Side of Psychoanalysis: The Seminar of Jacques Lacan, Book XVII* (translated with notes by R. Grigg, originally published 1991). New York: W. W. Norton and Co.

Lasch, C. (1978) *The Culture of Narcissism: American Life in an Age of Diminishing Expectations*. New York: Norton.

Le Vine, P. (1998) 'Editor's introduction' in S. Morita, *Morita Therapy and the True Nature of Anxiety-Based Disorders (*Shinkeishitsu*)* (translated by A. Kondo, originally published 1928). New York: State University of New York Press.

Lee, A. (2005) 'Japan plays happily at "cute horror"', *Financial Times*, July 9–10, p. 7.

Lifton, R. J. (1989) *Thought, Reform and the Psychology of Totalism: A Study of "Brainwashing" in China*. Chapel Hill, NC: University of North Carolina Press.

Lifton, R. J. (1999) *Destroying the World to Save it: Aum Shinrikyō, Apocalyptic Violence and the New Global Terrorism*. New York: Henry Holt and Co.

Lindow, V. (1994) 'The Japanese psychiatric system survivor movement', *Changes*, 12 (2), pp. 141–144.

Longenbach, J. and Litz, W. A. (eds) (1991) *Ezra Pound's Poetry and Prose, Volume VIII*. New York: Garland.

Lusthaus, D. (2000) 'Buddhist philosophy, Chinese', in *Concise Routledge Encyclopedia of Philosophy*. London and New York: Routledge.

Mackie, V. (1988) 'Feminist politics in Japan', *New Left Review I*, 167, pp. 53–76.
Mandel, E. (1978) *From Stalinism to Eurocommunism: The Bitter Fruits of 'Socialism in One Country'*. London: New Left Books.
Maraldo, J. C. (2000) 'Buddhist philosophy, Japanese', in *Concise Routledge Encyclopedia of Philosophy*. London and New York: Routledge.
Maruyama, M. (1969) *Thought and Behaviour in Modern Japanese Politics (Second Edition)* (Translated by I. Morris). Oxford: Oxford University Press.
Matsuki, K. (2004) 'Guilt which is not conscious, and afterwards', in O. Kitayama (ed.) *Japanese Contributions to Psychoanalysis*. Tokyo: Japan Psychoanalytic Society.
Matsuki, K. (ed.) (2007a) *Japanese Contributions to Psychoanalysis, Volume 2*. Tokyo: Japan Psychoanalytic Society.
Matsuki, K. (2007b) 'The mind that does not sway, or the mind that sways: Transference – counter-transference and neutrality', in K. Matsuki (ed.) *Japanese Contributions to Psychoanalysis, Volume 2*. Tokyo: Japan Psychoanalytic Society.
Matsuyuki, M. (1988) 'Japanese feminist counseling as a political act', *Women & Therapy*, 21 (2), pp. 65–77.
McCargo, D. (2004) *Contemporary Japan (Second Edition)*. London: Palgrave.
McNicol, T. (2003) '"Shut-ins" turn backs on Japan: "Hikikomori" make a fresh start in foreign climes', *The Japan Times*, 16 December 2003, http://www. japan-times.co.jp/cgi-bin/getarticle.p15?fl20031216zg.htm (accessed 21 July 2004).
Miike, Y. (2003) 'Japanese *enryo-sasshi* communication and the psychology of *amae*: Reconsideration and reconceptualization', *Keio Communication Review*, 25, pp. 93–115.
Miller, J.-A. (1986) '*Extimité*', in M. Bracher, M. W. Alcorn, R. J. Corthell, R. J. and F. Massardier-Kenney (eds) (1994) *Lacanian Theory of Discourse: Subject, Structure and Society*. New York, New York University Press.
Miller, J.-A. (2002) 'Elements of epistemology', in J. Glynos and Y. Stavrakakis (eds) *Lacan and Science*. London: Karnac.
Miller, M. E. (2002) 'Zen and psychotherapy: From neutrality, through relationship, to the emptying place', in P. Young-Eisendrath and S. Muramoto (eds) *Awakening and Insight: Zen Buddhism and Psychotherapy*. East Sussex, UK: Brunner-Routledge.
Millett, K. (1977) *Sexual Politics*. London: Virago.
Minakawa, K. (2004) 'On the use of metaphor to establish therapeutic alliance with borderline and schizophrenic adolescents', in O. Kitayama (ed.) *Japanese Contributions to Psychoanalysis*. Tokyo: Japan Psychoanalytic Society.
Mishima, Y. (1990) *Confessions of a Mask* (translated by M. Weatherby, originally published 1949). London: Paladin.
Mitchell, J. (1974) *Psychoanalysis and Feminism*. Harmondsworth: Penguin.
Miya, Y. (1997) 'Excerpts from *Sexuality*', in S. Buckley (ed.) *Broken Silence: Voices of Japanese Feminism*. Berkeley: University of California Press.
Mizoguchi, H. (2005) 'Reception of Pavlov's theory in Japan', *Japanese Psychological Research*, 47 (2), pp. 95–105.
Moloney, J. C. (1953) 'Understanding the paradox of Japanese psychoanalysis', *International Journal of Psycho-Analysis*, 34 (4), pp. 291–303.
Morikawa, K. (2004) 'Otaku: personaspacecity: The birth of a personopolis', in *Catalogue of Padiglione Giappone, IX Mostra Internazionale di Architettura*. Venice: La Biennale di Venezia.

Morita Therapy Centre (2004) 'Treatment goals', http//www.morita-therapy.org/treatment.html (accessed 7 January 2008).

Morita, S. (1998) *Morita Therapy and the True Nature of Anxiety-Based Disorders (*Shinkeishitsu*)* (translated by A. Kondo, originally published 1928). New York: State University of New York Press.

Morsbach, H. and Tyler, W. J. (1986) 'A Japanese emotion: *amae*', in R. Harré (ed.) *The Social Construction of Emotions*. Oxford: Basil Blackwell.

Moses, R. (1992) 'A short history of psychoanalysis in Palestine and Israel', *Israel Journal of Psychiatry and Related Sciences*, 29 (4), pp. 229–238.

Motora, Y. (1905) *An Essay on Eastern Philosophy*. Leipzig: R. Voigtländer's Verlag.

Mukoda, K. (1994) *The Name of the Flower: Stories by Kuniko Mukoda* (translated by T. Matsumoto). Berkeley, CA: Stone Bridge Press.

Murakami, H. (1987) *Hear the Wind Sing* (translated by A. Birnbaum, originally published 1979). Tokyo: Kodansha International.

Murakami, H. (2002) *Sputnik Sweetheart* (translated by P. Gabriel, originally published 1999). London: Vintage.

Murakami, H. (2003a) *Norwegian Wood* (translated by J. Rubin, originally published 1987). London: Vintage.

Murakami, H. (2003b) *Underground: The Tokyo Gas Attack and the Japanese Psyche* (translated by A. Birnbaum and P. Gabriel, originally published 1997–1998). London: Vintage.

Murakami, H. (2003c) *The Wind-Up Bird Chronicle* (translated by J. Rubin, originally published 1994–1995). London: Vintage.

Murakami, H. (2003d) *A Wild Sheep Chase* (translated by A. Birnbaum, originally published 1982). London: Vintage.

Murakami, H. (2003e) *Dance Dance Dance* (translated by A. Birnbaum, originally published 1988). London: Vintage.

Murakami, H. (2003f) *Hard-boiled Wonderland and the End of the World* (translated by A. Birnbaum, originally published 1985). London: Vintage.

Murakami, H. (2003g) *After the Quake* (translated by J. Rubin, originally published 2000). London: Vintage.

Murakami, H. (2003h) *South of the Border, West of the Sun* (translated by P. Gabriel, originally published 1992). London: Vintage.

Murakami, H. (2005) *Kafka on the Shore* (translated by P. Gabriel, originally published 2002). London: Vintage.

Murakami, R. (2005) *In the Miso Soup* (translated by R. McCarthy, originally published 1997). London: Bloomsbury.

Muramoto, K. (2001) *Women's Trauma and Healing in Japanese Culture*, unpublished PhD thesis, The Union Institute Graduate College.

Muramoto, S. (2002) 'Jung and Buddhism', in P. Young-Eisendrath and S. Muramoto (eds) *Awakening and Insight: Zen Buddhism and Psychotherapy*. East Sussex, UK: Brunner-Routledge.

Muramoto, S. and Hoffman, E. (2005) 'Humanistic psychology in Japan', *Journal of Humanistic Psychology*, 45 (4), pp. 465–482.

Murata, S. (2007) '"Yaoi" phenomenon: An introduction', seminar presentation, University of Kyoto, March. Available at http://www.psy.jinkan.kyoto-u.ac.jp/20070322.htm (accessed 7 January 2008).

Nagatomo, S. (1994) 'Review of Kawai Hayao's *The Buddhist Priest Myoe: A Life of Dreams*', *Philosophy East and West*, 44 (3), pp. 582–586.

Nakakuki, M. (1994) 'Normal and developmental aspects of masochism: Transcultural and clinical implications', *Psychiatry*, 57, pp. 244–257.

Nakakuki, M. (1997a) '"Amae" and "Shibumi" in a healthy personality development of Japanese', American Psychoanalytic Association Annual Meeting, San Diego, May.

Nakakuki, M. (1997b) 'Psychodynamics and psychotherapy of "Taijin Kyofu", culture-bound neurosis in Japan: "Corrective relational experience" vs. interpretation of amae conflict', American Psychoanalytic Association Annual Meeting, San Diego, May.

Nakane, C. (1970) *Japanese Society*. Berkeley: University of California Press.

Nakanishi, T. (1997) 'Interview', in S. Buckley (ed.) *Broken Silence: Voices of Japanese Feminism*. Berkeley: University of California Press.

Nishikawa, M. (2003) 'The basic axis of the group psychotherapy technique on the adolescent identity crisis in Japan: A case study of the intensive-multi-dimensional, concurrent-conjoint identity group psychotherapy' (in Japanese, English ms.), *International Journal of Counseling and Psychotherapy*, 1, 49–68.

Nishikawa, M. (2007) 'Ground matrix, space making and analysis in the psychotherapy process of a Japanese adult woman', Japan in Analysis Video Conferencing Symposium, Institute for Advanced Studies of Clinical Psychology, International Christian University, Tokyo, Japan, April.

Nishikawa, Y. (2005) 'An overview of the history of psychology in Japan and the background to the development of the Japanese Psychological Association', *Japanese Psychological Research*, 47 (2), pp. 63–72.

Nishimura, K. (2007) 'School counseling on the basis of psychoanalytic systems theory', Japan in Analysis Video Conferencing Symposium, Institute for Advanced Studies of Clinical Psychology, International Christian University, Tokyo, Japan, April.

Nishizono, M. (2004a) 'Child-rearing in Japan in transition', in O. Kitayama (ed.) *Japanese Contributions to Psychoanalysis*. Tokyo: Japan Psychoanalytic Society.

Nishizono, M. (2004b) 'A message to the world from the Japan Psychoanalytic Society that celebrates the 50th anniversary of its founding', in O. Kitayama (ed.) *Japanese Contributions to Psychoanalysis*. Tokyo: Japan Psychoanalytic Society.

Nishizono (2007a) 'Preface', in K. Matsuki (ed.) *Japanese Contributions to Psychoanalysis, Volume 2*. Tokyo: Japan Psychoanalytic Society.

Nishizono (2007b) 'Issues of psychoanalysis in the 21st century: From some experiences in Japan', in K. Matsuki (ed.) *Japanese Contributions to Psychoanalysis, Volume 2*. Tokyo: Japan Psychoanalytic Society.

Nobus, D. (2002) 'Illiterature', in L. Thurston (ed.) *Re-inventing the Symptom: Essays on the Final Lacan*. New York: Other Press.

Nobus, D. (2005) 'Lacan in Japan – 2', *Journal for Lacanian Studies*, 3 (1), pp. 125–128.

Nobus, D. and Quinn, M. (2005) *Knowing Nothing, Staying Stupid: Elements for a Psychoanalytic Epistemology*. London: Routledge.

Numazaki, I. (2003) '(De-)sexualizing gender relationships: Sexual harassment as modern and as a critique of modernity', in Y. Hayami, A. Tanabe and Y. Tokita-Tanabe (eds) *Gender and Modernity: Perspectives from Asia and the Pacific*. Kyoto and Melbourne: Kyoto University Press and Trans Pacific Press.

Ochiai, K. (1997) 'Interview', in S. Buckley (ed.) *Broken Silence: Voices of Japanese Feminism*. Berkeley: University of California Press.

Ōe, K. (1996) *Nip the Buds, Shoot the Kids* (translated by P. St. John Mackintosh and M. Sugiyama, originally published 1958). New York: Grove Press.

Ogura, K. (2004) 'A 7-year- and 2-month-old depressed boy who asked profound philosophical questions – a clinical vignette', in O. Kitayama (ed.) *Japanese Contributions to Psychoanalysis*. Tokyo: Japan Psychoanalytic Society.

Okano, K. (1994) 'Shame and social phobia: A transcultural viewpoint', *Bulletin of the Menninger Clinic*, 58 (3), pp. 323–338.

Okimoto, J., Settlage, C., Freed, W., Klein, K., Dao, E., Campbell, J., Yoshiike, Y., Lui, B. and Mason, C. (2007) 'The appeal cycle phenomenon in three cultures: An exploratory cultural comparison of child development in the second year of life', in K. Matsuki (ed.) *Japanese Contributions to Psychoanalysis, Volume 2*. Tokyo: Japan Psychoanalytic Society.

Okonogi, K. (1995) 'Japan', in P. Kutter (ed.) *Psychoanalysis International: A Guide to Psychoanalysis Throughout the World, Volume 2*. Stuttgart-Bad-Canstatt: Fromman-Holzboorg.

Okonogi, K. (2004a) 'A history of psychoanalysis in Japan', in O. Kitayama (ed.) *Japanese Contributions to Psychoanalysis*. Tokyo: Japan Psychoanalytic Society.

Okonogi, K. (2004b) 'Ajase complex and its implications', in O. Kitayama (ed.) *Japanese Contributions to Psychoanalysis*. Tokyo: Japan Psychoanalytic Society.

Okuyama, M. (2001) 'Spiritual quests in contemporary Japanese writers before and after the Aum affair: Ōe Kenzaburō and Murakami Haruki around 1995', *Nanzan Bulletin*, 25, pp. 33–42.

OMF International (2006) 'Japan', http://www.omf.org.uk/content.asp?id8509& cachefixer (accessed 27 December 2006).

Onda, A. (2002) 'The development of Buddhist psychology in modern Japan', in P. Young-Eisendrath and S. Muramoto (eds) *Awakening and Insight: Zen Buddhism and Psychotherapy*. East Sussex, UK: Brunner-Routledge.

Ooshima, Y. (2004) 'Arina Shinyokohama in Akihabara', in *Catalogue of Padiglione Giappone, IX Mostra Internazionale di Architettura*. Venice: La Biennale di Venezia.

Orbach, S. (2003) 'Therapy from the left: Interview with Susie Orbach', *European Journal of Psychotherapy, Counselling and Health*, 6 (1), pp. 75–85.

Oyama, T., Sato, T. and Suzuki, Y. (2001) 'Shaping of scientific psychology in Japan', *International Journal of Psychology*, 36 (6), pp. 396–406.

Parker, I. (1997) *Psychoanalytic Culture: Psychoanalytic Discourse in Western Society*. London and Thousand Oaks, CA: Sage.

Parker, I. (2003) 'The Label 'UKCP Registered Psychoanalyst': Diversity of practice inside and outside the International Psychoanalytical Association IPA', *The Psychotherapist*, 20, pp. 10–11.

Parker, I. (2004a) 'Review essay: Rakan no seishin-bunseki', *Journal for Lacanian Studies*, 2 (2), pp. 318–328.

Parker, I. (2004b) *Slavoj Žižek: A Critical Introduction*. London: Pluto Press.

Parker, I. (2006) 'Helplessness in an Adjacent Psychoanalytic Culture, Japan', *Psychodynamic Practice*, 12 (1), pp. 87–90.

Parker, I. (2007a) 'Psychoanalytic Cyberspace, Beyond Psychology', *The Psychoanalytic Review*, 94 (1), pp. 63–82.

Parker, I. (2007b) 'The Phallus is a Signifier', *The Symptom, Online Journal for Lacan.com, 8,* www.lacan.com/symptom8_articles/parker8.html (accessed 7 January 2008).

Parker, I. and Revelli, S. (eds) (2008) *Psychoanalytic Practice and State Regulation*. London: Karnac.

Penley, C. (1997) *Nasa/Trek: Popular Science and Sex in America*. London: Verso.
Phillips, A. (1988) *Winnicott*. London: Fontana.
Radich, M. (2004a) 'Translator and editor notes', in Shingu, K. (2004) *Being Irrational: Lacan, the Objet a, and the Golden Mean* (translated and edited by M. Radich, originally published 1995). Tokyo: Gakuju Shoin, Tokyo.
Radich, M. (2004b) personal communication, 17 August.
Rees, P. (2002) 'Japan: the missing million', *BBC News Correspondent*, http://news.bbc.co.uk/1/hi/progammes/correspondent/2334893/stm (accessed 21 July 2004).
Richards, G. (2000) 'Britain on the couch: The popularization of psychoanalysis in Britain 1918–1940', *Science in Context*, 13 (2), pp. 183–230.
Richie, D. (2004) *The Japan Journals 1947–2004*. Berkeley: Stone Bridge Press.
Rogers, C. R. (1951) *Client-Centred Therapy*. Boston: Houghton-Mifflin.
Roland, A. (1996) *Cultural Pluralism and Psychoanalysis: The Asian and North American Experience*. New York and London: Routledge.
Rothbaum, F., Weisz, J., Pott, M., Miyake, K. and Morelli, G. (2000) 'Attachment and culture: Security in the United States and Japan', *American Psychologist*, 55 (10), pp. 1093–1104.
Roudinesco, E. (1990) *Jacques Lacan and Co.: A History of Psychoanalysis in France, 1925–1985*. London: Free Association Books.
Said, E. (1985) *Orientalism*. Harmondsworth: Penguin.
Said, E. (2004) *Freud and the Non-European*. London: Verso.
Saitō, C. (1997) 'What is Japanese feminism?', in S. Buckley (ed.) *Broken Silence: Voices of Japanese Feminism*. Berkeley: University of California Press.
Saito, T. (2004a) 'Otaku sexuality', in *Catalogue of Padiglione Giappone, IX Mostra Internazionale di Architettura*. Venice: La Biennale di Venezia.
Saito, T. (2004b) 'Sexuality of Otaku: In the light of psychoanalysis', The Unconscious of Cultures Day Seminar, Shiran-Kaikan, University of Kyoto, October.
Sakiyama, Y. and Koch, N. (2003) 'Touch in dance therapy in Japan', *American Journal of Dance Therapy*, 25 (2), pp. 79–95.
Sakuta, T., Shiratsuchi, T., Kimura, Y. and Abe, Y. (1996) 'Psychotherapies originated in Japan', http//www.jicef.or.jp/wahec/ful319.htm (accessed 7 January 2008).
Samuels, A. (1985) *Jung and the Post-Jungians*. London: Routledge & Kegan Paul.
Samuels, A. (1992) 'National psychology, National Socialism, and analytical psychology: Reflections on C. G. Jung and anti-Semitism', *Journal of Analytical Psychology*, 37, pp. 23–64.
Santner, E. (1996) *My Own Private Germany*. Princeton: Princeton University Press.
Sato, K. (1997) '"Same language, same race": The dilemma of *Kanbun* in modern Japan' in F. Dikötter (ed.) *The Construction of Racial Identities in China and Japan: Historical and Contemporary Perspectives*. London: Hurst & Company.
Sato, T. (2002) 'Nihon ni okeru Shinrigaku no Juyo to Tenkai', *Kitaohji Shobo* (English manuscript 'Acceptance and development of psychoanalysis in Japan').
Sato, T. (2005) 'The history of psychology in Japan', *Japanese Psychological Research*, 47 (2), pp. 47–51.
Sato, T. (2007) "Rises and falls of clinical psychology in Japan: A perspective on the status of Japanese clinical psychology', *Ritsumeikan Journal of Human Sciences*, 13, pp. 133–144.
Sato, T. and Fumino, Y. (2005) 'Psychology in Japan', *The Psychologist*, 18 (3), pp. 156–157.

Sato, T. and Sato, T. (2005) 'The early 20th century: Shaping the discipline of psychology in Japan', *Japanese Psychological Research,* 47 (2), pp. 52–62.

Sato, T., Namiki, H., Ando, J and Hatano, G. (2004) 'Japanese conception of and research on human intelligence', in R. J. Sternberg (ed.) *International Handbook of Intelligence,* Cambridge: Cambridge University Press.

Seon, J. (2004) 'Otaku frontiers', in *Catalogue of Padiglione Giappone, IX Mostra Internazionale di Architettura.* Venice: La Biennale di Venezia.

Shi, J. (2004) 'Diligence makes people smart: Chinese perspectives of intelligence', in R. J. Sternberg (ed.) *International Handbook of Intelligence,* Cambridge: Cambridge University Press.

Shingu, K. (2004) *Being Irrational: Lacan, the Objet a, and the Golden Mean* (translated and edited by M. Radich, originally published 1995). Tokyo: Gakuju Shoin, Tokyo.

Shingu, K. (2005a) 'Freud, Lacan and Japan', *The Letter: Lacanian Perspectives on Psychoanalysis,* 34, pp. 48–62.

Shingu, K. (2005b) 'A history of the self-containing structure of the mind', *The Letter: Lacanian Perspectives on Psychoanalysis,* 34, pp. 63–69.

Shingu, K. (2006) 'Japanese myth, Buddhist legend and the structural analysis of clinical dreams in relation to the mourning process', *The Letter: Lacanian Perspectives on Psychoanalysis,* 37, pp. 93–113.

Shingu, K. (2007) personal communication, 12 May.

Shingu, K. (2008) 'Psychoanalysis, psychotherapy and psychiatry in Japan', in I. Parker and S. Revelli (eds) *Psychoanalytic Practice and State Regulation.* London: Karnac.

Shingu, K. and Funaki, T. (2008) '"Between two deaths": The intersection of psychoanalysis and Japanese Buddhism', *Theory & Psychology,* 18 (2), pp. 253–267.

Shuo, W. (2000) *Please Don't Call Me Human* (translated by H. Goldblatt). Harpenden, Herts: No Exit Press.

Siddle, R. (1997) 'The Ainu and the discourse of "race"', in F. Dikötter (ed.) *The Construction of Racial Identities in China and Japan: Historical and Contemporary Perspectives.* London: Hurst & Company.

Sōseki, N. (1957) *Kokoro* (translated by E. McClellan, originally published 1914). Washington DC: Regnery Publishing Inc.

Sōseki, N. (2002) *I Am a Cat* (translated by A. Ito and G. Wilson, originally published 1905–1906). Boston: Tuttle Publishing.

Spence, D. P. (1982) *Narrative Truth and Historical Truth.* New York: W. W. Norton.

Spradlin, S, J. (1998) 'Review of Kawai Hayao's *Buddhism and the Art of Psychotherapy*', *Journal of Analytical Psychology,* 43, pp. 413–422.

Sternberg, R. J. (ed.) (2004) *International Handbook of Intelligence,* Cambridge: Cambridge University Press.

Strachey, J. (1934) 'The nature of the therapeutic action of psycho-analysis', *International Journal of Psycho-Analysis,* 15, pp. 127–159.

Sugamura, G. and Warren, E. S. (2006) 'Conjoining paradigms: A dissolution-oriented approach to psychotherapy', in M. G. T. Kwee, K. J. Gergen and F. Koshikawa (eds) *Horizons in Buddhist Psychology: Practice, Research and Theory.* Chagrin Falls, OH: Taos Institute.

Sugamura, G., Haruki, Y. and Koshikawa, F. (2006) 'Mindfulness and bodyfulness in the practices of meditation: A comparison of Western and Eastern theories of mind-body', First Convention of the Asian Psychological Association, Bali, Indonesia, August.

Sugiman, T. (2006) 'Theory in the context of collaborative inquiry', *Theory & Psychology*, 16 (3), pp. 311–325.
Sugiman, T. (2007) 'A theory of construction of norm and meaning: Osawa's theory of the body', in T. Sugiman, K. Gergen, W. Wagner and Y. Yamada (eds) *Meaning in Action*. Tokyo: Springer-Verlag.
Sullivan, H. S. (1962) *Schizophrenia as a Human Process*. New York: W.W. Norton & Co.
Suzuki, K. (2002) 'Social-phobia and "Witz" in Japan', presented at XII World Congress of Psychiatry, Yokohama.
Suzuki, T. (2007) 'The dream as countertransference: Its therapeutic applications', in K. Matsuki (ed.) *Japanese Contributions to Psychoanalysis, Volume 2*. Tokyo: Japan Psychoanalytic Society.
Suzuki, Y. (2005) 'An historical examination of the concept of *jiga* (ego) in Japanese psychology, particularly as employed in a dissertation by Yujiro Motora and in Ladd's psychological theory', *Japanese Psychological Research*, 47 (2), pp. 115–124.
Swift, J. (1967) *Gulliver's Travels* (originally published 1726). Harmondsworth: Penguin.
Takahashi, T. (2004) 'Boundary as a guiding principle in comprehensive group treatment – interface between intrapsychic, interpersonal, and system issues', in O. Kitayama (ed.) *Japanese Contributions to Psychoanalysis*. Tokyo: Japan Psychoanalytic Society.
Takahashi, T. (2007) 'Sexuality if paranoid schizophrenics in object relations group psychotherapy: Freud's theory on paranoia revisited', in K. Matsuki (ed.) *Japanese Contributions to Psychoanalysis, Volume 2*. Tokyo: Japan Psychoanalytic Society.
Takano, A. (2004) 'Encounter and prenatal rancour', in O. Kitayama (ed.) *Japanese Contributions to Psychoanalysis*. Tokyo: Japan Psychoanalytic Society.
Takano, Y. and Osaka, E. (1999) 'An unsupported common view: Comparing Japan and the U.S. on individualism/collectivism', *Asian Journal of Social Psychology*, 2, pp. 311–341.
Tamari, T. (2006) 'Reflections on the development of cultural studies in Japan', *Theory, Culture & Society*, 23 (7–8), pp. 293–304.
The Week (2007) 'It must be true…I read it in the tabloids', *The Week*, 6 January, p. 11.
ToDo Institute (2004) 'ToDo Institute: Mindfulness, procrastination, and gratitude using Morita and Naikan therapy', http://www.todoinstitute.org/index.html (accessed 7 January 2008).
Tsuji, K., Miyasaki, L. S., Otsuka, K., Honda, G., Kato, S. and Abe, K. (2001) 'Panic disorder cases in Japanese-Brazilians in Japan: Their ethnic and cultural confusion', *Psychiatry and Clinical Neurosciences*, 55, pp. 127–130.
Tsutsui, William (2004) *Godzilla on my Mind: Fifty years of the King of the Monsters*. London: Palgrave.
Tsutsumi, S. (2004) 'Adolescents with developmental psychopathology in adulthood', in O. Kitayama (ed.) *Japanese Contributions to Psychoanalysis*. Tokyo: Japan Psychoanalytic Society.
Ueno, C. (1997) 'Are the Japanese feminine? Some problems of Japanese feminism in its cultural context', in S. Buckley (ed.) *Broken Silence: Voices of Japanese Feminism*. Berkeley: University of California Press.
Ueno, C. (2004) *Nationalism and Gender* (translated by B. Yamamoto). Melbourne: Trans Pacific Press.

Ueno, C. (2005) 'In the feminine guise: A trap of reverse orientalism', in R. F. Calichman (ed.) *Contemporary Japanese Thought*. New York: Columbia University Press.

United Nations (2004) 'Dr Hayao Kawai', http://www.un.org/Dialogue/kawai.html (accessed 7 January 2008).

Ushijima, S. (2004) 'The narcissism and death of Yukio Mishima – from the object relational point of view', in O. Kitayama (ed.) *Japanese Contributions to Psychoanalysis*. Tokyo: Japan Psychoanalytic Society.

Van Waning, A. (2007) 'NAIKAN, a Buddhist approach to self-reflection in Japan: Experiences, psychoanalytical and cultural reflections', in K. Matsuki (ed.) *Japanese Contributions to Psychoanalysis, Volume 2*. Tokyo: Japan Psychoanalytic Society.

Van Wolferen, K. (1990) *The Enigma of Japanese Power: People and Politics in a Stateless Nation*. New York: Vintage.

Varley, P. (2000) 'Shintō', in *Concise Routledge Encyclopedia of Philosophy*. London and New York: Routledge.

Wachs, S. (2007) 'Questioning gender: An interview with Japan-based psychotherapist Kim Oswalt', *Kyoto Journal*, 64, pp. 10–13.

Wallace, B. A. and Shapiro, S. L. (2006) 'Mental balance and well-being: Building bridges between Buddhism and western psychology', *American Psychologist*, 61 (7), pp. 690–701.

Watanabe, K. (1994) 'Japanese women's studies', *Women's Studies Quarterly*, 3/4, pp. 73–88.

Welch, P. (2005) 'Haruki Murakami's storytelling world', *World Literature Today*, January–April, pp. 55–59.

Winnicott, D. W. (1947) 'Hate in the countertransference', in D. W. Winnicott (1958) *Collected Papers: Through Paediatrics to Psycho-Analysis*. London: Tavistock.

Winnicott, D. W. (1974) *Playing and Reality*. Harmondsworth: Penguin.

Wishart, I. (2003) 'Lost in the matrix', *Investigate*, June 2003, http://www.investigatemagazine.com/june03matrix.htm (accessed 21 July 2004).

Wolfenstein, E. V. (1990) 'Group phantasies and "the individual": A critical analysis of psychoanalytic group psychology', *Free Associations*, 20, pp. 150–180.

Xun, Z. (1997) '*Youtai*: The myth of the "Jew" in modern China' in F. Dikötter (ed.) *The Construction of Racial Identities in China and Japan: Historical and Contemporary Perspectives*. London: Hurst & Company.

Yamaguchi, M. (2004) '"Burakumin" descendants still suffering', *The Japan Times*, 5 June 2004, http://202.221.217.59/print/news/nn06–2004/nn20040605f1.htm (accessed 14 December 2004).

Yamaguchi, S. (2004) 'Further clarification of the concept of *amae* in relation to dependence and attachment', *Human Development*, 47, pp. 28–33.

Yan, M. (2003) *Red Sorghum* (translated by H. Goldblatt). London: Arrow.

Yokoyama, T. (1987) *Japan in the Victorian Mind: A Study of Stereotyped Images of a Nation, 1850–80*. London: Palgrave.

Yonezawa, Y. (2004) 'Dojinshi as otaku expression: The state of Japanese fanzindoms', in *Catalogue of Padiglione Giappone, IX Mostra Internazionale di Architettura*. Venice: La Biennale di Venezia.

Yoshimoto, B. (1993) *Kitchen* (translated by M. Backus, originally published 1988). London: Faber & Faber.

Yoshimoto, B. (2002) *Asleep* (translated by M. Emmerich, originally published 1992). London: Faber & Faber.
Yoshimoto, B. (2003) *Goodbye Tsugumi* (translated by M. Emmerich, originally published 1989). London: Faber & Faber.
Yoshino, K. (1997) 'The discourse on blood and racial identity in contemporary Japan', in F. Dikötter (ed.) *The Construction of Racial Identities in China and Japan: Historical and Contemporary Perspectives*. London: Hurst & Company.
Žižek, S. (1991) *Looking Awry: An Introduction to Jacques Lacan through Popular Culture*. Cambridge, MA: MIT Press.
Žižek, S. (2004) 'The parallax view', *New Left Review*, 25, pp. 121–134.
Žižek, S. (2006) *The Parallax View*. Cambridge, MA: MIT Press.

Index